OXFORD MONOGRAPHS IN INTERNATIONAL LAW

The aim of this series is to publish important and original pieces of research on all aspects of international law. Topics that are given particular prominence are those which, while of interest to the academic lawyer, also have important bearing on issues which touch the actual conduct of international relations. Nonetheless, the series is wide in scope and includes monographs on the history and philosophical foundations of international law.

RECENT TITLES IN THE SERIES

Treaties on Transit Pipelines and Countermeasures
Danae Azaria

Corporate Obligations under International Law
Markos Karavias

A Contemporary Concept of Monetary Sovereignty
Claus D Zimmermann

Formalism and the Sources of International Law
A Theory of the Ascertainment of Legal Rules
Jean d'Aspremont

Extraterritorial Application of Human Rights Treaties
Law, Principles, and Policy
Marko Milanovic

Applicable Law in Investor-State Arbitration
The Interplay Between National and International Law
Hege Elisabeth Kjos

Disobeying the Security Council
Countermeasures against Wrongful Sanctions
Antonios Tzanakopoulos

The International Minimum Standard and Fair and Equitable Treatment
Martins Paparinskis

Maritime Security and the Law of the Sea
Natalie Klein

The Margin of Appreciation in International Human Rights Law
Deference and Proportionality
Andrew Legg

Complicity in International Law

Complicity in International Law

MILES JACKSON

OXFORD
UNIVERSITY PRESS

OXFORD
UNIVERSITY PRESS

Great Clarendon Street, Oxford, OX2 6DP,
United Kingdom

Oxford University Press is a department of the University of Oxford.
It furthers the University's objective of excellence in research, scholarship,
and education by publishing worldwide. Oxford is a registered trade mark of
Oxford University Press in the UK and in certain other countries

First Edition published in 2015

Published in the United States of America by Oxford University Press
198 Madison Avenue, New York, NY 10016, United States of America

British Library Cataloguing in Publication Data
Data available

Library of Congress Control Number: 2014959893

ISBN 978–0–19–873693–6

Jacket illustration: Getty Images © Arrville

Acknowledgements

Complicity is a subject that lends itself to an appreciation of assistance and encouragement. This book, which grew out of the doctoral thesis I defended at the University of Oxford in November 2013, depended on a great deal of both.

First and foremost, I would like to thank Professor Dapo Akande for his direction and advice on the thesis, both of which were indispensable, and for his warm support and friendship beyond it. I owe him a great deal.

I owe an intellectual debt to those who taught me international law, in particular Professor Stefan Talmon, for his rigour and inspiration many years ago, and Professors Ryan Goodman and William Alford. In addition, I am immensely grateful, both personally and professionally, to Professor Liora Lazarus.

I am also thankful to my examiners, Professors Andrew Ashworth and André Nollkaemper, and all at the University of Oxford and elsewhere who discussed drafts, chapters, and ideas with me: Sir Frank Berman, Professor Michael Bohlander, Professor Sandra Fredman, Professor John Gardner, Professor Guy Goodwin-Gill, Professor Imogen Goold, Professor Doug Husak, Professor Nina Jørgensen, Dr Maris Köpcke Tinturé, Professor Vaughan Lowe, Professor Catherine Redgwell, Professor Antonios Tzanakopoulos, and Professor Stefan Vogenauer.

I would like to thank Farid Ahmadov, Nick Friedman, Ryan Goss, Claire Hewer, Sotirios-Ioannis Lekkas, Thomas Liefländer, Kubo Mačák, Travers McLeod, Dhvani Mehta, Rob Mullins, Brid Ni Ghráinne, Nikki Palmer, and Laith Tapper for their friendship, help, and advice along the way. I am also immensely grateful to Anna Begemann, Caitlin Goss, and Natasha Simonsen, all of whom read the entire draft and for whose comments it is vastly better.

I am thankful to Oxford University Press and its Delegates, and personally to Emma Endean, Merel Alstein, and John Louth for their support and work in turning the draft into a book. In addition, I appreciate all of the work that Dhanuj Nair of Newgen put into shepherding the project to completion and Cheryl Prophett's excellent copy-editing.

This project would not have commenced without the generosity of the Rhodes Trust. I am grateful to all at Rhodes House, especially Mary Eaton, John Gee, Don Markwell, Colin Page, and Bob Wyllie. In turning my thesis into this book, I was supported by the Global Justice Research Fellowship at

St Anne's College; I am grateful to Don Ferencz of the Global Institute for the Prevention of Aggression for his support for the fellowship.

I am also indebted to the staff of the Law Faculty at the University of Oxford, the University's many libraries and librarians, and to University College, Oxford, and St Anne's College, Oxford.

Finally, I am deeply grateful to my family for their love and support, and to Emily Uecker for those and much more.

MMJ
Oxford, September 2014

Table of Contents

PART D. CONCLUSION

Table of Cases

INTERNATIONAL COURTS AND TRIBUNALS

International Court of Justice

Permanent Court of International Justice

International Criminal Court

Special Court for Sierra Leone

Post-Second World War Trials

Germany

United States of America

The Netherlands

Table of Treaties

OTHER PRIMARY AUTHORITIES

RESOLUTIONS OF THE UNITED NATIONS SECURITY COUNCIL

Resolution 418 (1977) of 4 November 1977
Resolution 822 (1993) of 30 April 1993
Resolution 827 (1993) of 25 May 1993
Resolution 853 (1993) of 29 July 1993
Resolution 874 (1993) of 14 October 1993
Resolution 884 (1993) of 12 November 1993
Resolution 955 (1994) of 8 November 1994
Resolution 1368 (2001) of 12 September 2001
Resolution 1373 (2001) of 28 September 2001

RESOLUTIONS OF THE UNITED NATIONS GENERAL ASSEMBLY

Resolution 174 (II) (21 November 1947)
Resolution 498 (V) (1 February 1951)
Resolution 2625 (XXV) (24 October 1970)
Resolution 3314 (XXIX) (14 December 1974)
Resolution 36/27 (13 November 1981)
Resolution 37/123 (16 December 1982)
Resolution 40/61 (9 December 1985)
Resolution 41/38 (20 November 1986)
Resolution 44/29 (4 December 1989)
Resolution 49/60 (9 December 1994)
Resolution 51/210 (17 December 1996)
Resolution 53/108 (26 January 1999)
Resolution 56/1 (18 September 2001)
Resolution 56/83 (12 December 2001)

UNITED NATIONS INTERNATIONAL LAW COMMISSION

Special Rapporteurs

Ago R, 'Second Report on State Responsibility—the Origin of International Responsibility' (1970) UN Doc A/CN.4/233 (1970) II YILC 177
Ago R, 'Fourth Report on State Responsibility—The Internationally Wrongful Act of the State, Source of International Responsibility' (1978) UN Doc A/CN.4/264 (1978) II YILC 72
Ago R, 'Seventh Report on State Responsibility—the Internationally Wrongful Act of the State, Source of International Responsibility' (1978) UN Doc A/CN.4/307 (1978) I(1) YILC 31
Crawford J, 'Second Report on State Responsibility' (1999) UN Doc A/CN.4/498/Add.1 (1999) II(1) YILC 3

Documents

'Observations and Comments from Governments on Chapters I, II, and III of Part I of the Draft Articles on State Responsibility for Internationally Wrongful Acts' (1980) UN Doc A/CN.4/328

'State Responsibility—Comments and Observations Received from Governments' (1998) UN Doc A/CN.4/488
'State Responsibility—Comments and Observations Received from Governments' (1999) UN Doc A/CN.4/492
'State Responsibility—Comments and Observations Received From Governments' (2001) UN Doc A/CN.4/515
'Responsibility of International Organizations—Texts and Titles of Draft Articles 1 to 67 adopted by the Drafting Committee on Second Reading in 2011' (2011) UN Doc A/CN.4/L.778

UNITED NATIONS TREATY BODIES

UNHRC, 'General Comment 20' (10 March 1992) UN Doc HRI/GEN/1/Rev.1 30 (1994)
UNHRC, 'General Comment 31' (29 March 2004) UN Doc CCPR/C/21/Rev.1/Add.13 (2004)
UNHRC, 'Report of the Special Rapporteur on the Promotion and Protection of Human Rights and Fundamental Freedoms while Countering Terrorism' (4 February 2009) UN Doc A/HRC10/3
UNHRC, 'Joint Study on Global Practices in relation to Secret Detention in the Context of Countering Terrorism' (19 February 2010) UN Doc A/HRC/13/42
UNHRC, 'Report of the Independent International Commission of Inquiry on the Syrian Arab Republic' (4 June 2013) UN Doc A/HRC/23/58

OTHER

Allied Control Council Law No 10, Punishment of Persons Guilty of War Crimes, Crimes against Peace and Humanity (20 December 1945) 3 Official Gazette Control Council for Germany 50–55 (1946)
Charter of the International Military Tribunal (Nuremberg) annexed to Agreement for the Prosecution and Punishment of the Major War Criminals of the European Axis (signed in London, 8 August 1945) 82 UNTS 279
Charter of the International Military Tribunal for the Far East (19 January 1946, amended 25 April 1946) TIAS No 1589
Report of the Preparatory Committee for the Establishment of an International Criminal Court—Draft Statute for the International Criminal Court (14 April 1998) UN Doc A/Conf.183/2/Add.1
Resolution RC.Res.6 adopted at the 13th Plenary Meeting, Review Conference of the Rome Statute, Kampala, Uganda (11 June 2010)
International Commission of Jurists, 'Report of the Expert Panel on Corporate Complicity in International Crimes' (Geneva 2008)
United Kingdom Parliament Joint Committee on Human Rights, *Allegations of UK Complicity in Torture* (2008-09 HL Paper 152 HC 230)
European Commission for Democracy through Law, 'Opinion on the International Legal Obligations of Council of Europe Member States in Respect of Secret Detention Facilities and Inter-State Transport of Prisoners' adopted by the Venice Commission at its 66th Plenary Session (17 March 2005), Op No 363/2005

DOMESTIC LEGISLATION

Austria

StGB § 12

United States of America

18 USC § 2 (1994)
Mo Rev Stat § 575.230 (Mo)
Mo Rev Stat § 575.210 (Mo)
Model Penal Code § 2.06 (Proposed Official Draft 1962)
New York Penal Law § 115 (NY)
W Va Code § 61–3-1 (1977) (W Va)

Canada

Crimes against Humanity and War Crimes Act 2000, s 5

England

Statute of Labourers (1349) 23 Edw III

England and Wales

Accessories and Abettors Act 1861, as amended by Sch 12 to the Criminal Law Act 1977, s 8
International Criminal Court Act 2001, s 65
Merchant Shipping Act 1995, s 93
Serious Crime Act 2007, s 44
Serious Crime Act 2007, s 45
Serious Crime Act 2007, s 46

Germany

StGB § 25
StGB § 26
StGB § 27
StGB § 49

Scotland

International Criminal Court (Scotland) Act 2001, s 5

List of Abbreviations

ARSIWA	Articles on Responsibility of States for Internationally Wrongful Acts
CIA	Central Intelligence Agency
DRC	Democratic Republic of the Congo
ECHR	European Convention on Human Rights
EHRR	European Human Rights Reports
FARC	Revolutionary Armed Forces of Colombia
FRG	Federal Republic of Germany
FRY	Federal Republic of Yugoslavia
GCIII	Convention (III) Relative to the Treatment of Prisoners of War (adopted 12 August 1949, entered into force 21 October 1950) 75 UNTS 135
ICC	International Criminal Court
ICCPR	International Covenant on Civil and Political Rights
ICJ	International Court of Justice
ICTR	International Criminal Tribunal for Rwanda
ICTY	International Criminal Tribunal for the former Yugoslavia
ILC	International Law Commission
IMT	International Military Tribunal
JCE	Joint Criminal Enterprise
JNA	Yugoslav People's Army
LQR	Law Quarterly Review
LRTWC	Law Reports of Trials of War Criminals
NATO	North Atlantic Treaty Organization
OAS	Organization of American States
PCIJ	Permanent Court of International Justice
PKK	Kurdistan Workers' Party
RIAA	Reports of International Arbitral Awards
SCSL	Special Court for Sierra Leone
StGB	Strafgesetzbuch
TO	Territorial Defense Forces, Yugoslavia
UAE	United Arab Emirates
UK	United Kingdom
UN	United Nations
UNGA	United Nations General Assembly
UNHRC	United Nations Human Rights Committee
UNSC	United Nations Security Council
UNTS	United Nations Treaty Series

US	United States of America
USC	United States Code
USSR	Union of Soviet Socialist Republics
VCLT	Vienna Convention on the Law of Treaties
VRS	Army of the Republika Srpska
YILC	Yearbook of the International Law Commission

PART A
A THEORY OF COMPLICITY

1

Introduction

1.1. Introduction

Allegations of complicity are pervasive: France has been accused of complicity in the Rwandan genocide,[1] China of complicity in atrocities in Darfur,[2] Pakistan of complicity in the sheltering of Osama Bin Laden,[3] and the United Kingdom of complicity in torture during the war on terror.[4] If these allegations tell us anything about the nature of complicity, it is that to be complicit one must be complicit *in* something. That something is the commission of wrongdoing by another actor.

This work is concerned with the ways in which international law responds to individual and state complicity in wrongdoing committed by another actor. Complicity rules take a variety of forms, ranging in source, content, and structure. This work provides an analytical account of these rules, locating them within a single framework. The framework assumes that no matter the legal subject of the complicity rule, certain issues of scope and form must be confronted.

Beyond this analytical account is a normative claim about the structure of complicity rules. Complicity is a particular way of contributing to wrongdoing. This requires that responsibility be attributed to accomplices *for* their acts of complicity. Rules of complicity structured in this way may be termed 'non-imputational' complicity rules. A state that assists another state's

[1] Mike Pflanz, 'French Leaders Accused of Complicity in Rwanda Genocide' *The Telegraph* (London, 5 August 2008) <http://www.telegraph.co.uk/news/worldnews/2506150/France-accused-of-complicity-in-Rwanda-genocide.html> accessed 18 December 2014.

[2] Eric Reeves, 'Arming Khartoum: China's Complicity in the Darfur Genocide' *Sudan Tribune* (Paris, 19 October 2010) <http://www.sudantribune.com/spip.php?article36644> accessed 18 December 2014.

[3] Robert Baer, 'Finding Bin Laden Raises Questions About Pakistan's Complicity' *Time* (New York, 2 May 2011) <http://www.time.com/time/world/article/0,8599,2069012,00.html> accessed 18 December 2014.

[4] United Kingdom Parliament Joint Committee on Human Rights, *Allegations of UK Complicity in Torture* (2008–09) HL Paper 152 HC 230.

commission of genocide should be held responsible for assisting genocide. It should not be held responsible for genocide. An individual who instigates another individual to commit war crimes should be held responsible for instigating war crimes and not be held responsible for war crimes themselves. This is the normative claim of the work.

1.2. The Structure of the Work

The work is divided into four parts, which together comprise ten chapters. Part A contains Chapters 1 and 2. Chapter 1, the present chapter, is a general introduction. Chapter 2 addresses some matters of foundational concern for a study of complicity. It provides a definition of complicity, considers why complicity rules exist, defends the work's normative claim concerning the structure of complicity, and builds an analytical framework in which complicity rules may be understood. That framework structures the analysis along three axes: the forms of complicity prohibited, the nexus between the accomplice's act and the principal's wrong, and the fault required of the accomplice.

Thereafter, the work is organized around the status of the complicit actor. Part B (Chapters 3–5) addresses individual complicity in international criminal law. After a brief assessment in Chapter 3 of the principle of individual criminal responsibility in international law, Chapter 4 analyses the two central complicity doctrines of instigation and aiding and abetting, placing them within the analytical framework of the work and evaluating their structure against the normative claim noted above. Chapter 5 assesses two ways that international criminal law deals with complicit omissions. First, it is now established that in a limited set of circumstances, an omission may fulfil the conduct element of aiding and abetting as a mode of responsibility. Second, some complicit omissions give rise to liability under the doctrine of command responsibility.

Part C (Chapters 6–9) addresses state complicity. As will become clear, the idea of state complicity historically had an uneasy relationship with the basic structures and assumptions of international law and state responsibility. These difficulties are noted in Chapter 6. To explain this uneasy relationship and understand how international law has developed, it is helpful to distinguish (a) state participation in the conduct of another state and (b) state participation in the conduct of a non-state actor.

In respect of the former, moving away from a historical absence of complicity rules, international law now prohibits various forms of state complicity in the wrongful conduct of another state. These are addressed in Chapter 7. Initially, *specific* complicity rules arose concerning state participation in a particular international wrong. This work analyses the specific complicity rule prohibiting state participation in the wrong of aggression. Subsequently, a *general* complicity rule arose prohibiting states from aiding or assisting another state in the commission of any international wrong. This is the rule reflected in Article 16 of the International Law Commission's Articles on Responsibility of States for Internationally Wrongful Acts (ARSIWA).[5] Although one element of the general rule unduly limits its scope, it represents a leap in the 'moral sophistication of international law'.[6]

In respect of the latter—state participation in the conduct of non-state actors—there has historically been a conceptual difficulty in assessing the state's participation as a form of *complicity*. Complicity is essentially derivative: it requires wrongdoing by the principal actor.[7] Without any such wrongdoing, there is nothing for the complicit state to be complicit in.[8] Even if the state is no longer the exclusive subject of international law, it has long been its primary subject.[9] That is to say, the predominant bearer of rights and duties within the international legal system has traditionally been the state.[10] The absence of direct regulation of the conduct of non-state actors robbed international law of the possibility of state responsibility for complicity in that conduct. De Frouville takes up this point in explaining that the rejection of complicity 'simply follows from the classical structure of normativity in international law which is articulated around the obligations, the only subjects of which are States'.[11]

It will be seen that some instances of state participation in the conduct of non-state actors will give rise to state responsibility under various broader due diligence obligations that require states to protect against certain harms. These are not complicity rules, for there is no principal wrong

[5] International Law Commission, 'Responsibility of States for Internationally Wrongful Acts' annexed to UNGA Res 56/83 (12 December 2001) UN Doc A/Res/56/83.

[6] Vaughan Lowe, 'Responsibility for the Conduct of Other States' (2002) 101 Japanese J Intl L 1, 12.

[7] Sanford Kadish, 'Complicity, Cause and Blame' (1985) 73 Calif L Rev 323, 337.

[8] Robert Weisberg, 'Reappraising Complicity' (2000–2001) 4 Buff Crim L Rev 217, 224; John Quigley, 'Complicity in International Law: A New Direction in the Law of State Responsibility' (1986) 57 British YB Intl L 77, 86.

[9] Robert Jennings and Arthur Watts, *Oppenheim's International Law—Volume 1: Peace—Introduction and Part 1* (9th edn. Longman 1996) 16.

[10] James Crawford, *Brownlie's Principles of Public International Law* (OUP 2012) 115.

[11] Olivier de Frouville, 'Attribution of Conduct to the State: Private Individuals' in James Crawford, Alain Pellet, and Simon Olleson (eds.) *The Law of International Responsibility* (OUP 2010) 257, 276.

on the international plane from which the state's responsibility is derived.[12] Obligations of this kind are not of primary concern; there is an extensive literature assessing their content and source.[13] Instead, this work assesses two developments that affect the ways in which international law regulates the participation of states in the harms caused by non-state actors.

First, Chapter 8 addresses the claim that the idea of complicity has penetrated the rules of attribution in international law. In customary international law, the attribution of conduct of a non-state actor to the state is marked by the search for an agency relationship. A complicit relationship—one falling short of the direction and/or control required for agency—is ordinarily insufficient to attribute the conduct of a non-state actor to the state.[14] In two contexts—terrorist attacks and human rights violations in the Inter-American system—there is a claim that a complicit relationship is sufficient for attribution. The work argues that this claim should be rejected.

Second, Chapter 9 explains that as international law has come to recognize conduct other than state conduct as internationally wrongful, so the conceptual possibilities for complicity have expanded. To put it bluntly, now that non-state actors can commit principal wrongs on the international plane, there is principal wrongdoing by non-state actors for states to be complicit in.[15] On this basis, international law is able to articulate and condemn state complicity *qua* complicity. The best example of this development is the prohibition on state complicity in genocide. Chapter 9 also raises the possibility that a non-state analogue to Article 16 ARSIWA will develop.

Together, Parts B and C (Chapters 3–9) provide an analytical account of complicity in international law and a critique of the structure of the rules in accordance with the normative claim of the work. As a broad narrative, the ease with which international criminal law has sanctioned individual complicity may be contrasted with the historical inadequacy of international law's regulation of state complicity. That inadequacy is (almost) a thing of

[12] De Frouville, 'Attribution of Conduct' 276–7.

[13] See Riccardo Pisillo-Mazzeschi, 'Due Diligence and the International Responsibility of States' (1992) 35 German YB Intl L 9; Robert Barnidge, *Non-State Actors and Terrorism: Applying the Law of State Responsibility and the Due Diligence Principle* (TMC Asser 2008); Sarah Heathcote, 'State Omissions and Due Diligence: Aspects of Fault, Damage and Contribution to Injury in the Law of State Responsibility' in Karine Bannelier, Theodore Christakis, and Sarah Heathcote (eds.) *The ICJ and the Evolution of International Law: The Enduring Impact of the Corfu Channel Case* (Routledge 2012) 295.

[14] Art 8 ARSIWA; *Application of the Convention on the Prevention and Punishment of the Crime of Genocide (Bosnia and Herzegovina* v. *Serbia and Montenegro)* (Merits) [2007] ICJ Rep 43 [398]–[407]; Tal Becker, *Terrorism and the State* (Hart 2006) 43–79; Christine Chinkin, *Third Parties in International Law* (OUP 1993) 142.

[15] De Frouville, 'Attribution of Conduct' 277.

the past, at least with respect to state complicity in the wrongdoing of other states. Part D (Chapter 10) draws these threads together.

1.3. The Scope of the Work

As noted above, complicity is essentially derivative; its logic is to tie the participatory conduct of the accomplice to the wrongdoing of the principal actor.[16] There is some terminological confusion in the literature on this point. Scholars sometimes use the term derivative to mean that the acts of the principal are imputed to the accomplice.[17] Complicity rules structured in this way are better described as *imputational* complicity. Although complicity rules are always derivative in that for every act of complicity there must be an act of principalship, they are not necessarily imputational.[18] Accomplices may (and, in terms of the normative claim of the work, should) be held responsible for their own contribution to the principal wrong.

The essential derivative character of complicity explains the exclusion of certain related forms of responsibility from this work. Consider the obligation of *non-refoulement* in international law. The obligation commonly arises in respect of the prohibition of torture in international human rights law.[19] Article 3 of the European Convention on Human Rights, for instance, prohibits deportation or extradition where there are substantial grounds for believing that the individual faces a real risk of torture or inhuman and degrading treatment in the receiving state.[20] The breach of Article 3 arises at the moment of the deportation or extradition. Whether the wrongful treatment later occurs is immaterial to the Article 3 violation. For this reason, *non-refoulement* is not a derivative form of responsibility and, consequently, is not a form of complicity per se. Instead, it may be thought of as a kindred

16 Kadish, 'Complicity, Cause and Blame' 337.

17 See George Fletcher, 'Complicity' (1996) 30 Isr L Rev 140.

18 Cf Markus Dubber, 'Criminalizing Complicity: A Comparative Analysis' (2007) 5 J Intl Crim Justice 977, 993.

19 Art 3(1) Convention against Torture and Other Cruel, Inhuman or Degrading Treatment or Punishment (adopted 10 December 1984, entered into force 26 June 1987) 1465 UNTS 85; UNHRC, 'General Comment 20' (10 March 1992) UN Doc HRI/GEN/1/Rev.1 30 (1994) [9]. See generally Elihu Lauterpacht and Daniel Bethlehem, 'The Scope and Content of the Principle of *Non-Refoulement*' in Erika Feller, Volker Türk, and Frances Nicholson (eds.), *Refugee Protection in International Law – UNHCR's Global Consultations on International Protection* (CUP 2003) 87.

20 See (European) Convention for the Protection of Human Rights and Fundamental Freedoms (adopted 4 November 1950, entered into force 3 September 1953; as amended) 213 UNTS 222; *Soering* v. *United Kingdom* (App 14038/88) (1989) 11 EHRR 439.

form of responsibility[21] that seeks to prevent contributions to wrongful conduct by introducing a general rule that responds to a risk of harm.[22]

Likewise, what might otherwise fulfil an ordinary mode or form of complicity may itself be prohibited directly. UN Security Council Resolution 418 of 1977 imposed an arms embargo on South Africa: 'all States shall cease forthwith any provision to South Africa of arms and related *matérial* of all types'.[23] Any such provision, which may also constitute aid or assistance under conventional doctrines of complicity where it is linked to a subsequent wrongful act, would give rise to direct state responsibility for breach of that obligation.[24] This is not a form of derivative liability. Obligations of this kind are not the focus of this work.

In addition, for reasons of scope, this work does not address a number of emerging topics and areas in international law related to, or even falling within, the idea of complicity. It does not address corporate complicity.[25] It does not deal with the responsibility of international organizations.[26] Although, of course, heightened forms of complicity at some point cross over into joint perpetration or commission, this work does not address the ways in which international law holds states or individuals jointly responsible.[27]

[21] KJM Smith, *A Modern Treatise on the Law of Complicity* (Clarendon 1991) 7.

[22] This is not to say that a state that deports or extradites an individual knowing that he or she will be tortured would not be complicit in torture by the recipient state should the torture occur. In all likelihood, the state would be responsible for complicity, in addition to its responsibility under the principle of *non-refoulement*. The point is that a breach of the *non-refoulement* obligation does not require the commission of wrongdoing by another actor.

[23] UNSC Res 418 (4 November 1977) UN Doc S/Res/418.

[24] See Roberto Ago, 'Seventh Report on State Responsibility—the Internationally Wrongful Act of the State, Source of International Responsibility' (1978) UN Doc A/CN.4/307 (1978) I(1) YILC 31 [72].

[25] See generally International Commission of Jurists, 'Report of the Expert Panel on Corporate Complicity in International Crimes' (Geneva 2008); Andrew Clapham, 'Extending International Criminal Law beyond the Individual to Corporations and Armed Opposition Groups' (2008) 6 J Intl Crim Justice 899.

[26] See generally International Law Commission, 'Responsibility of International Organizations—Texts and Titles of Draft Articles 1 to 67 adopted by the Drafting Committee on Second Reading in 2011' (2011) UN Doc A/CN.4/L.778; August Reinisch, 'Aid or Assistance and Direction and Control between States and International Organizations in the Commission of Internationally Wrongful Acts' (2010) 7 Intl Org L Rev 63; Pierre Klein, 'Attribution of Acts to International Organizations' in Crawford et al. *The Law of International Responsibility* 297; Nataša Nedeski and André Nollkaemper, 'Responsibility of International Organizations "in Connection with Acts of States"' (2012) 9 Intl Org L Rev 33.

[27] See generally Smith, *A Treatise on Complicity* 209–34; Jens Ohlin, 'Joint Intentions to Commit International Crimes' (2010–2011) 11 Chicago J Intl L 693; Jens Ohlin, Elies van Sliedregt, and Thomas Weigend, 'Assessing the Control Theory' (2013) 26 Leiden J Intl L 725; John Noyes and Brian Smith, 'State Responsibility and the Principle of Joint and Several Liability' (1998) 13 Yale J Intl L 225; Stefan Talmon, 'A Plurality of Responsible Actors—International Responsibility for Acts of the Coalition Provision Authority in Iraq' in Phil Shiner and Andrew Williams (eds.) *The*

This work does not deal with situations where a state directs and controls the commission of an internationally wrongful act by another state,[28] or indeed coerces such an act.[29] Moreover, it does not provide a comprehensive overview of state practice relating to state complicity[30] or of the modes of responsibility in international criminal law.[31]

Instead, this work seeks to understand *how* international law prohibits core instances of state and individual complicity. It places the rules into a single analytical framework based on the kinds of complicit conduct prohibited, the nexus between the accomplice's acts and the principal's wrong, and the fault required of the accomplice; and evaluates the structure of the accomplice's responsibility against the work's normative claim. In doing so, it also provides a narrative account of how international law increasingly regulates different forms of individual and state complicity.

Iraq War and International Law (Hart 2008) 185; Francesco Messineo, 'Multiple Attribution of Conduct' SHARES Research Paper No 2012-11; André Nollkaemper and Dov Jacobs, 'Shared Responsibility in International Law: A Conceptual Framework' (2012/2013) 34 Mich J Intl L 359.

[28] See Art 17 ARSIWA. [29] See Art 18 ARSIWA.

[30] See Quigley, 'Complicity in International Law' 81–107; Helmut Aust, *Complicity and the Law of State Responsibility* (CUP 2011) 97–191.

[31] See Gideon Boas, James Bischoff, and Natalie Reid, *Forms of Responsibility in International Criminal Law—International Criminal Law Practitioner Library Series: Volume I* (CUP 2007); Elies van Sliedregt, *Individual Criminal Responsibility in International Law* (OUP 2012).

2

The Structure of Complicity

2.1. Introduction

This chapter addresses four matters of foundational concern for a study of complicity. First, it provides a definition of complicity. Second, it explores the wrongness of complicity. Third, it considers the different ways that legal systems prohibit complicit conduct; that is to say, it assesses how complicity rules may be structured. That assessment gives rise to a preference for non-imputational complicity rules, which is the normative claim of the work. Fourth, it builds an analytical framework in which the rules arising in international law will be discussed. The framework consists of three issues that must be resolved whenever complicity is prohibited: the forms of complicity proscribed, the nexus between the accomplice's conduct and the principal's wrong, and the fault required of the accomplice.

2.2. A Definition of Complicity

In conventional usage, the idea of complicity is widely understood. At root, it concerns an actor's participation in wrongdoing committed by another actor.[1] In building a definition of complicity, it is helpful to look to criminal law, for it is here that complicity receives most attention.[2]

In criminal law, a common approach to complicity is to proscribe certain kinds of behaviour that constitute participation in another person's criminal acts. A range of terms is used to sanction participation in this way. The federal complicity rule in the United States refers to those who aid, abet,

[1] Smith, *A Treatise on Complicity* 1–2.

[2] See Smith, *A Treatise on Complicity*; Kadish, 'Complicity, Cause and Blame'; Joshua Dressler, 'Reassessing the Theoretical Underpinnings of Accomplice Liability: New Solutions to an Old Problem (1985–1986) 37 Hastings LJ 91; Weisberg, 'Reappraising Complicity'; Andrew Simester, 'The Mental Element in Complicity' (2006) 122 LQR 578; Robert Sullivan, 'Conduct and Complicity: Liability based on Omission and Risk' (2008) 39 Cambrian L Rev 60.

counsel, command, induce, or procure the commission of an offence.[3] In England and Wales, the Accessories and Abettors Act of 1861 refers to aiders, abettors, counsellors, and procurers.[4] Older sources reveal prohibitions on helping, giving comfort, and assisting.[5] There is also reference to advising, persuading, inducing, and soliciting.[6] These may be termed modes or forms of complicity.[7] There is a risk of spending too much time on a literal construction of these terms.[8] Rather, it should be recognized that together these terms attempt to prohibit complicity as a particular way of contributing to wrongdoing.

That contribution is best thought of as comprising two kinds of action: intentionally *helping* the principal to commit wrongdoing and intentionally *influencing* the decision of the principal to commit the wrong.[9] There is a temporal issue here. Despite linguistic similarities, the doctrine of accessory after the fact should not be regarded as a form of complicity.[10] This form of liability is a remnant of an ancient concern with receiving a felon or shielding him from justice.[11] Even in Blackstone's time, the crime of being an accessory after the fact was 'always an offence of a different species of guilt, principally tending to evade the public justice…'.[12] Accessories after the fact do not help or influence the principal in his commission of wrongdoing—they make no contribution to the wrong itself.[13]

That criminal law is the context in which ideas of complicity usually arise should not be seen to exclude their application to other areas of law. At root, complicity is simply a derivative form of responsibility for participation in wrongdoing committed by another actor. Wrongdoing, in this sense, may refer to the commission of any legal wrong, whether equitable, criminal, civil, or international. This definition frames the work's account of complicity in international law.

[3] 18 USC § 2 (1994) (USA).

[4] Accessories and Abettors Act 1861, as amended by Sch 12 to the Criminal Law Act 1977, s 8.

[5] Smith, *A Treatise on Complicity* 31.

[6] Kadish, 'Complicity, Cause and Blame' 343.

[7] Smith, *A Treatise on Complicity* 20.

[8] Ibid 33.

[9] Kadish, 'Complicity, Cause and Blame' 342.

[10] Smith, *A Treatise on Complicity* 7.

[11] Glanville Williams, *Criminal Law—The General Part* (2nd edn. Stevens & Sons 1961) 409–10.

[12] 4 Bl Comm 40. See also Smith, *A Treatise on Complicity* 7–8.

[13] The boundary between accomplice liability and liability as an accessory after the fact in international criminal law is explored in section 4.3.2. See *Blagojević, Jokić* (Trial Chamber Judgment) IT-02-60-T (17 January 2005) and *Strugar* (Trial Chamber Judgment) IT-01-42-T (31 January 2005).

2.3. The Wrongness of Complicity

2.3.1. Moral and Legal Wrongs

On one level, the case for complicity is a moral case. It rests on the claim that if it is wrong to do something, it is wrong to help or encourage others to do it. Gardner argues that:

> I am responsible for what I do, and you are responsible for what you do. But on any credible view I need to give attention, in what I do, to what you will do in consequence. And you need to give attention, in what you do, to what I will do in consequence. In that sense, there are two parts of morality. There is what I should do *simpliciter*, and then there is what I should do by way of contribution to what you do. If I fail in the first I am a principal. If I fail in the second I am an accomplice.[14]

On this account, the wrongness of the principal's act justifies a prohibition of complicity. A justification of this kind is most easily understood in the context of criminal law. Clearly, a number of criminal offences prohibit conduct that is morally wrong: murder, for instance, is *malum in se*.[15] More than simply justifying the existence of a complicity rule, the wrongness of the principal act requires it. Here, a prohibition of complicity—concern not just with what subjects do to each other but with what they help or encourage others to do—is a sign of the moral sophistication of a legal system.[16]

The justification of, and demand for, complicity rules on a basis other than the moral wrongness of the principal act requires further thought. In these cases, we are confined to saying that the principal, helped or encouraged by the accomplice, committed a *legal* wrong against the victim. Here, it is helpful to distinguish two different relationships among the three parties (V being the victim, P the principal, and A the accomplice):

A. V has a right exigible against both P and A. P, helped or encouraged by A, violates the correlative duty;
B. V has a right exigible against P only. P, helped or encouraged by A, violates the correlative duty.[17]

[14] John Gardner, 'Complicity and Causality' (2007) 1 Crim L & Phil 127, 132.
[15] See Bl Comm 54.
[16] Lowe, 'Responsibility for the Conduct of Other States' 12. See also Gardner, 'Complicity and Causality' 132.
[17] This distinction borrows from, but does not match, Hohfeld's distinction between paucital and multital rights. See Wesley Hohfeld, 'Fundamental Legal Conceptions as Applied in Judicial Reasoning' (1916–1917) 26 Yale L J 710, 718–19.

In both cases P violates the duty, though only in the former was the correlative right held by V also exigible against A. This distinction is important in considering whether complicity rules are justified and/or required.

In the former case, the shared legal obligation owed by P and A to V itself demands that A does not help or encourage P's violation of that obligation. There is an intuitive plausibility to this claim—as the International Law Commission puts it, one 'cannot do by another what [one] cannot do by [oneself]'.[18] As a general principle, this holds across the range of obligations arising in domestic and international law. It should be noted, however, that the exact content of the complicity prohibition might vary according to the nature of the principal obligation. A useful illustration in this regard is the difference between complicity in municipal criminal law and the law of torts.[19] In England and Wales, for instance, accomplice liability in tort law requires a higher form of participation in the wrong than criminal law; knowing assistance is insufficient.[20]

The second situation—where only P is under a duty to V—is more complicated. It is best illustrated through contractual duties in municipal law. Imagine P and V contract. P is under a contractual duty to refrain from building any structure within view of V's property. A, who is aware of the contract, then helps or encourages P to build such a prohibited structure. In a general sense, we may say that A is complicit in P's violation of his legal duty.

Whether this is the kind of complicity that the legal system ought to prohibit is a difficult question. It is fundamental that a contract does not impose obligations on third parties. P's voluntary assumption of a duty towards V does not give rise to a duty owed by A (or B, C, or D) to V.[21] Correlatively, V has no right arising under the contract exigible against A (or B, C, or D). This rule of privity flows from the consensual nature of contractual obligations.[22] In the context of treaties in international law, the same idea is captured by the *pacta tertiis* rule—a treaty does not create obligations on a third state without its consent.[23] However, appeals to privity or the *pacta tertiis* rule should not

[18] ARSIWA Commentary on Art 16 [6].

[19] See Hazel Carty, 'Joint Tortfeasance and Assistance Liability' (1999) 19 Legal Stud 489; Paul Davies, 'Accessory Liability for Assisting Torts' (2011) 70 Camb L J 353; Joachim Dietrich, 'Accessorial Liability in the Law of Torts' (2011) 31 Legal Stud 231. See also Robert Stevens, *Torts and Rights* (OUP 2007) 275–83.

[20] Davies, 'Accessory Liability for Assisting Torts' 357–8; Dietrich, 'Accessorial Liability in the Law of Torts' 239.

[21] See Wesley Hohfeld, 'Some Fundamental Legal Conceptions as Applied in Judicial Reasoning (1913–1914) 23 Yale L J 16, 36–7.

[22] See Edwin Peel, *Treitel's Law of Contract* (13th edn. Sweet and Maxwell 2011) 621.

[23] Art 34 Vienna Convention on the Law of Treaties (adopted 23 May 1969, entered into force 27 January 1980) 1155 UNTS 331 (VCLT). See Vaughan Lowe, *International Law* (OUP 2011) 81–6.

be the end of the matter. As Hohfeld puts it: 'Whether there should be such concomitant rights (or claims) is ultimately a question of justice and policy; and it should be considered, as such, on its merits.'[24]

2.3.2. An Analogy to Inducing Breach of Contract in England and Wales

Whether or not public international law should prohibit state complicity in the breach by another state of an international obligation binding only it (and not the potentially complicit state) is a central question in Chapter 7. It will be seen that the rule reflected in Article 16 ARSIWA denies the existence of any such prohibition. At this point, a tentative analogy might be drawn to the tort of inducing breach of contract in England and Wales.[25] It is tentative because of differences between the legal subjects of the rules, the nature of responsibility, and the underlying principles, structures, and purposes of the legal systems. Nonetheless, the analogy is helpful in illustrating how questions of justice and policy that inform the desirability of a complicity rule play out in a particular legal context.

Although the inducement tort's antecedents may be traced to the Roman *actio indirecta*,[26] in England and Wales the Statute of Labourers of 1349 is a more interesting starting point. Issued by Edward III in the midst of the Black Death, the statute sought to compel labourers to work at fixed prices.[27] In addition, it provided:

> [i]f any reaper, mower, or other workman or servant, of what estate or condition that he be, retained in any man's service, do depart from the said service without reasonable cause or license, before the term agreed, he shall have pain of imprisonment. And that none under the same pain presume to receive or to retain any such in his service.[28]

As Sayre explains, one effect of this provision was to create a new statutory remedy available against a third party for enticing another man's servant away from his service, the prevailing concern being the labour shortage

[24] Hohfeld, 'Some Fundamental Legal Conceptions' 36.

[25] For a comparative perspective, see Peter Eulau, 'Inducing Breach of Contract: A Comparison of the Laws of the United States, France, The Federal Republic of Germany and Switzerland' (1978) 2 Boston College Intl & Comp L Rev 41; James Crawford, 'Second Report on State Responsibility—Annex: Interference with Contractual Rights: A Brief Review of the Comparative Law Experience' (1999) UN Doc A/CN.4/498/Add.3.

[26] See Francis Sayre, 'Inducing Breach of Contract' (1922–1923) 36 Harv L Rev 663; Hazel Carty, *An Analysis of the Economic Torts* (2nd edn. OUP 2010) 30.

[27] (1349) 23 Edw III.

[28] Ibid.

caused by the Black Death.[29] This is to say that at the time, the relationship between master and labourer was thought by the law-giver to be of such importance that third party interference with that relationship warranted an additional remedy.[30]

This history is helpful in understanding the landmark case of *Lumley* v. *Gye*, which is the foundation of the modern common law tort of inducing breach of contract.[31] In *Lumley*, Johanna Wagner, a famous opera singer, contracted with Lumley, the manager of Her Majesty's Theatre, Haymarket, to perform exclusively at his theatre.[32] Gye, the manager of a rival opera house, made Wagner a more attractive offer. Wagner accepted the offer. Lumley brought suit against Gye.

In his dissenting judgment, Coleridge J denied the possibility of an action in tort in the following terms:

> ... in respect of breach of contract the general rule of our law is to confine its remedies by action to the contracting parties...; that, as between master and servant, there is an admitted exception; that this exception dates from the Statute of Labourers, 23 Edw. 3, and both on principle and according to authority is limited by it.[33]

Coleridge's dissent represented conventional understandings of the law in 1853: other than the master and servant cases deriving from the Statute of Labourers, no remedy lay against a complicit third party to a breach of contract.[34] The majority disagreed, holding that principle and public policy demanded that Lumley's contractual relations with Wagner be protected even against a third party.[35] As Crompton J put it, 'it would seem unjust, and contrary to the general principles of law, if such wrongdoer were not responsible for the damage caused by his wrongful and malicious act'.[36] The court thereby 'freed the old enticement action from its roots in status relations'.[37]

To emphasize, the reading of *Lumley* v. *Gye* presented here sees the tort of inducing breach of contract as a way to sanction an accomplice's participation in the breach of a legal duty owed by the principal. It sanctions a particular

[29] Sayre, 'Inducing Breach of Contract' 665–6.

[30] See *Lumley* v. *Gye* [1853] 118 ER 749, 765 (Coleridge J). This is to say nothing of the morality or wisdom of the statute.

[31] [1853] 118 ER 749.

[32] For a historical account, see SM Waddams, 'Johanna Wagner and the Rival Opera Houses' (2001) 117 LQR 431.

[33] *Lumley* (Coleridge J) 760.

[34] Sayre, 'Inducing Breach of Contract' 666.

[35] *Lumley* (Crompton J) 755. See Waddams, 'Johanna Wagner' 450.

[36] *Lumley* (Crompton J) 755. It should be noted that in the end Lumley did not prevail in his action. See Waddams, 'Johanna Wagner' 456–6.

[37] John Danforth, 'Tortious Interference with Contract: A Reassertion of Society's Interest in Commercial Stability and Contractual Integrity' (1981) 81 Colum L Rev 1491, 1495.

form of complicity—inducement or procurement—with a particular fault element—knowledge of the contract and intention to cause a breach of that contract.[38] It is derivative, in the sense that without the breach of contract committed by the principal there can be no liability for tortious inducement of that breach.[39] It is a private law analogue of doctrines of complicity in criminal law.

So complicity rules arise in surprising places. There is another lesson in the inducement cases, one relevant to the evaluation of Article 16 ARSIWA in Chapter 7. It is that the desirability of a prohibition of complicity outside of criminal law cannot be settled by appeals to privity of contract or the *pacta tertiis* rule.[40] Instead, we should weigh up principled and policy reasons, specific to the particular legal system, for and against holding the putative accomplice responsible.[41]

In respect of inducing breach of contract, these are manifold. Some argue that the value of the primary contractual relationship between P and V is so great as to require special protection from third parties.[42] This protection may be explained by analogy to the law of property, such that V's right under the contract is treated 'as a species of property which deserve(s) special protection…'.[43] An alternative conception is that the power to contract itself gives rise to a secondary right against all third parties that they not induce a breach of the contract.[44] Other arguments look to the wrongdoing of the complicit third party[45] or a broader societal interest in the integrity of contractual relations in a market economy.[46] As Danforth puts it:

> By extending the enticement action to allow tort protection against interference with contract, the court in *Lumley* v. *Gye* implicitly recognized that in 1853 society's interest in a stable foundation for economic activity had shifted from a concern for stability in status relations to a concern for stability in contractual relations.[47]

[38] See Carty, *An Analysis of the Economic Torts* 35–45.

[39] *OBG Limited and Others* v. *Allan and Others* [2008] 1 AC 1 [8] (Lord Hoffmann): '…*Lumley* v. *Gye* created accessory liability, dependent upon the primary wrongful act of the contracting party.'

[40] See Hohfeld, 'Some Fundamental Legal Conceptions' 36; Waddams, 'Johanna Wagner' 451.

[41] Sayre, 'Inducing Breach of Contract' 687; Andrew Simester and Winnie Chan, 'Inducing Breach of Contract: One Tort or Two' (2004) 63 Camb L J132, 139.

[42] See Roderick Bagshaw, 'Can the Economic Torts be Unified' (1998) 18 OJLS 729, 735; Carty, *An Analysis of the Economic Torts* 55.

[43] *OBG* v. *Allan* [32] (Lord Hoffmann). See Richard Epstein, 'Inducement of Breach of Contract as a Problem of Ostensible Ownership' (1987) 16 J Legal Stud 1; Pey-Woan Lee, 'Inducing Breach of Contract, Conversion and Contract as Property' (2009) 29 OJLS 511; Carty, *An Analysis of the Economic Torts* 55.

[44] Stevens, *Torts and Rights* 281.

[45] See *Lumley* (Crompton J) 755; Sayre, 'Inducing Breach of Contract' 672–86.

[46] Danforth, 'Tortious Interference with Contract' 1509.

[47] Ibid.

Against these justifications is the claim that the tort action unduly limits the interests of third parties in ordinary commercial activities.[48] More broadly, in Sayre's phrasing, at stake here is the 'very freedom of individual action which the common law exists largely to secure'.[49] On an efficient breach theory of contract, it is argued, though not without contestation,[50] that the tort liability of the third party inducer limits the efficient allocation of resources.[51] Others look to how the tort plays out in the particular context of labour relations.[52]

This is not the place to judge the desirability of the inducement tort. Instead, the tort serves to illustrate how ideas of complicity arise outside of criminal law and that the desirability of and demand for complicity rules turn on conflicting rationales shaped by the needs and purposes of the legal system or regime itself.[53] In addition, these conflicting rationales shape the breadth of the complicity rule, determining the forms of complicity prohibited, the requisite nexus between the accomplice's act and the principal's wrong, and the fault required of the accomplice. Complicity rules are not monolithic. Moreover, they may not be required to prohibit every form of participation in every legal wrong. These two points are important in considering the existence and forms of complicity appropriate to the international legal system.

2.4. Structuring Complicity Rules

2.4.1. Participation in Wrongdoing

States cooperate with each other and with non-state actors all the time, often virtuously but sometimes wrongfully. Likewise, international crimes are marked by their collectivity; orders are given, plans made, weapons provided, detainees rounded up, and only then does someone pull the trigger.[54] There are many ways to participate in wrongdoing. This much is beyond dispute.

[48] Sayre, 'Inducing Breach of Contract' 687; Harvey Perlman, 'Interference with Contract and Other Economic Expectancies: A Clash of Tort and Contract Doctrine' (1982) 49 Uni Chicago L Rev 61, 78–9.

[49] Sayre, 'Inducing Breach of Contract' 687. See also Dan Dobbs, 'Tortious Interference with Contractual Relationships' (1980) 34 Ark L Rev 335, 350.

[50] See generally Fred McChesney, 'Tortious Interference with Contract versus "Efficient" Breach: Theory and Empirical Evidence' (1999) 28 J of Legal Stud 131.

[51] Perlman, 'Interference with Contract' 78–87.

[52] David Howarth, 'Against *Lumley* v. *Gye*' (2005) 68 MLR 195.

[53] See Pey-Woan Lee, 'Inducing Breach of Contract, Conversion and Contract as Property' (2009) 29 OJLS 511, 522.

[54] See *Tadić* (Appeals Chamber Judgment) IT-94-1A (15 July 1999) [191]; Mark Osiel, 'The Banality of Good: Aligning Incentives Against Mass Atrocities' (2005) 105 Colum L Rev 1751.

What is in dispute is how to hold those participants responsible. Here, again, it makes sense to look to criminal law, where questions of participation have long been in issue.[55] The conventional theoretical framework in criminal law distinguishes two basic models: unitary and differentiated participation.[56] The unitary model is constituted by an expansive notion of principalship, imposing that label on all those who make a causal contribution to the crime.[57] Section 12 of the Austrian Penal Code, for instance, provides that an act is committed not only by the physical perpetrator but also by those who instigate or contribute to it.[58] Other than at sentencing, the unitary model denies any need for distinguishing between participants in wrongdoing. There are no accomplices; all are principals.

A unitary model of participation is inconsistent with how we do, and ought to, think about responsibility. To borrow Darryl Robinson's example, the groom, bartender, and guest are all participants in a wedding. Indeed, they may all causally contribute to it. But we would not deny profound differences in their roles.[59] Likewise, in the context of wrongdoing, complicity is a necessary element of a complete account of morality and responsibility. Gardner argues that 'the distinction between principals and accomplices is embedded in the structure of rational agency. As rational beings we cannot live without it'.[60] There are two elements to Gardner's account. The first concerns the wrongness of complicity: we should be concerned with not only the harms we do ourselves but also those we help or influence others to do.[61] The second concerns the scope of that wrong: both principals and accomplices should be responsible for their own actions.[62]

Another way of putting this is that the principal's wrong should not be imputed to the accomplice. Imputational complicity rules hold

[55] For a recent discussion of participation in crime in England and Wales, Germany, and the Netherlands see Johannes Keiler, *Actus Reus and Participation in European Criminal Law* (Intersentia 2013).

[56] Albin Eser, 'Individual Criminal Responsibility' in Antonio Cassese, Paola Gaeta, and John Jones (eds.), *The Rome Statute of the International Criminal Court: A Commentary—Vol 1* (OUP 2002) 767, 781–3.

[57] Ibid 781.

[58] StGB § 12 (Austria). See Kai Ambos, 'Is the Development of a Common Substantive Criminal Law for Europe Possible? Some Preliminary Reflections' (2005) 12 Maastricht J of Eur & Comp L 173, 184.

[59] Darryl Robinson, 'Comment on *Opinio Juris* LJIL Symposium on James Stewart, The End of "Modes of Liability" for International Crimes—James Stewart Responds to Darryl Robinson' (*Opinio Juris*, 21 March 2012) <http://opiniojuris.org/2012/03/21/ljil-stewart-responds-to-robinson/> accessed 18 December 2014.

[60] Gardner, 'Complicity and Causality' 132.

[61] See also Lowe, 'Responsibility for the Conduct of Other States' 13.

[62] See Gardner, 'Complicity and Causality' 136.

accomplices responsible *for* the wrongs of their principals. As discussed below, this is the approach in the United States and England and Wales.[63] It should be conceded that complicity rules structured in this way offer certain advantages. For one, they provide a forensic benefit,[64] as it can sometimes be difficult to identify the precise contribution made by each one of a number of participants in a certain wrong.[65] Although a robust doctrine of joint venture may mitigate this difficulty, there may still be uncertainty as to the particular roles played by the various participants.[66] Imputational complicity renders this uncertainty less consequential in that it need only be established that a particular participant aided or encouraged the commission of the wrong. In addition, imputational rules more directly connect accomplices to the harm that they help to bring about. In doing so, the condemnatory element of the law is heightened.[67]

However, these advantages cannot overcome principled objections to imputational complicity. Where the subject of the rule is a person, decisions about responsibility implicate the principle of autonomy—recognition of moral agency.[68] In this context, autonomy sustains a principle of culpability, which demands that agents are held responsible for their own wrongdoing.[69]

Where the subject of the rule is a state, the recognition of international legal personality is premised on an analogous idea. It is foundational in international law that state responsibility requires that conduct (i) is attributable to the state, and (ii) constitutes a breach of the state's international obligations.[70] This flows from the principle of sovereignty in international law. As Nollkaemper and Jacobs explain:

> Sovereignty implies that a state is not responsible for acts of another state (or more generally another legal person). Just as international criminal law rejects the concepts

[63] See section 2.4.2 below.

[64] William Wilson, 'A Rational Scheme of Liability for Participating in Crime' (2008) Crim L Rev 3.

[65] Law Commission, *Inchoate Liability for Assisting and Encouraging Crime* (Law Com No 300, 2006) [2.10].

[66] See Smith, *A Treatise on Complicity* 27–30.

[67] KJM Smith, 'The Law Commission Consultation Paper on Complicity: Part 1: A Blueprint for Rationalism' (1994) Crim L Rev 239, 244.

[68] Andrew Ashworth, *Principles of Criminal Law* (6th edn. OUP 2009) 23–4.

[69] Mirjan Damaška, 'The Shadow Side of Command Responsibility' (2001) 49 Am J of Comp L 455, 464; Joshua Dressler, 'Reforming Complicity Law: Trivial Assistance as a Lesser Offence' (2008) 5 Ohio State J of Crim L 427, 434–5.

[70] Art 2 ARSIWA.

of collective responsibility or guilt by association, instead relying on the principle of individual autonomy to limit responsibility to individuals only for their actual conduct, states resist principles of responsibility that require them to be responsible for conduct other than their own.[71]

States are right to resist such principles of responsibility. In addition, holding accomplices responsible for the principal's wrong conflicts with the principle of fair labelling.[72] In terms of the law's declarative function, it is crucial to accurately label wrongdoing.[73] Moreover, it is a matter of fairness to wrongdoers that their conduct is accurately labelled and condemned.[74] In imputational systems, an accomplice who knowingly gives a victim's whereabouts to a murderer is held responsible as a murderer, even though she did not, in fact, commit murder.[75] A more accurate description of her wrongdoing might be defined as assisting murder or facilitating murder.[76] A state that knowingly provides weapons to the principal state to commit an act of genocide would be held responsible for that act of genocide, rather than for its own wrong of assisting or facilitating genocide.

So complicity is a particular way of contributing to wrongdoing—a way of participating in a wrong committed by another actor. In accounting for complicity in law, there are principled reasons for holding accomplices responsible for their own contribution to the principal's wrong, rather than for the wrong itself. In criminal law, the central means of achieving this end is through a differentiated model of participation in wrongdoing. A differentiated model of participation distinguishes principals from other participants in the wrong.[77] The German Criminal Code is illustrative. Section 25 encompasses three forms of principalship.[78] The central form is direct perpetration—the person commits the offence himself.[79] Related to this is co-perpetration—two or more people jointly engage in the proscribed conduct.[80] The third form is indirect perpetration—a person commits the crime through another person.[81] Underpinning the three categories is the concept

[71] Nollkaemper and Jacobs, 'Shared Responsibility in International Law' 386.

[72] For an in-depth discussion, see James Chalmers and Fiona Leverick, 'Fair Labelling in Criminal Law' (2008) 71 MLR 217.

[73] Ashworth, *Principles of Criminal Law* 78.

[74] Ibid.

[75] Dressler, 'Reforming Complicity Law' 433.

[76] See Daniel Yeager, 'Helping, Doing, and the Grammar of Complicity' (1996) 15 Crim Just Eth 25.

[77] Eser, 'Individual Criminal Responsibility' 782.

[78] StGB § 25.

[79] StGB § 25(1).

[80] StGB § 25(2); Dubber, 'Criminalizing Complicity' 979.

[81] StGB § 25(1).

of *Tatherrschaft*—dominion over the act.[82] Dominion over the act is used to draw the line between principals and accomplices.[83]

The concept of *Tatherrschaft* is not the only way to distinguish principalship from secondary participation. *Tatherrschaft* is a normative model of principalship, its organizing device a judgment about responsibility.[84] Other normative models exist, with varying considerations built into the theory of agency. At the other end of a continuum is a naturalistic model, which looks to the actual course of events in the natural world.[85] The principal is she who does the deed or causes the proscribed result. In assigning individual criminal responsibility, a naturalistic model starts with the person who pulls the trigger and considers the range of reprehensible relationships to that crime.[86] It should be conceded, however, that a naturalistic model is still faced with difficult questions about what it means to 'do the deed' or 'cause the result'.

The role of accomplice liability obviously shifts in accordance with the breadth of principalship. In the German system, complicity is predominantly accounted for in two provisions. Section 26 establishes the responsibility of instigators—those who induce another to commit an unlawful act.[87] Complicity in this form is a matter of psychological influence.[88] Section 27 establishes the responsibility of aiders.[89] Here, the concern is primarily with the provision of assistance, though residual forms of psychological influence also fall within Section 27.[90] So the German differentiated model of participation comprises three forms of principalship, bounded by a theory of dominion over the act, and two forms of accomplice liability. This is not the only way to define either principalship or accomplice liability in criminal law. Conceptually, a differentiated model is limited only by the variety of words we have to describe the ways we might participate in crime. Crimes

[82] Dubber, 'Criminalizing Complicity' 981. For wider discussion of the concept of *Tatherrschaft* in the works of its originator, see Claus Roxin, *Täterschaft und Tatherrschaft* (1st edn. Cram, De Gruyter & Co 1963); Claus Roxin, 'Crimes as Part of Organized Power Structures' (Belinda Cooper tr.) (2011) 9 J Intl Crim Just 193.

[83] Ibid.

[84] Van Sliedregt, *Individual Criminal Responsibility* 72; Joachim Vogel, 'How to Determine Individual Criminal Responsibility in Systemic Contexts: Twelve Models' (2002) Cahiers de Défense Sociale 151, 155.

[85] Van Sliedregt, *Individual Criminal Responsibility* 71.

[86] Vogel, 'Twelve Models' 154–5. Of course, the substantive crime—or the deed—may itself be defined broadly, rendering participants principals in terms of its definition.

[87] StGB § 26.

[88] See Nigel Foster and Satish Sule, *German Legal System and Laws* (4th edn. OUP 2010) 375. Instigating 'means to evoke another person's intent to commit an offence'.

[89] StGB § 27.

[90] Foster and Sule, *German Legal System and Laws* 376.

may be ordered, solicited, or induced, facilitated, aided, or abetted, procured, advised, or assisted. Crimes may be tolerated, sanctioned, or permitted.

The ways in which different forms of complicity are ordinarily proscribed are assessed in section 2.5.2 below. What is important is the structure of the differentiated system. A pure differentiated model of participation in crime distinguishes among participants at the level of the attribution of responsibility.[91] That is to say, there is a normative distinction within the code between principalship and accomplice liability. In Germany, under StGB § 26 the participant is held responsible for instigating the underlying offence; under StGB § 27 the participant is held responsible for assisting the commission of the underlying offence.[92] Accomplices are held responsible for complicity; the acts of their principals are not imputed to them. This is a conceptually coherent and normatively desirable approach to participation in wrongdoing.

2.4.2. Different Stages of Differentiation

To give a richer account of participation in wrongdoing, it is helpful to distinguish three kinds of differentiation:

A. doctrinal differentiation;
B. differentiation in the attribution of responsibility;
C. differentiation in the consequences of responsibility.

Doctrinal differentiation distinguishes among participants in wrongdoing at the level of legal doctrine. In the context of complicity, the law recognizes the category of accomplice, and with it certain doctrinal requirements of conduct and fault. Differentiation in the attribution of responsibility distinguishes among participants in wrongdoing at the stage of conviction or responsibility. An accomplice is not held responsible for the wrong of the principal but for her own contribution to that wrong. Differentiation in the consequences of responsibility distinguishes among participants at the sentencing or remedial stage of the system.

In criminal law, the principles of culpability and fair labelling require, ideally, differentiation amongst participants at each of the three stages. Where the subject of the rule is a state, the principle of sovereignty similarly demands differentiation at each of the three stages. In assessing the approach of various legal systems to the issue of differentiation, a lesson may be drawn from Anglo-American complicity law. Doctrinally, Anglo-American law does not follow a unitary model of participation in crime. The federal complicity rule in the United States speaks of aiders, abettors, counsellors, commanders,

[91] Van Sliedregt, *Individual Criminal Responsibility* 70. [92] StGB § 26; StGB § 27.

inducers, and procurers.[93] In England and Wales, the Accessories and Abettors Act of 1861 refers to aiders, abettors, counsellors, and procurers.[94] Thus judgments are littered with assessments in these terms. In other words, there is doctrinal differentiation among participants in crime.

However, both the federal complicity rule in the US and the Accessories and Abettors Act in England and Wales are unitary at the level of responsibility and punishment.[95] In the US, 18 USC § 2 makes an accomplice punishable as a principal.[96] Although the provision refers only to punishment, it is rarely suggested that there is differentiation in the attribution of responsibility.[97] Accomplices are not convicted of abetting murder or assisting a robbery, but of murder or robbery.[98] This point is made more explicit in the American Law Institute's Model Penal Code. Section 2.06 provides that an accomplice 'is legally accountable for the conduct of another person . . . '.[99] In England and Wales, the Accessories and Abettors Act renders accomplices liable to be indicted, tried, and punished as principals.[100] Despite doctrinal differences between different forms of complicity, each leads to the same verdict—conviction of the principal's offence.

The lesson here is that we should look beyond the fact of doctrinal recognition of complicity to understand how the accomplice is held responsible and

[93] 18 USC § 2 (1994). See also Model Penal Code § 2.06(2) and (3) (Proposed Official Draft 1962):

(2) A person is legally accountable for the conduct of another person when:

. . .

(c) he is an accomplice of such other person in the commission of the offense.

(3) A person is an accomplice of another person in the commission of an offense if:

(a) with the purpose of promoting or facilitating the commission of the offense, he

(i) solicits such other person to commit it, or

(ii) aids or agrees or attempts to aid such other person in planning or committing it, or

(iii) having a legal duty to prevent the commission of the offense, fails to make proper effort so to do.

[94] Accessories and Abettors Act, s 8: 'Whosoever shall aid, abet, counsel, or procure the commission of any indictable offence . . . shall be liable to be tried, indicted, and punished as a principal offender.'

[95] Van Sliedregt, *Individual Criminal Responsibility* 70–1.

[96] 18 USC § 2 (1994).

[97] See Weisberg, 'Reappraising Complicity' 224: 'Thus, the modern view is that complicity is not a distinct crime, but a way of committing a crime'; Dressler, 'Reforming Complicity Law' 433.

[98] Dressler, 'Reassessing the Theoretical Underpinnings of Accomplice Liability' n 3.

[99] Model Penal Code § 2.06(2)(c) (Proposed Official Draft 1962).

[100] Accessories and Abettors Act, s 8. See PR Glazebrook, 'Structuring the Criminal Code: Functional Approaches to Complicity, Incomplete Offences, and General Defences' in Andrew Simester and ATH Smith (eds.) *Harm and Culpability* (Clarendon 1996) 195, 200: 'The basic principle underlying the modern law of complicity is, thus, quite simply, that a person may commit an offence in one or other of two ways. He may do so either by doing what has been declared to be an offence or by helping or encouraging someone else to do that.'

punished. In assessing different rules, we should also be aware that the same result—imputation of the conduct of a principal to an accomplice—may also be achieved through the definitional trick of including complicit conduct within the terms of the substantive offence.[101] For instance, the West Virginia Code criminalizes arson in the following manner:

> Any person who willfully and maliciously sets fire to or burns, or who causes to be burned, *or who aids, counsels, procures, persuades, incites, entices or solicits any person to burn*, any dwelling, whether occupied, unoccupied or vacant, or any outbuilding, whether the property of himself or herself or of another, *shall be guilty of arson in the first degree* and, upon conviction thereof, be sentenced to the penitentiary for a definite term of imprisonment which is not less than two nor more than twenty years.[102]

Evidently, the definition of the substantive offence does the work of imputation in respect of arson. The aider, the counsellor, the procurer—each is responsible for the substantive offence of arson in the first degree. In this case, there is most likely overlap with the general complicity rule operating in West Virginia.[103] Nonetheless, the rule demonstrates another way of achieving the same result: the responsibility of a participant for wrongdoing committed by the principal.[104]

Where a legal system differentiates between principals and accomplices at the level of the attribution of responsibility, it will ordinarily follow that the accomplice is punished for her own contribution to the principal's wrong rather than for the acts of the principal. That is to say, there will ordinarily be differentiation in the consequences of responsibility. In criminal cases this does not mean that the tariff will not be set by reference to the principal's crime—it is, of course, more reprehensible to aid murder than to aid robbery. In Germany, aiders under StGB § 27 receive at least a discount of a quarter vis-à-vis the principal.[105] It also does not mean that certain accomplices will not be punished to the same extent as the principal. Those convicted as instigators under StGB § 26 are liable to be sentenced as if they were principals.[106]

[101] See Vogel, 'Twelve Models' 160–1.

[102] W Va Code § 61-3-1 (1977) cited in Paul Robinson, 'Imputed Criminal Liability' (1984) 93 Yale L J 609, n 6 (emphasis added).

[103] The orthodox approach to accomplice liability in West Virginia may be found in *State* v. *Fortner*, 182 W Va 345, 387 S.E.2d 812 (1989).

[104] See George Fletcher, *Rethinking Criminal Law* (first published 1978, OUP 2000) 649–50: 'Aiding another person to commit a crime renders one an accomplice, and being an accomplice is simply one way of "being guilty of an offence." This way of approaching the problem of what the code calls "liability for conduct of another" is but a technique for rounding out the definition of particular offences. Every offence has built into it a penumbral orbit of liability for those who aid others in committing the offence.'

[105] StGB § 27, 49(1)(2). See also Dubber, 'Criminalizing Complicity' 984.

[106] StGB § 26.

More interesting are the practices of legal systems that use imputational complicity rules. Even if an accomplice is held responsible for murder rather than for complicity in murder, judicial discretion might enable an accomplice's lower degree of participation to be taken into account at the sentencing stage.[107] The obvious temptation is to suggest that it does not matter that accomplices are held responsible as principals if differences in culpability can be reflected at sentencing.[108] Such a suggestion is unwarranted. No doubt variations in sentencing do denote important assessments regarding the culpability of participants in crime. However, where the accomplice is actually held responsible for the principal's wrong, sentence variations at best mitigate the violation of the principles of culpability and fair labelling. The accomplice is still held responsible for murder and labelled as a murderer.

The question of sentencing is linked to another point. The principled concerns about culpability and fair labelling are sometimes obscured by arguments about the relative blameworthiness of accomplices and principals. Generally, those who assist or encourage wrongdoing are less culpable that those who commit it.[109] Of course, as we move up the scale of influence from encouragement, to instigation, to ordering, the picture becomes cloudier.[110] In part, by capturing within principalship those who control the commission of the offence, a normative model of perpetration addresses these concerns.[111] But more generally, even if there are situations in which an instigator or facilitator is as blameworthy as (or more blameworthy than) the principal, she still did not commit the principal wrong. The principles of culpability and fair labelling require that instigators and facilitators are held responsible and punished for instigation and facilitation. Increased blameworthiness vis-à-vis the principal may be expressed at sentencing.

In sum, then, there are two points here. First, we should not let doctrinal differentiation of participation in wrongdoing blind us to what is happening

[107] See Fletcher, *Rethinking Criminal Law* 636–7.

[108] See James Stewart, 'The End of "Modes of Liability" for International Crimes' (2012) 25 Leiden J Intl L 165, 171: 'I argue that whatever moral significance there might be between making a difference to a crime and "making a difference to the difference that principals make", this discrepancy can be adequately accounted for at the sentencing stage of a criminal trial.' (footnote omitted).

[109] Ashworth, *Principles of Criminal Law* 406.

[110] In the context of mass atrocity, this point is sometimes seen to raise what is called the Hitler-as-accomplice problem—see Stewart, 'The End of Modes of Liability' 166–7; Osiel, 'Making Sense of Atrocity' 85. This problem, to the extent it is a problem, may be resolved in a number of ways, including by the adoption of a normative model of principalship, through the use of ordering as a heightened mode of participation, or by precise definition of the wrong in question.

[111] Of course, we should be careful of over-refined distinctions in separating various forms of participation. For a related discussion, see section 2.5.2 below.

at the level of responsibility and punishment. Second, differentiation in the consequences of responsibility, often obtained through judicial discretion, mitigates but does not obviate principled concerns about holding an accomplice responsible for a wrong she did not commit. In Austin's term, the pronouncement of a court or tribunal is verdictive; it is an official judgment, in this case concerning responsibility.[112] Where accomplices are held responsible as though they committed the wrong, there is verdictive congruence where there ought to be none. A principled scheme of participation in wrongdoing would hold accomplices responsible for, and label them in terms of, their own contribution to the principal's wrong.

2.4.3. Substantive Complicity Rules

The discussion up to this point on structuring complicity rules has assessed complicity as it is accounted for in the general part of the criminal law. In this context, there are principled reasons for preferring differentiation between principals and accomplices in the attribution of responsibility. Another way to reach the same result is through substantive complicity rules. Rules of this kind sanction complicity as its own substantive wrong.[113] Some scholars implicitly assume that these rules are not a form of complicity because there is no imputation of the conduct of the principal to the accomplice.[114] This assumption is unfounded. Although the prevailing approach to complicity in some systems is imputational, other forms of derivative liability that hold actors responsible for helping or influencing another actor to commit wrongdoing are still complicity rules. Although complicity rules are always derivative, they are not always imputational.

In the US, concerns with imputational criminal complicity have provoked tentative moves towards the substantive complicity model. An example may be found in New York State's facilitation laws.[115] Facilitation, rather than denoting a form of assistance for the purposes of imputational complicity liability, constitutes a criminal offence per se. The New York Penal Law creates four degrees of the offence of criminal facilitation.[116] Criminal facilitation in the second degree is illustrative of the statute's approach:

> A person is guilty of criminal facilitation in the second degree when, believing it probable that he is rendering aid to a person who intends to commit a class A felony, he engages in conduct which provides such person with means or opportunity for

112 JL Austin, *How to Do Things with Words* (OUP 1962) 150.

113 See Vogel, 'Twelve Models' 160–1 for a framing of 'general part' versus 'special part' models.

114 See Dubber, 'Criminalizing Complicity' 993.

115 Weisberg 'Reappraising Complicity' 261.

116 New York Penal Law § 115.

the commission thereof and which in fact aids such person to commit such class A felony.

Criminal facilitation in the second degree is a class C felony.[117]

This is a substantive complicity rule. Criminal facilitation rules of this kind avoid both the problem of exclusively inchoate offences[118] and the principled objections to imputational complicity.[119] In respect of the former, they impose a sanction that responds to the additional responsibility of the accomplice where the principal wrong occurs.[120] In respect of the latter, the facilitator is held responsible only for his own contribution to the principal wrong.

New York State's compromise facilitation laws hint at another advantage accruing to non-imputational complicity rules. The use of complicity as an imputational doctrine denies any normative difference between different forms of complicity. Aiders, counsellors, encouragers, and facilitators are all responsible for the principal's wrong. Imputation prevents distinctions from being drawn not only between principals and accomplices but also among different kinds of accomplices, at least at the stage of the attribution of responsibility. For instance, those who incite or induce another to commit crime may bear greater responsibility than those who simply advise on, say, the possibilities of escape.[121] The German Criminal Code recognizes this distinction by refusing to allow to instigators the sentencing discount available to facilitators.[122] Other differences among modes of complicity are imaginable. This point is taken up in section 2.5.2 below.

Substantive complicity rules open up the possibility of drawing distinctions in terms of both the forms of complicity prohibited and the wrongdoing committed by the principal actor.[123] Many jurisdictions have created a substantive offence of assisting the escape of a prisoner.[124] For instance, Section 575.230 of the Missouri Revised Statutes provides that aiding the escape of a prisoner being held on a felony charge or conviction is itself

117 New York Penal Law § 115.05.

118 See section 2.4.4 below.

119 See section 2.4.1 above.

120 Legal systems may also proscribe failed attempts at complicity. In England and Wales, inchoate crimes of assisting or encouraging crime were introduced by ss 44–46 of the Serious Crime Act 2007. See Andrew Simester, John Spencer, Robert Sullivan, Graham Virgo, *Simester and Sullivan's Criminal Law: Theory and Doctrine* (4th edn. Hart 2010) 253–4; Fletcher, *Rethinking Criminal Law* 680–1.

121 See Fletcher, *Rethinking Criminal Law* 671–2.

122 StGB § 26; StGB § 27.

123 Weisberg 'Reappraising Complicity' 264.

124 Offences of this kind may have been introduced to remedy (incorrectly) perceived difficulties arising on the basis that the status of the principal—in this case, a prisoner—meant that others could not be complicit in his crime. Although a non-prisoner cannot commit the crime of escaping from prison, it is not the case that a non-prisoner cannot contribute to—that is, be complicit in—such an escape. See Kadish, 'Complicity, Cause and Blame' 372–4.

a class B felony.[125] Of course, the escape is itself a crime for which the prisoner is liable.[126] However, the aider is responsible for his own actions. Here we see the prohibition of a general form of complicity—aiding—in a specific crime.

A rule might be specific at both the level of the complicit conduct and in terms of the assisted wrong. In international law, the rule reflected in Article 3(f) of the Definition of Aggression prohibits states from allowing their territory to be used by another state to commit an act of aggression against a third state.[127] The rule does not prohibit states from aiding acts of aggression in ways other than the provision of territory. Likewise, it does not prohibit states from allowing their territory to be used in the commission of any internationally wrongful act other than aggression. It prohibits a specific kind of complicit conduct in a specific wrong.

So there are two ways that a legal system may prohibit complicity without imputing the conduct of the principal to the accomplice. The first, often found in the general part of the criminal law, uses a model of participation in wrongdoing that distinguishes amongst participants at the level of the attribution of responsibility. The second uses specific substantive complicity rules. Both may be termed non-imputational complicity. In each case, accomplices are held responsible in terms of their own fault and conduct; that is to say, for their contribution to the principal's wrong. In contrast to imputational complicity rules, both approaches reflect in law that complicity is a particular way of contributing to wrongdoing.

2.4.4. Inchoate Liability: Getting Rid of Complicity?

So far, this chapter has set out a definition of complicity, assessed the wrongness of complicity, and considered the ways in which complicity rules may be structured, the last-mentioned giving rise to a preference for non-imputational complicity. Before setting out the analytical framework of the work, it is important to consider a challenge to complicity emanating from another direction. This challenge proposes a shift away from complicity as a derivative form of responsibility, instead establishing inchoate wrongs of

[125] Mo Rev Stat § 575.230.1:

> A person commits the crime of aiding escape of a prisoner if the person:
>
> . . .
>
> (2) Assists or attempts to assist any prisoner who is being held in custody or confinement for the purpose of effecting the prisoner's escape from custody or confinement.

See also Weisberg, 'Reappraising Complicity' 221.

[126] Mo Rev Stat § 575.210.

[127] UNGA Res 3314 (XXIX) (14 December 1974) (Definition of Aggression).

assisting and encouraging wrongdoing.[128] Under such a scheme, the responsibility of the complicit actor is founded in law at the moment she performs her culpable acts of assistance or encouragement.[129] In England and Wales, this shift was evident in the development of the common law offence of incitement. Incitement, in this context, is essentially synonymous with encouragement.[130] The inciter's liability is fixed at the moment of incitement, regardless of whether the incited party perpetrates the crime.

Crucially, under such a scheme it does not matter for the purposes of the participant's responsibility whether or not the wrong is committed.[131] Responsibility is entirely inchoate rather than derivative. The adoption of inchoate responsibility of this kind would signal the end of complicity as a legal doctrine.

There is a principled attraction to the inchoate model. In many cases, once the complicit actor has performed her acts of assistance or encouragement with the requisite culpability, the occurrence of the harm is outside of her control. It is an instance of moral luck.[132] Consider these examples:

1. D, knowing that P intends to burgle V's premises, leaves a ladder outside V's house in order to assist P to enter the premises. On learning that V has returned from holiday earlier than expected, P abandons the project.
2. D, knowing that P intends to burgle V's premises, leaves a ladder outside V's house to assist P to enter the premises. P, unaware that D has left the ladder, commits the burglary without using the ladder.
3. D, knowing that P intends to burgle V's premises, leaves a ladder outside V's house to assist P to enter the premises. P uses the ladder to commit the burglary.[133]

In the first example, the burglary is not committed. In the second, the burglary is committed without D's assistance. In the final example, D successfully assists in the commission of the offence. If we think the defendant in the final example should be treated equivalently to the first two then a system of inchoate responsibility should be adopted.

This issue forms part of a larger philosophical debate concerning the roles of harm and moral luck in assessing the gravity of wrongdoing, a debate prominent in the theory of liability for attempts in criminal law. Criminal

128 See Law Commission, *Assisting and Encouraging Crime* (Law Com CP No 131, 1993).

129 Ibid [4.24].

130 Law Com No 300 [3.19]; *Marlow* [1998] 1 Cr App R (S) 273, 275.

131 In this sense, an analogy may be drawn to the obligation of *non-refoulement* in international law—responsibility is not contingent on subsequent wrongdoing by the receiving state.

132 Andrew Ashworth, 'Belief, Intent, and Criminal Liability' in John Eekelaar and John Bell (eds.) *Oxford Essays in Jurisprudence—Third Series* (Clarendon 1987) 1, 16–20.

133 See Law Com No 300 [3.2]–[3.5].

liability is ordinarily based on (i) the harm caused and (ii) the culpability of the perpetrator.[134] The classic example in attempts liability concerns two people, both of whom intend to kill their victim by shooting.[135] In the first case, the victim is hit and dies. In the second case, the bullet misses. Subjectivist theorists advance a thesis that the moral position of the two shooters is no different.[136] Taken a step further, judgments as to their culpability, and thus as to criminal responsibility and punishment, should be alike.[137]

Although alluring, the subjectivist thesis is not entirely convincing. One objection focuses on the expressive goals of the criminal law. For the law to embrace the subjectivists' moral equivalence thesis is for it to say that it does not matter to the law whether or not the harm results.[138] But harm should matter to the perpetrator, to the law, and to us.[139] A second objection, in cases of attempted complicity, concerns the reach of the criminal law and its effect on individual liberty in the absence of behaviour that causes harm. Strictly speaking, these objections are more accurately located in the realm of legal theory than moral theory, for the concerns are grounded explicitly in the role and effects of the criminal law itself.[140]

At the level of moral theory, it should be conceded that arguments based on respective culpability are not conclusive in either direction.[141] Nonetheless, there is intuitive appeal to the claim that luck rightly influences judgments about morality. As Nagel puts it:

> Whether we succeed or fail in what we try to do nearly always depends to some extent on factors beyond our control. This is true of murder, altruism, revolution, the sacrifice of certain interests for the sake of others—almost any morally important act. What has been done, and what is morally judged, is partly determined by external factors... [T]here is a morally significant difference between reckless driving and manslaughter. But whether a reckless driver hits a pedestrian depends on the presence of the pedestrian at the point where he recklessly passes a red light.[142]

[134] Ashworth, *Principles of Criminal Law* 438; JC Smith, 'Some Problems of the Reform of the Law of Offences against the Person' (1978) 31 CLP 15; Ashworth, 'Belief, Intent, and Criminal Liability' 4.

[135] Ashworth, 'Belief, Intent, and Criminal Liability' 16.

[136] Ibid.

[137] See Antony Duff, *Criminal Attempts* (OUP 1996) 335.

[138] Antony Duff, *Intention, Agency and Criminal Liability—Philosophy of Action and the Criminal Law* (Blackwell 1990) 191.

[139] Ibid.

[140] Andrew Ashworth, 'Taking the Consequences' in Stephen Shute, John Gardner, and Jeremy Horder (eds.) *Action and Value in Criminal Law* (Clarendon 1993) 107, 113.

[141] For a recent discussion, see Susan Wolf, 'The Moral of Moral Luck' (2013) 31 Philosophic Exchange 5.

[142] Thomas Nagel, *Mortal Questions* (CUP 1979) 25.

On this account, consequences matter. Accounting for the harm (and good) we bring about is an essential part of morality, responding to our capacity as causal agents. Nagel's moral claim is generally upheld in contemporary assessments of the gravity of offences.[143] In the context of criminal attempts, it seems right that we hold the murderer more blameworthy than the attempted murderer, even though it may be a matter of luck that one is not the other, or vice versa. So it should be in complicity. Successful attempts at assistance or encouragement are more reprehensible than unsuccessful attempts, for successful attempts actually contribute to wrongdoing. A system of inchoate liability that treats the two alike does not accurately reflect the increased culpability of those who successfully help or influence principal wrongdoers.

2.4.5. Conclusion

Complicity is a particular way of contributing to wrongdoing. In reflecting this, legal systems should hold accomplices responsible for their own contribution to the principal's wrong, rather than for the wrong of their principal. This is the normative claim of the work. In this form, complicity avoids the principled objections to imputational responsibility as well as the inadequate attention to consequences inherent in an inchoate model. This normative claim is used to evaluate the ways in which international law prohibits state and individual complicity.

2.5. Prohibiting Complicity: An Analytical Framework

2.5.1. Introduction

The argument thus far has sought to establish the normative claim of the work; namely, that doctrines of complicity ought to give rise to responsibility and sanction for the accomplice's contribution to the principal's wrong. It is against this standard that the complicity rules binding states and individuals in international law will be assessed.

Any attempt to prohibit complicit conduct must resolve at least three issues. The first concerns the forms of complicity prohibited. Between and within the categories of help and influence, legal systems take different approaches. It is conceivable that one legal system prohibits only help and another only influence. Moreover, within the category of influence, certain

[143] See Paul Robinson and John Darley, 'Objectivist v. Subjectivist Views of Criminality: A Study in the Role of Social Science in Criminal Law Theory' (1998) 18 OJLS 409.

modes of complicity may be specifically incorporated or rejected. This issue relates to the second—the required nexus between the assistance or influence provided and the principal's wrong. How do we account for that relationship? Should there be a substantiality criterion limiting the reach of accomplice liability? The third issue concerns the fault required of the accomplice. What forms of fault are appropriate for complicity?

The rest of this section constructs a framework around these three issues, using domestic criminal law and criminal law theory to give colour to these questions as they arise in Parts B and C of the work. In this respect, a few caveats are necessary. First, the analytical framework constituted by these three elements is not the only way to structure an assessment of complicity. Other approaches are conceivable. The present framework simply draws out commonly occurring questions arising across legal systems seeking to prohibit complicity and provides a general assessment of the normative choices at stake.

Second, it should be borne in mind that the framework is exactly that—a framework, in this case set up to serve the analysis of how complicity might be prohibited. It does not itself prescribe a singular conception of complicity that ought to apply across international law as a whole. In evaluating the rules, attention must of course be paid to the nature of the legal subject bound by the rule and to the heterogeneity of interests at stake in different areas of international law.

Third, and related to the second point, it should be emphasized that the three elements of the analytical framework are inter-dependent—the appropriate nexus element may depend on the breadth of conduct sanctioned, which in turn may depend on the fault required of the accomplice. The three elements of complicity rules set out in the analytical framework work together to prohibit actors from participating in the wrongdoing of others.

2.5.2. Issue One: Forms of Complicity

2.5.2.1. Helping and Influencing

As noted above, the terms used in criminal law to prohibit complicity are numerous—aiding, abetting, assisting, facilitating, inciting, inducing, soliciting, encouraging, instigating, and so on. Each of these denotes a form of complicity, some of which overlap, at times entirely. The challenge for the law is to draw principled lines and establish workable doctrine. In terms of the principle of fair labelling, categories of wrongdoing should be differentiated to reflect morally significant differences in blameworthiness.[144] In addition,

[144] Ashworth, *Principles of Criminal Law* 78.

as Ashworth puts it, 'where people generally regard two types of conduct as different, the law should try to reflect that difference'.[145]

As a starting point, Kadish's division of complicity into cases of help and cases of influence is useful.[146] Of course, the distinction is not watertight. Although acts that influence the decision of the perpetrator to commit the wrong cannot generally be considered acts of help, the converse is not true.[147] Fletcher gives the example of a German case where the accomplice provided a key to the principal to facilitate his theft of wine from a cellar.[148] The key did not fit the lock so the principal broke into the cellar.[149] Nonetheless, it is easy to view the provision of the key—the help—as an act that influences the decision of the principal to commit the wrong.

Despite the overlap, a general division between help and influence makes sense. In criminal law, the doctrines of aiding and abetting are sometimes thought to map onto this distinction.[150] However, the gravity of different kinds of conduct falling within a single category of influence is too wide-ranging. Compare these two scenarios:

A. A local drug dealer, A1, is owed money by P1. P1 is broke. A1 tells P1 that if he beats up V the debt will be forgiven. P1 beats up V.
B. A2 sees P2 beating up V. He shouts encouragement to P2 from across the street. P2 continues to beat up V.

Both A1 and A2 are complicit in the assault but there is a morally significant difference in their culpability. A useful way to draw a line between instigation and encouragement turns on the provision by the accomplice of a *reason* for action.[151] A helpful formulation in this respect is Hart and Honoré's: the instigator 'should by his words or deeds have done something to render some course of action more *eligible* in the eyes of the [principal] than it would otherwise have been'.[152] So far as possible, the law should recognize this difference in culpability.

In this regard, the scheme envisaged in Article 25(3) of the Rome Statute of the International Criminal Court, for instance, makes sense.[153] Article 25(3)

145 Ibid 79.

146 Kadish, 'Complicity, Cause and Blame' 342. See also Smith, *A Treatise on Complicity* 33.

147 See Dressler, 'Reforming Complicity Law' 22.

148 Fletcher, *Rethinking Criminal Law* 677–8.

149 Ibid.

150 See *Mrkšić, Radić, Šljivančanin* (Trial Chamber Judgment) IT-95-13/1-T (27 September 2007) [551]; William A Schabas, *The International Criminal Court—A Commentary on the Rome Statute* (OUP 2010) 434; Eser, 'Individual Criminal Responsibility' 799.

151 HLA Hart and Tony Honoré, *Causation in the Law* (2nd edn. Clarendon 1985) 54.

152 Ibid.

153 Rome Statute of the International Criminal Court (adopted 17 July 1998, entered into force 1 July 2002) 2187 UNTS 90.

distinguishes between inducing and soliciting, on one hand, and abetment, on the other, as forms of influence on the decision of the perpetrator to commit the crime.[154] Inducing and soliciting wrongdoing may be regarded as synonymous with instigation. Abetment may be regarded as synonymous with encouragement. Once we divide cases of influence into instigation and encouragement, the respective label conveys, more or less, the degree of blameworthiness of the instigator or encourager.[155] Of course, there will still be some context-specific variance of culpability within each category, turning on the position of the accomplice, the relationship between the accomplice and the principal, and the force of the instigation or encouragement. But for the most part, the label gives a fair description of the wrongfulness of the accomplice's conduct.

The category of help or assistance presents a trickier challenge for the principle of fair labelling. Husak argues that 'almost no one would be inclined to use generalizations such as '"Bill aided a crime"...or "Howard helped Elizabeth commit a murder"'.[156] Moreover, there may be normatively significant differences between driving a getaway car, holding a ladder, providing a gun, and failing to lock a door.[157] If this is so, we may want these differences reflected in labelling.[158]

One solution may lie in the regulation of specific kinds of complicit conduct within the category of assistance. There is a potential red herring here. The required specialization does not (only) refer to the principal crime aided, but to the *kind* of complicit conduct. In other words, this challenge is not met by defining a specific crime of aiding in the escape of a prisoner. The law would need to differentiate among normatively different forms of aiding—perhaps financing, providing weapons, knowing failure to prevent in breach of a specific duty, and so on. There are risks here, though. The aforementioned kinds of complicit conduct are themselves liable for further sub-division, and they do not nearly account for the myriad ways we might assist another actor's commission of wrongdoing.[159] In addition, there are issues of over-complexity and accessibility in moving towards an ever more refined and differentiated code.[160]

[154] Art 25 Rome Statute. [155] See Hart and Honoré, *Causation in the Law* 378.

[156] See Doug Husak, 'Abetting a Crime' (2014) 33 L & Phil 41, 61. [157] Ibid.

[158] Ashworth, *Principles of Criminal Law* 78.

[159] Christopher Kutz, 'Causeless Complicity' (2007) 1 Crim L & Phil 289, 294.

[160] See Ashworth, *Principles of Criminal Law* 80–1; Chalmers and Leverick, 'Fair Labelling in Criminal Law' 23–8. See also Jeremy Horder, 'Rethinking Non-Fatal Offences against the Person' (1994) 14 OJLS 335, 339 for a framing of labelling as falling between particularism and moral vacuity.

This problem requires further work. One option might be to draw from the general barrel of assistance certain particularly culpable or easily differentiated kinds of complicit conduct. The proliferation of materials concerning financing of terrorism is a step in this direction.[161] In international law, an interesting example is again the rule reflected in Article 3(f) of the Definition of Aggression: the obligation imposed on states not to allow their territory to be used by another state for an act of aggression.[162] Here we see the prohibition of a very specific kind of complicit conduct.

Despite these difficulties, it remains useful to divide up complicity into two categories of influence—instigation and encouragement—and one form of assistance. A legal system may use a combination of these terms or their synonyms to prohibit complicity. It may prohibit one without the others or divide them further. At the top end of the culpability spectrum, forms of influence and assistance that cross into principalship are excluded from complicity. Assuming a normative model of perpetration, it is appropriate to assign principal responsibility to some secondary parties who do not physically do the deed.[163] This category includes at least those who order the commission of wrongdoing and those who use another as an innocent instrumentality.[164] Given the scalar quality of influence and assistance, there are no doubt difficult boundary decisions to be made.[165] But neither these boundary difficulties nor the challenge of labelling discussed above detracts from the broader normative claim of the work: the accomplice should not be held responsible for the principal's wrong.

2.5.2.2. Complicity and Omissions

2.5.2.2.1. Introduction

One recurring issue about the forms of conduct that constitute complicity concerns omissions. Given the range of preventive duties imposed on states, this issue resonates in international law and the law of state responsibility.[166] In addition, international criminal law is slowly coming to terms with omissions that help or encourage others to commit crimes.[167]

The central question is whether a failure to act may fulfil the conduct element of a particular rule of complicity. It is not controversial that an omission

[161] See Husak, 'Abetting a Crime' 63. [162] Art 3(f) Definition of Aggression.

[163] See section 2.4.1 above. [164] See Husak, 'Abetting a Crime' 57. [165] Ibid.

[166] See Art 2(1) Convention against Torture; Art I Convention on the Prevention and Punishment of the Crime of Genocide Convention (adopted 9 December 1948, entered into force 12 January 1951) 78 UNTS 277.

[167] See section 5.2 below; *Mrkšić, Šljivančanin* (Appeals Chamber Judgment) IT-95-13/1A (5 May 2009).

may be prohibited by a specific rule, the breach of which gives rise to direct liability.[168] In national legal systems, these offences are often statutory.[169] For instance, under the United Kingdom's Merchant Shipping Act of 1995, it is an offence for the master of a ship, on receiving at sea a signal of distress, to fail to assist an aircraft.[170] In international law, Article 85(4)(b) of Additional Protocol I to the Geneva Conventions requires the contracting parties to repatriate prisoners of war and civilians without unjustifiable delay, with the effect that failure to repatriate in good time engages the international responsibility of the state.[171]

These examples of direct responsibility are of less interest. More relevant are instances in which the omission might link the omitting party to the harm that results.[172] In criminal law, this may arise through principal omissions liability or accomplice omissions liability. In terms of principal liability, omissions may be a way of perpetrating the substantive offence. If, for instance, a parent allows his child to starve to death, this approach would categorize such conduct as murder.[173] This may be referred to as a prohibition of 'commission by omission',[174] and contrasted with the direct criminalization of an omission—in this case, perhaps, intentional neglect of a child. In terms of accomplice liability, an omission is a way in which the conduct element of complicity liability may be fulfilled. This may be thought of as commission of aiding and abetting by omission. Liability of this kind is underpinned by the same idea as commission by omission—an omission can be as wrongful as an act or, if not equally wrongful, sufficiently wrongful to justify criminal liability as though an act was committed.[175]

[168] Fletcher, *Rethinking Criminal Law* 422; Michael Duttwiler, 'Liability for Omission in International Criminal Law' (2006) 6 Intl Crim L Rev 1, 7–8.

[169] Fletcher, *Rethinking Criminal Law* 422. See generally Andrew Ashworth, 'The Scope of Criminal Liability for Omissions' (1989) 105 LQR 424.

[170] Merchant Shipping Act 1995, s 93. See Brian Hogan, 'Omissions and the Duty Myth' in Peter Smith (ed.) *Criminal Law: Essays in Honour of JC Smith* (Butterworths 1987) 85, 86.

[171] Art 85(4)(b) Protocol Additional to the Geneva Conventions of 12 August 1949, and relating to the Protection of Victims of International Armed Conflicts (adopted 8 June 1977, entered into force 7 December 1978) 1125 UNTS 3. See Duttwiler, 'Liability for Omission' 7–8.

[172] See Fletcher, *Rethinking Criminal Law* 423: 'The gravamen of liability for "breach of duty" is the breach itself; for commission by omission, the occurrence of a particular result.'

[173] See Ashworth, *Principles of Criminal Law* 98–9.

[174] Fletcher, *Rethinking Criminal Law* 422; Duttwiler, 'Liability for Omission' 5.

[175] Sanford Kadish, 'Act and Omission, *Mens Rea*, and Complicity: Approaches to Codification' (1989) 1 Crim L Forum 65, 70; Duttwiler, 'Liability for Omission' 5. See also StGB § 13; George Fletcher, 'Criminal Omissions: Some Perspectives' (1976) 24 Am J Comp L 703.

2.5.2.2.2. A Municipal Criminal Law Approach to Omissions

In criminal law, liability for a complicit omission is rare. In England and Wales, complicity through omission has most often arisen in the context of ownership or control of a vehicle or premises.[176] In *Rubie* v. *Faulkner*, for instance, a learner-driver was driving under the defendant's supervision in accordance with the Motor Vehicles (Driving Licenses) Regulations 1937.[177] The driver caused an accident and was convicted of driving without due care and attention. The defendant, who had sat passively in the front seat while the driver undertook a dangerous passing manoeuvre, was convicted at first instance of aiding and abetting by omission. The conviction was upheld on appeal on the basis of his failure to act in accordance with the duty imposed by the Regulations.[178] This approach has been applied in other cases of supervision of learner-drivers.[179]

The principle has also arisen in respect of motor vehicle owners who fail to intervene to prevent a principal from driving dangerously in their car[180] and licensees who fail to shut a public house as required, thereby aiding and abetting the consumption of intoxicating liquor outside of permitted hours.[181] Critically, in these cases the defendant was not under an independent duty to act but rather had a power of control.[182] Although there is some suggestion in other judgments that the defendant's complicity is founded on the encouragement that the principal receives from her inaction,[183] the better interpretation is that the failure to act where there is a power of control constitutes accomplice liability.[184] These cases might give us pause; it is an open question whether property ownership should itself be sufficient to ground a duty to act.[185]

Although the underlying theoretical bases of principal and accomplice liability are not the same,[186] in the absence of cases or scholarship on complicit omissions it makes sense to look to principal omissions liability. The key to understanding cases of commission by omission in England and Wales is the presence of a specific legal duty to prevent a particular result.[187]

176 Smith, *A Treatise on Complicity* 40. 177 [1940] 1 KB 571. 178 Ibid 574.

179 See *Harris* [1964] Crim LR 54; *Crampton* v. *Fish* [1969] 113 SJ 1003. See also Smith, *A Treatise on Complicity* 41.

180 *Du Cros* v. *Lambourne* [1907] 1 KB 40; *R* v. *Webster* [2006] EWCA Crim 415.

181 *Tuck* v. *Robson* [1970] 1 All ER 1171.

182 Ashworth, *Principles of Criminal Law* 411; Smith, *A Treatise on Complicity* 42–3.

183 See *Cassady* v. *Reg Morris (Transport) Ltd* [1975] RTR 470.

184 Smith, *A Treatise on Complicity* 42.

185 For discussion, see Ashworth, 'Criminal Liability for Omissions' 446–7.

186 Smith, *A Treatise on Complicity* 43–4.

187 Fletcher, *Rethinking Criminal Law* 611. In respect of Germany, see StGB § 13; Fletcher, 'Criminal Omissions' 703.

It is sufficient to sketch the common categories of duty.[188] First, the duty may arise on the basis of the relationship between the defendant and person suffering the harm. The relationship is usually one between parent and child or between spouses.[189] Second, duties may be imposed on the basis of the defendant's status. These are usually obligations of the kind imposed on doctors, nurses, and other professionals. Third, duties sufficient to give rise to criminal responsibility may be imposed on people who have a special relationship to the particular harm that arises.[190] The case of *Miller* is an apt illustration.[191] The defendant fell asleep with a lit cigarette. He awoke, and seeing the bed alight, simply moved to another room. The house caught fire. Miller's conviction for arson was upheld on the basis that he failed to take steps to avert the harm caused by his prior dangerous act.[192]

Finally, the duty may arise from the assumption of a specific responsibility or undertaking to act in a specific way.[193] In *Pittwood*, the defendant was employed by a railway company to control the gate at a crossing.[194] After he failed to do so a train struck a cart that was crossing the tracks, killing the victim. Pittwood was convicted of manslaughter. The exact source of the duty in *Pittwood* is not clear.[195] One possibility is that the source is the contract of employment itself.[196] A second possibility is that in cases of this kind, the *undertaking* to avert harm to someone or a class of people is an independent ground for imposing a duty.[197] In many cases, these two duties will arise together, and determining the exact source of the duty for the imposition of criminal responsibility will not matter.[198] For instance, a nurse may conclude a contract and undertake to care for a patient in her home.[199] If she fails to care for the patient, there is little doubt that a breach of contract arises. She will also have breached her undertaking to care for the patient. Whether the imposition of criminal liability is based on the contractual duty or the undertaking will not matter.

188 See generally Ashworth, 'Criminal Liability for Omissions' 439–59.

189 Ibid 612; Simester et al. *Simester and Sullivan's Criminal Law* 71.

190 Simester et al. *Simester and Sullivan's Criminal Law* 74–5.

191 *Miller* [1983] 2 AC 161.

192 Ibid. See Ashworth, 'Criminal Liability for Omissions' 439.

193 Fletcher, *Rethinking Criminal Law* 614–18; Simester et al. *Simester and Sullivan's Criminal Law* 73–4.

194 *Pittwood* [1902] 19 TLR 37.

195 Simester et al. *Simester and Sullivan's Criminal Law* 73.

196 See *Pittwood* [38].

197 Fletcher, *Rethinking Criminal Law* 615.

198 Ibid.

199 See *R* v. *Instan* [1893] 1 QB 450.

In other cases, however, determining the source of the duty might matter. As Fletcher puts it, in deciding whether the omission was sufficiently culpable for criminal liability 'it would hardly be helpful to get entangled in the intricacies of consideration and contractual validity'.[200] There might be difficult questions of third party reliance—say, for instance, where a drowning swimmer did not know that a lifeguard was hired for his protection—that do not necessarily affect any assessment of moral culpability.[201] A focus on the undertaking given by the defendant may remove some the vagaries of contract law and provide a more coherent basis for the imposition of omissions liability. Nonetheless, in the vast majority of cases the contract will still be the primary source in determining the existence and content of the duty.[202]

In each case, the defendant's capacity to have averted the harm is a required element of criminal liability. This is consistent with a basic principle of fairness.[203] Capacity also establishes that the omission was a factual cause of the harm—but for the failure to act the harm would not have resulted.[204] In this sense, capacity might relate to the ability of the defendant to have intervened. If a parent saw her child drowning but was unable to swim herself, no liability would arise for failing to dive in. Alternatively, capacity might relate more specifically to the underlying event. In *Morby*, for instance, the defendant failed to obtain medical treatment for his sick son because of his religious beliefs.[205] On appeal, his conviction was quashed on the basis that it was not shown that any such intervention would or would probably have prolonged the child's life.[206] In a drowning case, the same principle applies—liability

200 Fletcher, *Rethinking Criminal Law* 615. See also Bohlander, *Principles of German Criminal Law* 43.

201 See Larry Alexander, 'Criminal Liability for Omissions: An Inventory of Issues' in Stephen Shute and Andrew Simester (eds.) *Criminal Law Theory: Doctrines of the General Part* (OUP 2002) 121, 137–8.

202 Interestingly, in *Pittwood* counsel for the defendant argued that the duty under the contract was owed only to the railway company, the defendant's employer and party to the contract. That this was true under the law of contract did not affect the court's imposition of criminal responsibility on the defendant.

203 Ashworth, 'Criminal Liability for Omissions' 449–50.

204 Simester et al. *Simester and Sullivan's Criminal Law* 104; Ashworth, *Principles of Criminal Law* 111. The essence of this point holds on alternative explanations of the role of causation in omissions cases. For instance, in Moore's view, omissions liability in duty cases is non-causal. Instead, an independent ground of desert—counterfactual dependence—is the basis of liability. On such a theory, the ability or capacity of the defendant to have prevented the harm—the harm's counterfactual dependence on the omission—does the work of establishing responsibility. See Michael Moore 'Causing, Aiding, and the Superfluity of Accomplice Liability' (2007) 156 U Penn LR 395, 428.

205 *Morby* (1882) 8 QBD 571.

206 Ibid.

will not arise if the parent's intervention would not have made any difference to the resulting harm.

In the common law at least, these cases are exceptions to the foundational principle that criminal liability does not arise for failing to prevent a specific harm from occurring. The passer-by who watches a child drown is not liable for murder. The parent or lifeguard may be liable, as may be someone who inadvertently knocked the child into the water. This principle is rooted in concerns for individual autonomy and negative liberty,[207] and is one to which the common law has a longstanding attachment.[208] A duty to avert harm seeks to compel people to act in a particular way, potentially contrary to how they might ordinarily have chosen to act for themselves. With a typical incrementalism, the common law has carved out exceptions to this general principle. Capacity establishes that the failure to act is a factual cause of the harm.[209] As is the case with actions, not all factual causes are seen as the legal cause of the harm. This is the role of the duty. In each case, the failure to act to avert the harm is seen as so culpable that the omission may be treated as the legal cause of the harm.[210]

2.5.2.2.3. Principal Omissions and Complicit Omissions

To reiterate, these duty cases establish principalship—the failure to act is seen as the legal cause of the resulting harm.[211] The question, then, is whether a failure to act in accordance with a duty may give rise to accomplice liability. There is no reason that it should not. If we are willing to accept that certain omissions are the legal cause of a resulting harm, there is no reason that certain omissions should not be seen to constitute complicity in the bringing about of the harm by another actor. In some cases, distinguishing the two might be difficult. One way to determine whether the person who fails to perform his duty should be assessed as a principal or accomplice is the factual presence of another cause of the resulting harm. This point may be illustrated in the following scenarios:

A1. As in *Pittwood*, the defendant intentionally omits to close a railway gate and a train strikes the victim. The train driver is faultless.[212]

[207] Ashworth, 'Criminal Liability for Omissions' 427.

[208] Simester et al. *Simester and Sullivan's Criminal Law* 69.

[209] Ashworth, *Principles of Criminal Law* 111.

[210] See Fletcher, *Rethinking Criminal Law* 611; Helen Beynon, 'Causation, Omissions and Complicity' (1987) Crim L Rev 539; Arthur Leavens, 'A Causation Approach to Criminal Omissions' (1988) 76 Cal L Rev 547.

[211] A broader discussion of controversies around the concept of causation is beyond the scope of this work. See Ernest Weinrib, 'A Step Forward in Factual Causation' (1975) 38 MLR 518; Hart and Honoré, *Causation in the Law*; Michael Moore, 'The Metaphysics of Causal Intervention' (2000) 88 Cal L Rev 827.

[212] *Pittwood*.

A2. A cleaner intentionally omits to lock the doors of a bank in the knowledge that it will assist in a bank robbery.[213]

Under the duty analysis set out above, the railway gate attendant may be liable for the wrong defined by the resulting harm. In respect of A2, Ashworth suggests there is no difficulty in seeing the cleaner as an accomplice to the bank robbery.[214] This is surely correct—the cleaner was under a duty to lock the doors and his intentional failure to act rendered assistance to the principal perpetrators. Indeed, this case seems to epitomize and justify the recognition of a category of complicit omissions in criminal law.

In other situations, it might be more difficult to distinguish principals from accomplices. Compare the following scenarios:

B1. A child falls into a swimming pool. His father, a strong swimmer, watches him drown.

B2. A child is pushed into the swimming pool by his mother. Again, the father watches him drown.[215]

Under the duty analysis set out above, the father in B1 may be liable for the resulting harm. But what of the father in B2? It is difficult to distinguish the moral blameworthiness of the father's omission in B1 from that in B2. In both cases, he owed a duty to prevent harm to the child and failed to act accordingly. This might suggest treating both parents as principals. However, in the second scenario, we might also ask whether or not the father's omission aided the mother's act of murder. It would seem that it did.[216]

The answer probably lies in how we construct the father's duty. On one hand, the father's duty may be thought of as an obligation to prevent the child's death. On the other, it may be thought of as an obligation to prevent the child from being killed by another actor.[217] If we construct the duty along the former lines, the failure to prevent the child's death in breach of the duty constitutes principalship. If we construct it along the latter lines, the failure to prevent the other actor from killing the child gives rise to accomplice liability.

[213] See Ashworth, *Principles of Criminal Law* 410–11.

[214] Ibid.

[215] See generally Alexander, 'Criminal Liability for Omissions: An Inventory of Issues' 121.

[216] See *R* v. *Russell* (1933) VLR 59.

[217] See Gardner, 'Complicity and Causality' 134.

2.5.2.3. Conclusion on Issue One of the Analytical Framework: Forms of Complicity

It will be seen in Parts B and C that there is a disparity in the forms of complicity prohibited by complicity rules binding individuals and states, respectively, in international law. To some extent, these differences may be explained by reference to the formation and constitution of the rules in each regime. Like much domestic criminal law, international criminal law has benefited from the prescription of broad principles of criminal responsibility in the context of complicity. Courts and tribunals have thus had a chance to refine the doctrines in pursuit of a coherent approach to complicit conduct. The starting point in state complicity was quite different. Before the acceptance of the rule reflected in Article 16 ARSIWA, complicity rules arose on a very specific and ad hoc basis in response to particularly culpable forms of assistance in particular wrongs. Even with the acceptance of Article 16, doubts exist as to the inclusion of certain kinds of complicity within its scope.[218] Forms of complicity that are wrongful for individuals in international law are lawful for states.[219]

2.5.3. Issue Two: The Nexus Requirement

The first part of the analytical framework concerned the forms of complicity prohibited. The second concerns the nexus between the accomplice's acts and the principal's wrong. The term complicity itself denotes a relationship between the two. Here, there are two related questions. First, how should we understand the nature of that relationship? Second, should a certain level of contribution be required as a condition of responsibility?

In respect of the first question, the debate centres on role of causation. As it is in philosophy[220] and law[221] more generally, causation in accomplice liability is deeply contested.[222] Legal approaches to causation differ from legal

[218] See section 7.3.5 below.

[219] See André Nollkaemper, 'The Charles Taylor Judgment: Disconnecting the Responsibilities of Presidents and States' (*SHARES Blog*, 1 October 2013) available at <http://www.sharesproject.nl/the-charles-taylor-judgment-disconnecting-the-responsibilities-of-presidents-and-states/> accessed 19 December 2014.

[220] See generally Elizabeth Anscombe, *Causality and Determination* (CUP 1971); David Lewis, 'Causation' (1973) 70 Journal of Philosophy 556; John Mackie, *The Cement of the Universe: A Study of Causation* (Clarendon 1974); David Lewis, 'Causation as Influence' (2000) 97 Journal of Philosophy 182.

[221] See generally, Hart and Honoré, *Causation in the Law*; Richard Wright, 'Causation in Tort Law' (1985) 73 Calif L Rev 1735; Jane Stapleton, 'Law, Causation and Common Sense' (1988) 8 OJLS 111.

[222] See Kadish, 'Complicity, Cause and Blame'; Gardner, 'Complicity and Causality'; Moore, 'The Superfluity of Accomplice Liability'; Kutz, 'Causeless Complicity'.

system to legal system, as well as within legal systems. For this reason, this section does not attempt a detailed evaluation of competing positions or seek to prescribe a singular conception applicable to international criminal law and the law of state responsibility. Instead, it will propose Gardner's model as a helpful way to understand accomplice liability in general, with the caveat that different normative systems might draw lines in different ways.

Gardner's model seeks to account for accomplice liability as causal.[223] In doing so, it runs up against accounts that see the moral relevance of voluntary action on the part of the principal as precluding any causal role for accomplices.[224] Voluntary action, in this sense, often finds expression in the doctrine of *novus actus interveniens*—causal chains between actions and occurrences are said to be irrevocably split by the volitional conduct of a second actor.[225] One thing that is true in this account is that the *novus actus* doctrine is helpful in understanding how common law courts identify principal wrongdoers in criminal law; as Moore puts it, 'the doctrines of accomplice liability fit like soft clay around the shape of intervening causation'.[226]

But that itself does not show that complicity is non-causal. At root, causation entails 'making a difference to what happens in the world'.[227] At the top end of the spectrum, certain complicit relationships appear to be straightforwardly causal.[228] Gardner gives the following example:

> When I pay a hitman to kill an enemy it is a straightforward consequence of what I do that the hitman kills my enemy, and hence that my enemy dies... I procure the killing and I also cause, through the hitman, the death. There is a straightforward causal explanation of how it all unfolds, action and reaction, antecedent and consequent. None of this wipes out the hitman's part in the story as a responsible agent.[229]

In other situations, accomplices make a less direct, but still causal, contribution to the principal wrong. To understand this point, it is again useful to refer back to Kadish's distinction between two archetypal forms of complicity: *helping* the perpetrator to commit the wrong and *influencing* the decision of the perpetrator to do so.[230] When considering conduct that helps the perpetrator to commit the wrong, in the central case the accomplice makes a

[223] Gardner, 'Complicity and Causality' 136–41.

[224] See Kadish, 'Complicity, Cause and Blame' 334–5.

[225] Ibid 335.

[226] Moore, 'The Superfluity of Accomplice Liability' 409.

[227] Kutz, 'Causeless Complicity' 294.

[228] Gardner, 'Complicity and Causality' 137. See also Mackie, *The Cement of the Universe* 120–5.

[229] Gardner, 'Complicity and Causality' 136–7.

[230] Kadish, 'Complicity, Cause and Blame' 342.

different kind of causal contribution to the wrong from the principal.[231] The accomplice's causal contribution is indirect.[232] Imagine A gives P a knife and P uses the knife to cause result R. P causes the result R. A makes a causal contribution to P's causing of result R.[233] Accomplices make 'a difference to the difference that principals make'.[234]

The analysis is more complicated where the accomplice is said to have influenced the decision of the principal to commit the wrong.[235] Ordinary cases of instigation or encouragement are plagued by underdetermination—the inscrutability of the mind causes grave difficulties in determining whether the accomplice's conduct had an effect on the principal's decision.[236] In cases of instigation—where the accomplice has provided *a reason*[237] for action—it is not a great leap to infer that the instigation was causally relevant to the principal's deliberations.[238] Again, the accomplice makes an indirect causal contribution to the wrong.

Cases of encouragement are more difficult. Imagine a principal who has settled on a criminal course of action.[239] Before commencing, he is encouraged by A. In this instance, A's encouragement may be causally superfluous or causally relevant in strengthening P's faltering resolve.[240] It is difficult to tell.

These evidentiary difficulties are not easily overcome. The most convincing explanation is Smith's. In cases of influence, attempted acts of encouragement of which the principal is aware are assumed to act on his mind.[241] In other words, they are taken to have causally contributed to his decision. In some respects, the doctrine of presumed effect renders complicity by encouragement similar to attempts liability—a culpable mental state together with some minor conduct gives rise to liability.[242] Yet it is different in a crucial aspect. The presumption of causal contribution may be rebutted by evidence that the encouragement played no role in the principal's decision.[243] This

[231] John Gardner, 'Moore on Complicity and Causality' (2008) U Penn L Rev Pennumbra 432, 437–8. This point about causal pluralism, as Gardner calls it, is crucial to understanding the scheme set out here.

[232] Smith, *A Treatise on Complicity* 89.

[233] Gardner, 'Moore on Complicity and Causality' 438.

[234] Gardner, 'Complicity and Causality' 128.

[235] For discussion, see Hart and Honoré, *Causation in the Law* 52–7.

[236] Kutz, 'Causeless Complicity' 299.

[237] Hart and Honoré, *Causation in the Law* 54.

[238] See ibid 388.

[239] Smith, *A Treatise on Complicity* 85.

[240] Ibid.

[241] Ibid 87. See also Law Commission, *Participating in Crime* (Law Com No 305, 2007) [2.37]–[2.39].

[242] Weisberg, 'Reappraising Complicity' 231.

[243] Smith, *A Treatise on Complicity* 87.

would not be encouragement or abetment but a failed attempt at such. In other words, to be an accomplice, acts of assistance must actually assist and acts of encouragement must actually encourage.[244]

The first issue was to understand the nature of the relationship between accomplice's act and principal's wrong; the second is to set out the level of contribution required to inculpate the accomplice.[245] At a bare minimum, we know that the assistance or encouragement must be successful.[246] In some cases, it will be possible to categorize the accomplice's actions as a *sine qua non* of the principal's commission of wrongdoing—say, for instance, the cleaner who intentionally omitted to lock the door of the bank.[247] Here, the wrong would not have come into existence without the cleaner's omission.[248] There are plainly other cases in which the complicit conduct is not a *sine qua non* of the principal's wrong—for example, the principal would have been able to obtain the weapon from another seller if the putative accomplice had refused to sell.[249] However, the fact that certain assistance or encouragement was not a *sine qua non* of the principal wrong does not mean that it made no contribution to it at all.[250]

In general, complicity rules ought to be conditioned by a substantiality requirement.[251] How such a requirement should be formulated in practice might turn on the legal interests protected by the particular system and the breadth of the other elements of the complicity rule. At minimum, it seems clear that including trivial contributions with doctrines of complicity would result in over-criminalization for individuals[252] and an undue limitation on free intercourse among nations for states.[253]

Moreover, as the connection between the accomplice's act and the principal's wrong approaches a de minimis standard, it starts to become inconsistent with the essential derivative nature of complicity. The logic of complicity is to link the accomplice to the principal wrong itself, either through imputational responsibility or through a model of participation that renders the

244 Gardner, 'Complicity and Causality' 137.

245 See Smith, *A Treatise on Complicity* 82.

246 Kadish, 'Complicity, Cause and Blame' 357; Gardner, *Complicity and Causality* 137.

247 See Ashworth, *Principles of Criminal Law* 410–11.

248 Gardner, 'Complicity and Causality' 137.

249 Ibid 138. This point is affected by how stringently the wrongful event is defined. If the wrong is defined in terms of how *exactly* it occurred, then plainly any contribution is a *sine qua non* cause of that specifically defined wrong. See Dressler, 'Reforming Complicity Law' 441.

250 See Chiara Lepora and Robert Goodin, *On Complicity and Compromise* (OUP 2013) 60 n 4.

251 Smith, *A Treatise on Complicity* 86–8; Moore, 'The Superfluity of Accomplice Liability' 421.

252 Kadish, 'Complicity, Cause and Blame' 363.

253 Lowe, 'Responsibility for the Conduct of Other States' 5.

accomplice responsible for instigating torture or facilitating murder, as the case may be.[254] The defensibility of such a link is underpinned by requiring at least some more-than-marginal contribution by the accomplice.

2.5.4. Issue Three: The Fault of the Accomplice

2.5.4.1. Introduction

The third plank of the analytical framework concerns the fault required of the accomplice. By nature, the fault required in complicity is complicated—the presence of an accomplice adding another element to issues relating to the intersection of *actus reus* and *mens rea*.[255] Experience shows that accomplices may assist or encourage a principal with a spectrum of attitudes.[256] As Smith puts it:

> There is no natural or automatically ascertainable proper level of mental involvement or culpability; it is a normative issue of what mental states, bearing in mind the social circumstances and consequences and possibilities for control, ought to be taken as appropriate subjects of criminal sanctions.[257]

More fundamentally, how we think about the fault element may depend on the structure of the complicity rule at issue.[258] Where complicity rules are imputational, we should be concerned with the relationship between the fault required for the principal wrong and the fault required of the accomplice. Where complicity is not imputational, it is possible to conceive of a detailed scheme of responsibility, combining specific forms of complicity with specific forms of fault. We would be able to capture normatively significant differences among the different forms of fault with which accomplices act.

Nonetheless, no matter the structure of the rule, it is vital to determine what kinds of fault are appropriate for complicity. Two overriding concerns pervade the literature and domestic case law.[259] First, must accomplices share the purpose of the principal or is it sufficient that they know of that criminal purpose? Second, if knowledge is the appropriate standard, what exactly must the accomplice know? These two concerns merge to throw up a third issue: is there a role for reckless complicity?

254 See Smith, *A Treatise on Complicity* 88.

255 Sanford Kadish, 'Reckless Complicity' (1987) 2 J Crim L & Criminology 369.

256 Smith, *A Treatise on Complicity* 142.

257 Ibid 154.

258 Antony Duff, '"Can I Help You?" Accessorial Liability and the Intention to Assist' (1990) 10 Legal Stud 165, 167–8.

259 See Smith, *A Treatise on Complicity* 141–96.

2.5.4.2. *Purpose or Knowledge*

Intentional wrongdoing is more blameworthy than reckless wrongdoing.[260] At its core, to act intentionally is to act *in order to* bring about a particular result.[261] Here, the result obtained corresponds to the agent's purpose in acting.[262] Ordinarily, intention also includes virtually certain side-effects of action.[263] So if a villain blows up an aircraft in order to collect the insurance, we would still say that he intended the deaths of the passengers, even though this was not his purpose.[264] The lesson here is that the legal category of intention extends beyond the narrow linguistic sense of 'intending' to include an assessment of responsibility.[265] We are responsible not only for consequences we act in order to bring about but also for those we know will occur in the ordinary course of events.

The presence of the accomplice makes the distinction between knowledge (that wrongdoing will occur) and purpose (to assist in the commission of wrongdoing) more salient. It is easy to think of cases where an accomplice's purpose or motive is to assist in the perpetration of the principal wrong. Duff gives the example of a supplier who sells materials to the principal and who will be paid from the proceeds of crime.[266] A good way to identify this category of purposeful assisters is to ask if their action would have failed if the principal wrong were not committed.[267] But what about the independent supplier who, purely in pursuit of profit, sells a gun to the principal in the knowledge of the principal's intentions,[268] or the businessman who, bearing no ill will towards a particular ethnic group, knowingly sells chemical weapons to a dictator who commits genocide?[269]

In the United States, this question is sometimes cast as the 'true purpose' debate, anchored between Judge Learned Hand's opinion in *Peoni* and Judge Parker's in *Backun*.[270] In *Peoni*, Judge Hand held that the words used to prohibit various modes of complicity—aid, abet, counsel, procure, etc—'carry

[260] See Fletcher, *Rethinking Criminal Law* 442–9.

[261] Duff, *Intention, Agency and Criminal Liability* 72.

[262] Glanville Williams, 'Oblique Intention' (1987) 46 Camb L J 417, 418. See also Ashworth, *Principles of Criminal Law* 171–2.

[263] Simester et al. *Simester and Sullivan's Criminal Law* 132.

[264] Williams, 'Oblique Intention' 423. See also *Hyam* v. *DPP* [1975] AC 55, 77 (Lord Hailsham).

[265] Duff, *Intention, Agency and Criminal Liability* 72–3; Ashworth, *Principles of Criminal Law* 172.

[266] Duff, 'Can I Help You?' 169. [267] Ibid.

[268] See Weisberg, 'Reappraising Complicity' 217–22.

[269] See *Frans van Anraat* (Dutch Supreme Court) (30 June 2009) LJN: BG4822, 07/10742. See also Harmen van der Wilt, 'Genocide, Complicity in Genocide and International v. Domestic Jurisdiction: Reflections on the *van Anraat* Case' (2006) 4 J Intl Crim Just 239.

[270] Weisberg, 'Reappraising Complicity' 236.

an implication of purposeful attitude . . . '.[271] In other words, accomplices must provide their aid in order to assist the principal. This is the approach of the American Law Institute's Model Penal Code.[272] In *Backun*, Judge Parker held that an otherwise lawful transaction could give rise to accomplice liability where the seller was advised of the purchaser's criminal intent; the seller cannot wash his hands of his aid.[273] This is the prevailing approach in England and Wales: purpose is not required for complicity.[274]

Resolving this issue is difficult for just as we might think that not every knowing assister should be liable, so is it difficult to argue that no such knowing assister should be liable.[275] As noted above, non-imputational complicity rules might allow a narrow tailoring of conduct and culpability.[276] But even in systems using non-imputational complicity rules, we need some sense of when the provision of help or influence should give rise to responsibility, even if we then provide a grading of culpability.

This issue cannot be settled by reference only to the words at issue.[277] The usual argument against a standard of knowledge suggests that it is too burdensome to impose on actors carrying out their own lawful business an obligation to cease their activities to prevent harm carried out by another actor.[278] Just as you are not an accomplice to murder if you walk past a stranger bleeding to death from a gunshot wound, so continuing your ordinary lawful activities in the knowledge of another's criminal intention should not make you an accomplice to their wrong.[279]

This argument is not conclusive. In the first place, even if we think that philosophical concerns for individual autonomy mean that there should be no legal duty to save the stranger, these concerns are diminished when the duty simply demands that a shopkeeper refrain from making a sale. Second, concerns regarding the excessive hampering of trade are overstated. It will be a rare case that an ordinary shopkeeper *knows* that his customer intends to commit a crime. This is true whether she is selling screwdrivers, cricket bats, or cleaning materials. In situations where the object of trade is more likely to be connected to crime—substances often used as poisons, for instance—it

[271] *United States* v. *Peoni* (1938) 100 F.2d 401 (2nd Cir).

[272] Model Penal Code S2.06(3)(a). See Weisberg, 'Reappraising Complicity' 239; Robinson, 'Imputed Criminal Liability' n 100.

[273] *Backun* v. *United States* (1940) 112 F.2d 635 (4th Cir).

[274] *DPP for Northern Ireland* v. *Lynch* [1975] AC 653. See Smith, *A Treatise on Complicity* 143–50.

[275] Duff, 'Can I Help You?' 177.

[276] Ibid 181; Smith, *A Treatise on Complicity* 157–60; Weisberg, 'Reappraising Complicity' 264.

[277] Smith, *A Treatise on Complicity* 33; Ashworth, *Principles of Criminal Law* 99. Cf *Peoni* 402.

[278] Smith, *A Treatise on Complicity* 153; Duff, 'Can I Help You?' 178.

[279] Duff, 'Can I Help You?' 178.

is not over-burdensome to require that the seller refrain from assisting those who she knows intend to commit a crime. The culpability of a businessman who sells chemical weapons for profit in the knowledge of the buyer's criminal intention is not significantly lower than the purposeful supplier.[280]

It should be conceded that this might bring into the ambit of complicity certain knowing assisters who act with benevolent intentions. In *Gillick*, for instance, a doctor prescribed contraception to a girl under the age of 16 on the basis of his medical judgment.[281] Presumably the doctor would have known that he would thereby be facilitating the commission of unlawful sexual intercourse even though this was not his purpose in prescribing the contraception.[282] In war, a prisoner might, under threats, inform his captors of the location of another soldier knowing that it would facilitate acts of ill-treatment.[283] These concerns can be largely alleviated through creative use of the defences of necessity and duress. In *Gillick*, the doctor's provision of contraception would thus be excused on the basis of his honest and reasonable judgment that doing so was necessary for the girl's health.[284] In the case of the prisoner threatened by his captors, the defence of duress might excuse his knowing assistance.[285] Many of the situations in which we intuitively think it unfair to punish a knowing assister can be accommodated within ordinary doctrines of duress and necessity.

So as a general position, intentional assistance provided in the knowledge that it assists the principal should be sufficient to inculpate the accomplice, as distinct from assistance given with the specific purpose of assisting in the wrong.[286] In the particular case, however, there may be complicating factors. For instance, the appropriate fault for accomplice liability may well depend on the strength of the nexus requirement between the help or influence and the principal's actions—the less stringent the connection, the more appropriate a demand for coincidence of purpose.[287] In addition, some scholars have argued that the nature of the principal's wrong might affect our determination of what it means to be complicit therein. In international law, this argument arises principally in the context of specific intent crimes. Mettraux has argued that the essential character of genocide demands that accomplices act

[280] Smith, *A Treatise on Complicity* 154.

[281] *Gillick* v. *West Norfolk and Wisbech Area Health Authority and the Department of Health and Social Security* [1986] AC 112.

[282] Simester et al. *Simester and Sullivan's Criminal Law* 221.

[283] See *Erdemović* (Appeals Chamber Judgment) IT-96-22-A (7 October 1997).

[284] JC Smith [1986] Crim LR 113, 117 (note); Duff, 'Can I Help You?' 167.

[285] Cf *Erdemović* (Appeals Chamber Judgment).

[286] For a wider discussion, see Lepora and Goodin, *On Complicity and Compromise* 78–96.

[287] See Duff, 'Can I Help You?' 166–8.

with the specific intent of destroying the protected group.[288] This issue will be addressed in Chapter 4.

It will be seen in Chapter 4 that the jurisprudence of the ad hoc tribunals shows a preference for a standard of knowledge.[289] This is consistent with customary international law.[290] The Rome Statute requires only knowledge for instigation under Article 25(3)(b) but demands that aiding and abetting under Article 25(3)(c) be done with the purpose of facilitating the commission of the crime.[291] In the law of state responsibility, Article 16 ARSIWA introduces ambiguity by referring to both a knowledge and purpose standard. On the one hand, the text of Article 16 requires that the aid or assistance be provided 'with knowledge of the circumstances of the internationally wrongful act' committed by the principal state.[292] On the other hand, the Commentary suggests that the rule is conditioned by a requirement that the aid or assistance 'be given with a view to facilitating the commission of the wrongful act…'.[293] The term 'with a view to facilitating' clearly contemplates purpose. In many cases, assisting states will act with both knowledge and purpose, but there will be instances where the difference is dispositive. This matter is addressed in Chapter 7.

2.5.4.3. Specificity of Knowledge

If accomplices must act with knowledge, what exactly must they know? In the common law, the classic formulation is Lord Goddard's in *Johnson* v. *Youden*: 'Before a person can be convicted of aiding and abetting the commission of an offence he must at least know the essential matters which constitute the offence'.[294] In many cases, this is a workable test: the accomplice stands guard while watching the principal break into a bank, or encourages the principal to vandalize a car. But in other cases, the relationship between the accomplice's knowledge and the crime that eventuates might be more complicated.[295] In this respect, four situations may be imagined:

1. A drives P to V's house knowing that he intends to commit a battery against V. P commits battery against V.

[288] Guénaël Mettraux, *International Crimes and the* Ad Hoc *Tribunals* (OUP 2005) 212.

[289] See *Blaškić* (Appeals Chamber Judgment) IT-95-14-A (29 July 2004) [49]; *Orić* (Appeals Chamber Judgment) IT-03-68-A (3 July 2008) [43]. Although knowledge is said to be the standard, at times it is reduced to recklessness. See section 4.3.3 below.

[290] See *Zyklon B—Trial of Bruno Tesch and Two Others* (8 March 1946) (1947) I LRTWC 93; *Taylor* (Appeals Chamber Judgment) SCSL-03-01-A (26 September 2013) [413]–[437]. See also Van Sliedregt, *Individual Criminal Responsibility* 128–30.

[291] Arts 25(3)(b), 25(3)(c) Rome Statute.

[292] Art 16 ARSIWA.

[293] ARSIWA Commentary on Art 16 [5].

[294] *Johnson* v. *Youden* [1950] 1 KB 544, 546. See Simester, 'The Mental Element in Complicity' 583.

[295] For comprehensive treatment, see Smith, *A Treatise on Complicity* 161–96.

2. A drives P to V's house knowing that he intends to commit a battery against V and/or rob him. P robs V.
3. A drives P to V's house knowing that he intends to commit an aggravated assault against him. Instead, P commits grievous bodily harm against V.
4. A drives P to V's house knowing that he intends to break into his house. P breaks into the house and murders V.

Situation 1 is the archetypal case of accomplice liability. Other cases are not quite as straightforward. In *Maxwell*, the defendant drove a lead car that guided another car to an inn that was to be attacked by members of the Ulster Volunteer Force.[296] The trial judge found an irresistible inference that Maxwell knew that the job he was contributing to involved an attack of violence in which people would be endangered *or* premises seriously damaged.[297] In response, Maxwell's counsel argued that on the basis of the 'essential matters' test, he did not know which crime was to be committed.

Maxwell's appeal was dismissed, though on the basis of different tests.[298] Lord Scarman proposed a test that asks whether the actual crime committed was at least one of a set of crimes within the accomplice's contemplation.[299] So in the second situation, A contemplated both robbery and battery in his provision of aid and would thus be responsible as an accomplice to the crime that occurred. In a sense, this standard requires knowledge that the aid will assist in the commission of crime, but a lower standard of fault as to the commission of the specific offence that actually occurs.[300]

Scarman's colleagues proposed a different test, sourced in Parker CJ's judgment in *Bainbridge*: 'there must be not merely suspicion but knowledge that a crime *of the type* in question was intended'.[301] This corresponds to the third situation: A believed that P intended to commit aggravated assault against V but he actually committed grievous bodily harm. Neither of the two tests in *Maxwell* would hold A responsible as an accomplice to murder in situation 4, where the accomplice assists, contemplating a burglary, but the principal commits murder.

[296] *Maxwell* v. *DPP for Northern Ireland* [1979] 68 Cr App R 128.
[297] *Maxwell* 132.
[298] See Smith, *A Treatise on Complicity* 165–9.
[299] *Maxwell* 153 (Lord Scarman).
[300] See Andrew Ashworth and Jeremy Horder, *Principles of Criminal Law* (7th edn. OUP 2013) 435–6.
[301] *Bainbridge* [1960] 1 QB 129, 133 (Lord Parker); *Maxwell* 148 (Lord Hailsham) (emphasis added).

The issue of specificity of knowledge arises in international law. In respect of international criminal law, the ICTY and ICTR have articulated an 'essential matters' test along the lines of *Johnson* v. *Youden*,[302] as well as a test that requires only that the accomplice contemplated that one of a number of crimes would be committed, of which the actual crime was one, even if he did not know exactly which it was to be.[303] In respect of state complicity, states' interactions with each other are often complex; aid may be provided without certainty as to the range or extent of the recipient state's intentions. Complicity rules must grapple with these complications.

2.5.4.4. *Reckless Complicity*

It makes sense at this point to consider a challenge to the orthodox framing of the debate about the fault element in complicity. James Stewart argues that knowledge/purpose dichotomy is doctrinally and conceptually misleading.[304] His doctrinal claim focuses on the standards applied by international criminal tribunals; this is a matter to be addressed in Part B. His conceptual claim has implications for complicity more generally.

In short, Stewart argues that knowledge simply cannot be the standard for complicity because accomplices cannot *know* that the principal crime will be committed:

> Even if member X of a criminal gang provides her terrorist colleague Y with a nuclear warhead for a specific terrorist mission, X cannot know with certainty that a crime will transpire. Short of knowing that water will flow downhill or that the sun will rise in the east, no one can know with certainty what the future will involve, and surely few human actions ever acquire a degree of predictability anywhere close to the direction of the Earth's rotation or laws of physics.[305]

This argument from 'epistemological impossibility'[306] may be right in a narrow sense. However, it glosses over the widespread use of the term knowledge, in both ordinary language and law, to include certain beliefs about what will happen in the future. In terms of ordinary language, Stewart's argument denies the conceptual coherence of the commonplace phrase: 'You knew that would happen.' In terms of law, as Stephen Shute puts it, the

[302] See *Haradinaj, Balaj, Brahimaj* (Appeals Chamber Judgment) IT-04-84-A (19 July 2010) [58]; *Orić* (Appeals Chamber Judgment) [43]; *Mrkšić, Šljivančanin* (Appeals Chamber Judgment) IT-95-13/1A (5 May 2009) [159]; *Simić* (Appeals Chamber Judgment) IT-95-9-A (28 November 2006) [86]; *Nahimana* (Appeals Chamber Judgment) [482].

[303] See *Haradinaj* et al. (Appeals Chamber Judgment) [58]; *Mrkšić, Šljivančanin* (Appeals Chamber Judgment) [159]; *Simić* (Appeals Chamber Judgment) [86].

[304] Stewart, 'The End of Modes of Liability' 192–3.

[305] Ibid 194.

[306] Ibid 195.

interpretation of the term knowledge may well be 'less demanding than our normal conceptual understandings would lead us to expect'.[307]

Leaving aside those objections, Stewart's main argument is that in many legal systems the conventional category of knowledge for accomplices 'surreptitiously dilute(s) into recklessness'.[308] The classic case of reckless complicity concerns the provision of assistance in situations where the accomplice is not practically certain that the principal is intending to commit the crime.[309] Kadish gives the example of a bed-ridden employee who gives the code to his employer's safe to a career criminal, P, so that P can bring him some documents from the safe.[310] The employee's purpose in giving the codes is not to help P to steal. Likewise, he does not know that P is intending to commit the crime. But knowing that his helper is a career criminal, the employee certainly is aware of a risk that his provision of the codes will assist in the commission of theft.[311]

Comparative analyses of recklessness are rendered difficult by subtle distinctions in how legal systems grade mental states short of actual knowledge.[312] Assessments of risk-taking ordinarily revolve around three foci: the gravity of the risk, the social utility of taking the risk, and the risk-taker's subjective posture towards that risk.[313] For current purposes, the American Law Institute's Model Penal Code's formulation will suffice: 'A person acts recklessly with respect to a material element of an offence when he consciously disregards a substantial and unjustifiable risk that the material element exists or will result from his conduct.'[314]

It is here where we should heed Stewart's lesson: where orthodox doctrinal accounts of complicity uphold a standard of knowledge but reject recklessness, we should attempt to figure out exactly when such knowledge is held to exist.[315] The distinction between acting intentionally and acting recklessly entails a critical judgment as to culpability, rendering demarcation of the boundary important.[316] Moreover, it is plainly inconsistent with the principal of culpability to hold an accomplice responsible for an intentional offence where she did not act intentionally.[317] Accomplices may assist the principal

307 Stephen Shute, 'Knowledge and Belief in Criminal Law' in Shute and Simester, *Criminal Law Theory* 171, 192.

308 Stewart, 'The End of Modes of Liability' 195.

309 This question also arises where assistance is provided for the purposes of the commission of a specific crime and additional crimes are committed. In this respect, there are links to the extended form of joint venture.

310 Kadish, 'Reckless Complicity' 371. 311 Ibid.

312 Fletcher, *Rethinking Criminal Law* 442–9. 313 Ibid 260–1.

314 MPC S2.02(2)(c). 315 Stewart, 'The End of Modes of Liability' 192–3.

316 See Fletcher, *Rethinking Criminal Law* 442–9.

317 Damaška, 'The Shadow Side of Command Responsibility' 463–4.

with the belief that that the occurrence of the principal crime is unlikely, possible, more likely than not, probable, highly likely, or practically certain.[318] At some point, what looks like the (extended) category of legal knowledge blurs into the culpable risk-taking entailed by recklessness.[319]

Somewhere around that blurred line is the doctrine of wilful blindness, defined by Glanville Williams in the following terms:

> A court can properly find wilful blindness only where it can almost be said that the defendant actually knew. He suspected the fact; he realised its probability; but he refrained from obtaining the final confirmation because he wanted in the event to be able to deny knowledge. This, and this alone, is wilful blindness.[320]

Williams notes that the rule is somewhat unstable and liable to unjustified extension.[321] It is not simply a judgment that the potential accomplice took an unjustifiable risk by not inquiring into the principal's intentions. This would render wilful blindness indistinguishable from the lower standard of recklessness.[322] Rather, it arises where the accomplice either (i) shuts his eyes because he is virtually certain of the answer that his enquiries would bring, or (ii) strongly suspects the truth of the principal's intentions but refuses to enquire so as not to know.[323] In both cases, the imposition of responsibility in a situation falling short of the ordinary fault element is justified by the accomplice's additional fault in deliberately shutting his eyes having been adverted to the risk.[324] If limited in this way, the doctrine of wilful blindness may be seen as a justified extension to the category of knowledge.

2.5.5. Analytical Framework: Conclusion

The work's analytical framework thus structures the analysis of complicity in international law around three questions any legal system must answer in order to prescribe a complicity rule: the forms of complicity prohibited, the

[318] See Shute, 'Knowledge and Belief in Criminal Law' 195. For a wider discussion of the difference between knowledge and belief, see Robert Sullivan, 'Knowledge, Belief, and Culpability' in Shute and Simester, *Criminal Law Theory* 207; Shute, 'Knowledge and Belief in Criminal Law' 171.

[319] Stewart, 'The End of Modes of Liability' 192. As the Law Commission points, in England and Wales courts have been willing to dilute the requirement of knowledge as to the principal offence to include, in different cases: (i) belief that P *might* commit the offence; (ii) foresight of the risk of a strong possibility that P will commit the offence; (iii) contemplation of the risk of a real possibility that P will commit the offence; and (iv) foresight that it is likely that P will commit the offence. See Law Commission, *Participating in Crime* [2.65]; Simester, 'The Mental Element in Complicity' 583–8.

[320] Williams, *The General Part* 159.

[321] Ibid.

[322] Simester et al. *Simester and Sullivan's Criminal Law* 150.

[323] Ibid.

[324] Martin Wasik and Mark Thompson, '"Turning a Blind Eye" as Constituting *Mens Rea*' (1981) 32 NILQ 328, 330–1.

nexus between the accomplice's acts and the principal's wrong, and the fault required of the accomplice. In each case, there are normative choices to be made—choices that depend, in part, on the structure of the complicity rule at issue as well as on the other elements of that rule. This framework is used throughout the work to provide an analytical account of the ways in which international law responds to state and individual complicity.

2.6. Conclusion

The definition of complicity provided in this chapter delimits the scope of the work. This definition views doctrines of complicity as establishing a derivative form of responsibility for participating in the wrongdoing of another actor. Where that principal wrongdoing is morally wrongful, it follows that we should not participate in its commission. In respect of legal wrongs, it is clear that the justification and/or demand for a complicity rule turns on conflicting rationales shaped by the needs and purposes of the legal system itself.

A central question in this work concerns the structure of complicity rules in international law. As a normative matter, complicity rules ought to hold accomplices responsible for their own contribution to the principal's wrong, rather than for the wrong committed by the principal. This normative claim is married to an analytical assessment of complicity rules structured around the forms of complicity prohibited, the nexus between the accomplice's acts and the principal's wrong, and the fault of the accomplice.

Part B (Chapters 3–5) provides an account of complicity rules binding individuals in international law. Part C (Chapters 6–9) provides an account of complicity rules binding states in international law. Each part is anchored by the normative claim and framework set out in above. This allows for an account of complicity that is both evaluative and analytical. Part D (Chapter 10) draws some conclusions.

PART B

COMPLICITY IN INTERNATIONAL CRIMINAL LAW

3

Individual Criminal Responsibility

3.1. Introduction

Part B (Chapters 3–5) provides an account of complicity in international criminal law. Complicity rules establish a derivative form of responsibility for participating in wrongdoing committed by another actor. That participation entails the provision of help to, or influence on, the principal wrongdoer.[1]

The present chapter (Chapter 3) defines the scope of Part B and briefly assesses the principle of individual criminal responsibility in international law. Chapter 4 analyses two paradigm doctrines of complicity in international criminal law: instigation and aiding and abetting. It also assesses the recent controversy over the criterion of specific direction in the jurisprudence of the ICTY and the dispute concerning the putative crime of complicity in genocide arising under the statutes of the ad hoc tribunals.[2] Its approach is to set out and address various doctrinal issues arising in the case law and scholarship, assess the rules within the analytical framework set out in Part A, and evaluate the rules against the work's normative claim as to the optimal structure of complicity rules. This framework centres the analysis on three axes: the forms of complicity prohibited, the nexus between the accomplice's act and the principal's wrong, and the fault required of the accomplice. The normative claim establishes a preference for non-imputational complicity rules.

Chapter 5 (the final chapter in Part B) addresses international criminal law's response to complicit omissions. That response takes two forms. First, the idea of aiding and abetting by omission has received increased attention and recognition in the jurisprudence of the ICTY and ICTR.

[1] Kadish, 'Complicity, Cause and Blame' 342.

[2] Statute of the International Criminal Tribunal for the Former Yugoslavia adopted by UNSC Res 827 (25 May 1993) UN Doc S/RES/827; Statute of the International Criminal Tribunal for Rwanda adopted by UNSC Res 955 (8 November 1994) UN Doc S/RES/955.

This recognition should be supported. As a matter of fact, certain omissions do help or influence the decision of a perpetrator to commit a crime. As a normative matter, omissions may be sufficiently wrongful so as to justify the imposition of accomplice liability. Second, international criminal law establishes, through the doctrine of command responsibility, a special form of responsibility for complicit omissions. Indeed, the most culpable form of command responsibility—a failure to prevent the perpetration of crimes by subordinates with actual knowledge of their intended commission—adds little, if anything, to the rule of aiding and abetting by omission. Command responsibility also establishes a rule of negligent complicity by imputing to superiors crimes of their subordinates about which they ought to have known.

3.2. The Scope of Part B

Part B assesses the criminal law doctrines of instigation and aiding and abetting, as well as international criminal law's response to complicit omissions. It does not discuss certain kindred forms of responsibility in international criminal law. These kindred forms of responsibility include the extended form of joint criminal enterprise liability and incitement to commit genocide.[3] The extended form of joint criminal enterprise should be seen as a complementary doctrine to complicity.[4] It replicates the structure of imputational complicity in providing a rule by which the acts of the principal perpetrator are attributed to the participant in a joint criminal enterprise.[5] In imputational complicity, the trigger for imputation is the accomplice's acts of help or encouragement. In joint criminal enterprise, the trigger is the defendant's participation in a common enterprise. Here, the law treats this decision to

[3] See generally Allison Danner and Jenny Martinez, 'Guilty Associations: Joint Criminal Enterprise, Command Responsibility, and the Development of International Criminal Law' (2005) 93 Calif L Rev 75; Attila Bogdan, 'Individual Criminal Responsibility in the Execution of a "Joint Criminal Enterprise" in the Jurisprudence of the ad hoc International Tribunal for the Former Yugoslavia' (2006) 5 Intl Crim L Rev 63; Kai Ambos, 'Joint Criminal Enterprise and Command Responsibility' (2007) 5 J Intl Crim J 159; Jens Ohlin, 'Incitement and Conspiracy to Commit Genocide' in Paola Gaeta (ed.) *The UN Genocide Convention: A Commentary* (OUP 2009) 207.

[4] See Smith, *A Treatise on Complicity* 209–34.

[5] See Kai Ambos, 'Amicus Curiae Brief in the Matter of the Co-Prosecutors' Appeal of the Closing Order against Kaing Guek Eav "Duch" Dated 8 August 2008' (2009) 20 Crim L Forum 353, 369 referring to JCE II and III as 'autonomous (systemic) concepts of imputation'. See also *Pinkerton* v. *United States* 328 US 640 (1946).

participate as significant enough to associate the defendant with the deviatory but foreseeable conduct of his confederates.[6]

Incitement to commit genocide refers to conduct that might constitute instigation or abetment of genocide under ordinary doctrines of complicity.[7] However, it is founded in law at the moment the incitement occurs and is not dependent on the subsequent commission of the incited offence—incitement to commit genocide may be committed without genocide being perpetrated.[8] For this reason, it is not a derivative form of responsibility, and is therefore not a doctrine of complicity, but is rather a supplementary inchoate crime.[9]

In addition to the exclusion of joint criminal enterprise and incitement to commit genocide, this chapter also does not discuss the prohibition on contributions to group crime set out in Article 25(3)(d) of the Rome Statute. In contrast to the first two doctrines, the reason for exclusion here is pragmatic rather than conceptual. Using language borrowed from Article 2(3)(c) of the International Convention for the Suppression of Terrorist Bombing,[10] the provision creates a complicated and much criticized mode of participating in one of the crimes within the jurisdiction of the court.[11] Although the cases of *Mbarushimana* and *Ruto* have clarified certain issues relating to the scope of the doctrine, notably that contributions by members of the group itself, as well as by non-group members, may give rise to liability,[12] responsibility pursuant to Article 25(3)(d) is somewhat residual.[13] For reasons of scope, the primary focus is on the doctrines of instigation and aiding and abetting, together with international law's response to complicit omissions.

[6] Simester, 'The Mental Element in Complicity' 598–9.

[7] See William Schabas, *Genocide in International Law: The Crime of Crimes* (2nd edn. CUP 2009) 319; *Akayesu* (Appeals Chamber Judgment) ICTR-96-4 (1 June 2001) [478].

[8] *Nahimana, Barayagwiza, Ngeze* (Appeals Chamber Judgment) ICTR-99-52-A (28 November 2007) [678].

[9] Ibid.

[10] Art 2(3)(c) International Convention for the Suppression of Terrorist Bombings (adopted 15 December 1997, entered into force 23 May 2001) 2149 UNTS 284.

[11] Eser, 'Individual Criminal Responsibility' 803; Kai Ambos, 'Article 25—Individual Criminal Responsibility' in Otto Triffterer (ed.) *Commentary on the Rome Statute of the International Criminal Court: Observers' Notes, Article by Article* (2nd edn. Hart 2008) 743, 757–9.

[12] *Mbarushimana* (Decision on the Confirmation of Charges) ICC-01/04-01/10 (16 December 2011) [268]–[292]. See also *Ruto, Kosgey, Sang* (Decision on the Confirmation of Charges) ICC-01/09-01/11 (23 January 2012) [350]–[354].

[13] See *Lubanga Dyilo* (Decision on the Confirmation of Charges) ICC-01/04-01/06 (29 January 2007) [337]. See though *Katanga* (Trial Chamber Judgment) ICC-01/04-01/07 (7 March 2014).

3.3. The Principle of Individual Criminal Responsibility

Part of Nuremberg's legacy is the entrenchment of the principle of individual criminal responsibility for violations of international law.[14] Article 6 of the Charter of the International Military Tribunal at Nuremberg, signed by the United Kingdom, France, the Union of Soviet Socialist Republics, and the United States and decreed on 8 August 1945, provided for individual criminal responsibility for crimes against peace, war crimes, and crimes against humanity.[15] It also set out the modes of participation in the crimes prohibited therein:

> Leaders, organizers, instigators and accomplices participating in the formulation or execution of a common plan or conspiracy to commit any of the foregoing crimes are responsible for all acts performed by any persons in execution of such plan.[16]

The purpose of criminal law provisions setting out the various modes of participation in crimes is to capture the range of ways that an individual may be culpable in relation to wrongdoing.[17] The language of this provision reflects the position and status of the defendants as high-ranking members of the Nazi party. Participation in (a) the formulation or execution of (b) a common plan or conspiracy to commit crimes against peace, war crimes, or crimes against humanity gave rise to responsibility for any acts performed in the execution of the plan.[18] The provision responds to the scale of the atrocities founding prosecutions for war crimes and crimes against humanity and the nature of crimes against peace as an offence of planning, preparing, and initiating certain conduct.

The scale of the atrocities and nature of the defendants' involvement make it difficult to glean much insight into the operation of complicity in

[14] For a historical discussion, including developments prior to the post-Second World War tribunals, see Andrea Gattini, 'A Historical Perspective: From Collective to Individual Responsibility and Back' in André Nollkaemper and Harmen van der Wilt (eds.) *System Criminality in International Law* (CUP 2009) 101.

[15] Art 6 Charter of the International Military Tribunal (Nuremberg) annexed to Agreement for the Prosecution and Punishment of the Major War Criminals of the European Axis (signed in London, 8 August 1945) 82 UNTS 279. See also *Judgment of the Nuremberg International Military Tribunal* (1 October 1946) (1947) 41 Am J Intl L 172.

[16] Art 6 Nuremberg Charter. See also Art 5(c) Charter of the International Military Tribunal for the Far East (19 January 1946, amended 25 April 1946) TIAS No 1589.

[17] See Boas et al. *Forms of Responsibility* 2.

[18] The Tribunal ruled that as a separate count the conspiracy charge was applicable only to crimes against peace. *Judgment of the Nuremberg IMT* 224

international law from the Nuremberg IMT.[19] On trial was systematic illegality, and the trial sought to establish the responsibility of the defendants in those terms. Likewise, the further trials carried out under Allied Control Council Order No 10 were marked by a tendency to consider each defendant's responsibility in general terms.[20] Although a number of doctrinal insights are evident in the judgments, including some bearing on complicity,[21] their value is primarily historical and foundational. In respect of the former, the trials contributed greatly to the historical record, producing a mass of documentary and other evidence detailing Nazi criminality.[22] In respect of the latter, the trials affirmed and developed principles on which international criminal law has been built.[23]

Individual criminal responsibility is reflected in identical terms in the statutes of the International Criminal Tribunals for the former Yugoslavia and Rwanda:

> A person who planned, instigated, ordered, committed or otherwise aided and abetted in the planning, preparation or execution of a crime referred to in articles 2 to 5 of the present Statute, shall be individually responsible for the crime.[24]

These are the forms of responsibility at the ad hoc tribunals—planners, instigators, orderers, perpetrators, and aiders and abettors bear individual criminal responsibility. On its face, at least, this entails a more sophisticated approach to participation in crime than at the post-Second World War tribunals.[25] The Rome Statute takes participation a step further in Article 25:

> 3. In accordance with this Statute, a person shall be criminally responsible and liable for punishment for a crime within the jurisdiction of the Court if that person:
>   (a) Commits such a crime, whether as an individual, jointly with another or through another person, regardless of whether that other person is criminally responsible;
>   (b) Orders, solicits or induces the commission of such a crime which in fact occurs or is attempted;

[19] See Kevin Heller, *The Nuremberg Military Tribunals and the Origins of International Criminal Law* (OUP 2011) 3.

[20] Ibid 252. See also Van Sliedregt, *Individual Criminal Responsibility* 18–37.

[21] See *Robert Wagner & Six Others* (24 July 1946) (1948) III LRTWC 23 (Permanent Military Tribunal, Strasbourg).

[22] Heller, *The Nuremberg Military Tribunals* 3–4.

[23] Ibid 3.

[24] Art 7(1) ICTY Statute, Art 6(1) ICTR Statute.

[25] Gerhard Werle, 'General Principles of International Criminal Law' in Antonio Cassese (ed.) *Oxford Companion to International Criminal Justice* (OUP 2009) 54, 58.

(c) For the purpose of facilitating the commission of such a crime, aids, abets or otherwise assists in its commission or its attempted commission, including providing the means for its commission;
(d) In any other way contributes to the commission or attempted commission of such a crime by a group of persons acting with a common purpose. Such contribution shall be intentional and shall either:
(i) Be made with the aim of furthering the criminal activity or criminal purpose of the group, where such activity or purpose involves the commission of a crime within the jurisdiction of the Court; or
(ii) Be made in the knowledge of the intention of the group to commit the crime.[26]

Although the many ways that people participate in wrongdoing will not always fall neatly into one category or another, the court ought to strive for precision in defining the elements of each sub-paragraph.[27] Nonetheless, there is inevitably interpretive scope for the court to emphasize and expand particular forms of responsibility. For instance, early indications suggest that many participants will be brought within the bounds of commission under Article 25(3)(a).[28] On its face, Article 25(3)(a) encompasses three kinds of perpetrators: individual perpetrators, co-perpetrators, and those who perpetrate through another person.[29] In each case, the essential characteristic is one of *control* over the crime.[30] Individual perpetrators are those who commit a crime by their own hands; they physically perpetrate the crime.[31] Responsibility for co-perpetration arises when an individual commits a crime jointly with another person. Finally, intermediary or indirect perpetration occurs where a person commits a crime through another person, regardless of whether the latter is criminally responsible. In this last case, the principal—or perpetrator-by-means—uses the actual physical executor as a tool or instrument for the commission.[32]

The use of control over the crime to define principalship denotes the adoption of a normative model of perpetration.[33] It brings into the ambit

[26] Art 25(3) Rome Statute.
[27] See Hans Vest, 'Problems of Participation—Unitarian, Differentiated Approach, or Something Else?' (2014) 12 J Intl Crim Just 295, 303. Cf *Lubanga* (Separate Opinion of Judge Fulford) [7]–[9].
[28] Schabas, *A Commentary on the Rome Statute* 431.
[29] See *Lubanga* (Trial Chamber Judgment) [977].
[30] *Lubanga* (Trial Chamber Judgment) [1005]; *Lubanga* (Decision on the Confirmation of Charges) [326]–[341]; *Katanga, Chui* (Decision on the Confirmation of Charges) ICC-01/04-01/07 (30 September 2008) [480]–[489].
[31] Eser, 'Individual Criminal Responsibility' 789.
[32] *Katanga* (Decision on the Confirmation of Charges) [495].
[33] Van Sliedregt, *Individual Criminal Responsibility* 86.

of principalship leaders and other superiors who might otherwise have been thought of as orderers or planners.[34] Responsibility on the basis of co-perpetration will arise where at least two individuals share essential tasks for the concerted purpose of committing a crime, each of them being able to frustrate the commission of the crime by failing to perform her task.[35] Responsibility on the basis of perpetration-by-means will arise not only where an innocent or incapable agent is used as a tool by the principal, but also where the principal controls the agent in an organizational context.[36] Here, international criminal law is attempting to capture within principalship the so-called perpetrator behind the perpetrator, where the tightly controlled and hierarchical apparatus of power is used to secure the indirect perpetrator's wishes.[37]

It is clear, then, that the boundaries of different forms of participation may shift. Moreover, the line between principalship and accomplice liability drawn by the control theory remains a matter of discussion in international criminal law practice and scholarship.[38] Wherever (and assuming) that line is drawn, doctrines of complicity will sit around principalship, inculpating those who help the principal to commit the wrong or influence her decision to do so.

3.4. Conclusion

The principle of individual criminal responsibility is firmly established in international law. The next two chapters analyse and evaluate the ways in which international criminal law prohibits complicity in the crimes of others. Chapter 4 assesses the doctrines of instigation and aiding and abetting, paradigm doctrines of complicity. Chapter 5 assesses complicit omissions. Together, these chapters illustrate that international criminal law proscribes complicity in a comprehensive way.

[34] See Schabas, *A Commentary on the Rome Statute* 428.

[35] *Lubanga* (Trial Chamber Judgment) [994]; *Lubanga* (Decision on the Confirmation of Charges) [342].

[36] *Katanga* (Decision on the Confirmation of Charges) [500]–[510].

[37] Ibid [514]. See Eser, 'Individual Criminal Responsibility' 795.

[38] See *Lubanga* (Trial Chamber Judgment) [917]–[1018]; *Lubanga* (Separate Opinion of Judge Fulford); *Chui* (Concurring Opinion of Judge Van den Wyngaert); Ohlin, van Sliedregt and Weigend, 'Assessing the Control Theory'; Thomas Weigend, 'Problems of Attribution in International Criminal Law' (2014) 12 J Intl Crim Just 253; Vest, 'Problems of Participation'; Jens Ohlin, 'Searching for the Hinterman: In Praise of Subjective Theories of Imputation' (2014) 12 J Intl Crim Just 325.

4

Archetypal Doctrines of Complicity in International Criminal Law

4.1. Introduction

Chapter 4 analyses the two archetypal doctrines of complicity in international criminal law: instigation and aiding and abetting. These are the central ways in which international law prohibits conduct that assists or influences the decision of a principal perpetrator to commit wrongdoing. It also considers the difficulties caused by the inclusion within the statutes of the ad hoc tribunals of a reference to 'complicity in genocide' as a punishable act. It takes the view that a distinct crime of complicity in genocide is inconsistent with the general structure of international criminal responsibility.

4.2. Instigation

The jurisprudence on instigation at the ad hoc tribunals has been relatively settled for some time.[1] The conduct element of instigation occurs when an individual urges, prompts, or encourages another person to commit a crime.[2] The fault element is fulfilled where the defendant either (i) acted with the intention that the crime be committed or (ii) was aware of the substantial likelihood that a crime would be committed in the execution of his prompting.[3] Although it need not be shown that the crime would not have occurred without the prompting of the accused, his actions must be a 'clear contributing factor to the conduct' of the principal.[4]

[1] Boas et al. *Forms of Responsibility* 344.

[2] *Semanza* (Trial Chamber Judgment) ICTR-97-20-T (15 May 2003) [381].

[3] *Kordić, Čerkez* (Appeals Chamber Judgment) IT-95-14/2-A (17 December 2004) [29], [32]; *Nahimana* (Appeals Chamber Judgment) [480].

[4] *Kvočka* (Trial Chamber Judgment) IT-98-30/1-T (2 November 2001) [252].

The Rome Statute does not refer specifically to instigation as a form of individual criminal responsibility. Instead, Article 25(3)(b) prohibits solicitation and inducement. Both solicitation and inducement refer to ways that an accomplice may influence a principal's decision to commit a crime.[5] Black's Law Dictionary defines solicitation as the 'criminal offence of urging, advising, commanding or otherwise inciting another to commit a crime'.[6] It defines inducement as the 'act or process of enticing or persuading another person to take a course of action'.[7] As is evident, it is difficult to draw exact lines between the doctrines.

The best approach in this regard is to treat solicitation and inducement under Article 25(3)(b) as broadly synonymous with the doctrine of instigation developed at the ad hoc tribunals.[8] Inducement does have a sense that the perpetrator was enticed into action, either by the promise of reward or forbearance of sanction. Early indications from the ICC suggest that the accomplice's instigation ought to have a 'direct effect' on commission of the principal crime.[9] Whether this means something different from a 'clear contributing factor' as required by the ad hoc tribunals is doubtful.

It is possible, however, that a stricter fault element will develop at the ICC. As noted above, instigation at the ad hoc tribunals requires only an awareness of the substantial likelihood that the crime will be committed.[10] In its Decision on the Confirmation of Charges in *Ntaganda*, the Pre-Trial Chamber held that inducing under Article 25(3)(b) requires that the accomplice is 'at least aware that the crimes will be committed in the ordinary course of events as a consequence…'.[11] This was said to be required by Article 30 of the Rome Statute.[12] Although in many cases of instigation it will be easy to infer intent (in the strict sense) from the accomplice's words, the tightening up of the fault element is still to be supported.

The Rome Statute's approach to instigation raises interesting questions about the culpability of an instigator vis-à-vis other participants in wrongdoing. Article 25(3)(b) establishes criminal responsibility for those who order, solicit, or induce another to commit wrongdoing. As a preliminary matter, immediately evident is the incongruity of the inclusion of ordering in the

[5] Kadish, 'Complicity, Cause and Blame' 343.

[6] Bryan Garner (ed.) *Black's Law Dictionary* (9th edn. West 2009) 1520.

[7] Ibid 845.

[8] Gerhard Werle, 'Individual Criminal Responsibility in Article 25 ICC Statute' (2007) 5 J Intl Crim Just 953, 966–7. See also Schabas, *A Commentary on the Rome Statute* 432.

[9] *Ntaganda* (Decision on the Confirmation of Charges) ICC-01/04-02/06 (9 June 2014) [153].

[10] *Kordić, Čerkez* (Appeals Chamber Judgment) IT-95-14/2-A (17 December 2004) [32]; *Nahimana* (Appeals Chamber Judgment) [480].

[11] *Ntaganda* (Decision on the Confirmation of Charges) [153].

[12] Ibid n 625.

provision, both with respect to ideas of solicitation and inducement and within the context of the Rome Statute's scheme of culpability as a whole. Soliciting and inducing denote a similar kind of participation—the wrong of persuading another to commit a crime. Ordering does not rest on persuasion, but on command. Moreover, it implicitly demands a relationship of authority between the person giving the order and the primary perpetrator.[13]

It is doubtful that the inclusion of ordering within Article 25(3)(b) fits with the culpability scheme of Article 25. This scheme seems to grade different forms of responsibility from most serious to least.[14] Those who order their subordinates to commit crimes are at least as culpable as, if not more culpable than, those who pull the trigger.[15] The Rome Statute itself recognizes this in the inclusion of indirect perpetration in Article 25(3)(a). In its Decision on the Confirmation of Charges in *Katanga*, the ICC Pre-Trial Chamber sought to distinguish 'ordinary cases of criminal ordering' under Article 25(3)(b) from intermediary perpetration through ordering under Article 25(3)(a). For the court, the difference lay in the notion of 'automatic compliance' in a hierarchical organization in the latter case.[16]

It remains to be seen how these two forms of ordering develop in the case law.[17] Two points may be made at this stage. First, so-called 'ordinary cases of criminal ordering' generally still imply at least an equivalent, if not greater, level of culpability to physical perpetration under Article 25(3)(a). Second, there is interpretive room within the idea of commission 'through another person' in the text of Article 25(3)(a) to accommodate most cases where a superior issues an order to a subordinate to commit a crime.[18] This would leave Article 25(3)(b) to address solicitation and inducement, or instigation, a classic form of complicity.

Other than the incongruity of ordering, a second noticeable aspect of Article 25(3)(b) is the heightened culpability of instigators vis-à-vis both those who provide physical assistance and ordinary abettors under Article 25(3)(c).[19] With respect to ordinary abettors, there is substantial overlap in

[13] Eser, 'Individual Criminal Responsibility' 796.

[14] See *Lubanga* (Trial Chamber Judgment) ICC-01/04-01/06 (14 March 2012) [996]–[998]; Werle, 'Individual Criminal Responsibility' 957; Eser, 'Individual Criminal Responsibility' 797. Cf *Katanga* (Trial Chamber Judgment) ICC-01/04-01/07 (7 March 2014) [1386]; *Lubanga* (Separate Opinion of Judge Fulford) [7]–[9]; *Chui* (Concurring Opinion of Judge Van den Wyngaert) ICC-01/04-02/12 (18 December 2012) [22]–[30]. This issue is discussed in section 4.4.2 below.

[15] See Eser, 'Individual Criminal Responsibility' 796.

[16] *Katanga* (Decision on the Confirmation of Charges) [517].

[17] See *Ntaganda* (Decision on the Confirmation of Charges) [145]–[152].

[18] See Ambos, 'Article 25' 747–52; Eser, 'Individual Criminal Responsibility' 797.

[19] For a discussion of the Rome Statute's culpability scheme, see section 4.4.2 below.

the conduct that each seeks to prohibit.[20] The difference between the two was addressed by the ICTY in *Orić*. According to the Trial Chamber, instigation does not require that the criminal idea originated with the instigator but that the decision of the perpetrator to commit the crime was 'brought about by persuasion or strong encouragement' by the instigator.[21] One way to draw a line distinguishing instigators from ordinary abettors is the provision by the former of a *reason* for action.[22] Encouragement short of this standard may still constitute abetment, though conviction in these cases will turn on the fulfilment of the nexus requirement.

Thus instigation may be thought of as a more serious form of complicity than simple abetment, distinguished by the strength of the influence. Under the Rome Statute, it also denotes a more serious form of responsibility than the provision of help.[23] This approach denies a singular conception of complicity liability that encompasses the ways that an accomplice may participate in wrongdoing. In doing so, it echoes the approach of the German Criminal Code. Under StGB § 26, instigators are punished to the extent of the principal's liability.[24] Under StGB § 27, the prohibition on the provision of aid, the aider's sentence may be mitigated pursuant to Section 49 of the Code.[25] This distinction makes sense. Once a principal makes up his mind to commit the crime, the exact manner of commission, in many cases, is really a matter of details. Influencing the decision of the perpetrator to commit the crime in the first place entails a closer connection to the wrong than simply helping along the way.

4.3. Aiding and Abetting

4.3.1. The Conduct Element

The second archetypal form of complicity in international criminal law is aiding and abetting.[26] Even though it is sometimes considered as a unitary doctrine, the terms mirror Kadish's distinction between helping the primary perpetrator to commit the crime and influencing his decision to do so.[27]

[20] Schabas, *A Commentary on the Rome Statute* 434.
[21] *Orić* (Trial Chamber Judgment) IT-03-68-T (30 June 2006) [271].
[22] HLA Hart and Tony Honoré, *Causation in the Law* (2nd edn. Clarendon 1985) 54.
[23] Werle, 'Individual Criminal Responsibility' 957. See though section 4.4.1 below.
[24] StGB § 26. [25] StGB § 27, 49(1)(2).
[26] Eser, 'Individual Criminal Responsibility' 798; Schabas, *A Commentary on the Rome Statute* 433–4.
[27] Kadish, 'Complicity, Cause and Blame' 342. See *Mrkšić* et al. (Trial Chamber Judgment) [551]; Schabas, *A Commentary on the Rome Statute* 434.

At the ad hoc tribunals, the conduct element of aiding and abetting liability is formulated to comprise 'acts specifically directed to assist, encourage or lend moral support to the perpetration' of the crime.[28] The formulation 'assist, encourage or lend moral support' reflects customary international law.[29] Article 25(3)(c) of the Rome Statute refers to those who aid, abet *or otherwise assist* in the commission or attempted commission of crime, and specifically includes the provision of means for the commission of crime.[30] The phrasing of the provision suggests that aiding and abetting are subsets of a wider category of assistance.[31] Too much time should not be spent on trying to explicitly delineate the meaning of each—'exchanging synonyms' is not helpful.[32] Instead, it is likely that the ICC will look to the ad hoc tribunals' jurisprudence on this issue.

Assistance, often termed 'practical' assistance by the tribunals,[33] is in many cases relatively straightforward, and encompasses the range of conduct envisaged in Kadish's category of helping the principal to commit crime.[34] Examples are the provision of weapons, transport, or information concerning the location of the potential victims to the principal perpetrator.[35] One complication has been added by the recent decision of the Appeals Chamber of the ICTY in *Perišić*;[36] this will be addressed in more detail below.[37]

Encouragement and the provision of moral support fall into Kadish's second category: influencing the decision of the principal to commit the crime.[38] Statements of support, cheering, or applause will suffice,[39] remembering that stronger forms of influence will be captured within the doctrine of instigation. Beyond outward expressions of encouragement, more difficult questions arise. One is whether liability for aiding and abetting may be founded on an individual's mere presence at the scene of the crime. In *Furundžija*, the Trial Chamber examined a long line of cases arising out of the Second World War. As a baseline, it found that presence alone was not sufficient to give rise to liability.[40] This is consistent with a long held common law position.[41]

[28] *Tadić* (Appeals Chamber Judgment) [229].
[29] See *Taylor* (Appeals Chamber Judgment) SCSL-03-01-A (26 September 2013) [362].
[30] Art 25(3)(c) Rome Statute.
[31] Eser, 'Individual Criminal Responsibility' 798.
[32] Ibid 799.
[33] See *Blaškić* (Appeals Chamber Judgment) [46].
[34] Kadish, 'Complicity Cause and Blame' 345.
[35] See *Ntakirutimana, Ntakirutimana* (Appeals Chamber Judgment) ICTR-96-10-A & ICTR-96-17-A (13 December 2004) [530], [532].
[36] *Perišić* (Appeals Chamber Judgment) IT-04-81-A (28 February 2013).
[37] See section 4.3.4.
[38] Kadish, 'Complicity, Cause and Blame' 342–4.
[39] See *Wilcox* v. *Jeffery* [1951] 1 All ER 464; *R* v. *Giannetto* [1997] 1 Cr App R 1. See also Ashworth, *Principles of Criminal Law* 408.
[40] *Furundžija* (Trial Chamber Judgment) IT-95-17/1-T (10 December 1998) [232].
[41] Smith, *A Treatise on Complicity* 35–9.

However, where the defendant's presence had a 'significant legitimizing or encouraging effect on the principal' responsibility may arise.[42] This is most often the case where the spectator occupies a position of authority vis-à-vis the principal perpetrator.

Exact formulations of the test for liability of the approving spectator have differed in judgments of the tribunals. A summation may be found in the judgment of the Appeals Chamber of the ICTY in *Brđanin*. Describing the situations where such conduct may amount to tacit approval or encouragement, the Appeals Chamber stated:

> In the cases where this category was applied, the accused held a position of authority, he was physically present [at] the scene of the crime, and his non-intervention was seen as tacit approval and encouragement.[43]

Although liability does not follow automatically on this basis where a superior officer is present at the scene of the crime, presence is 'an important *indicium* of encouragement or support'.[44] In the case of *Akayesu* at the ICTR, the defendant's status as mayor of the Taba commune and presence at the scene of the crimes 'sent a clear signal of official tolerance for sexual violence'.[45]

It is also possible that the category of the approving spectator encompasses situations other than those of a superior present at the scene of the subordinate principal's crime. A line of British cases suggests that in cases of non-accidental and continuing presence, liability may arise in the absence of any positive act where a spectator intended to encourage the principal and in fact did so.[46] This does not overly stretch the conceptual limits of the ICTY's holding in *Brđanin*. *Brđanin* and its antecedents establish that an inference of encouragement may be drawn from the defendant's status.[47] Although this is the most likely basis of the inference, it need not be seen as the only one. In situations where it becomes clear that the principal is deriving substantial encouragement from the spectator's presence, and it can be shown that such encouragement was intended, liability for aiding and abetting should arise.[48]

[42] *Furundžija* (Trial Chamber Judgment) [232].

[43] *Brđanin* (Appeals Chamber Judgment) IT-99-36-A (3 April 2007) [273].

[44] *Brđanin* (Trial Chamber Judgment) IT-99-36-T (1 September 2004) [271]. See also Boas et al. *Forms of Responsibility* 308–10.

[45] *Akayesu* (Trial Chamber Judgment) ICTR-96-4-T (2 September 1998) [693].

[46] *Coney* (1882) 8 QBD 534; *R* v. *Clarkson* (1971) 55 Cr App Rep 445.

[47] *Brđanin* (Appeals Chamber Judgment) [273]; *Akayesu* (Trial Chamber Judgment) [693]; *Aleksovski* (Trial Chamber Judgment) IT-95-14/1-T (25 June 1999) [65]; *Blaškić* (Trial Chamber Judgment) IT-95-14-T (3 March 2000) [284].

[48] See Smith, *A Treatise on Complicity* 35–9.

As explained in the next section, the crucial point, in this respect, is the demonstration of substantial effect.

4.3.2. The Nexus Requirement

The range of conduct that might help or encourage a principal's commission of crime is broad. Complicity rules ordinarily, and ought to, specify a minimum relationship between the accomplice's actions and the principal's crime.[49] International criminal law is no different. The ad hoc tribunals have held that the acts of assistance, encouragement, or support must have a substantial effect on the commission of the crime to attract liability for complicity.[50] This reflects customary international law.[51] The standard has also been expressed as one of substantial contribution,[52] though it is doubtful that this differs in a material respect from the standard of substantial effect.[53] Indeed, in *Mrkšić*, the ICTY Appeals Chamber articulated both tests in the same paragraph.[54] Permitting resources under one's control to be used for the perpetration of crime, guarding detainees, and controlling access to them are examples of conduct that may have a substantial effect on the principal's perpetration.[55] A similar requirement may be read into the Rome Statute.[56]

In determining what constitutes a 'substantial effect', it is helpful to distinguish different forms of aiding and abetting. Some forms of assistance may substantially contribute to the perpetration of crime without the principal being aware thereof.[57] The nineteenth century case of *State* v. *Tally* provides an example. Tally, a judge, prevented the transmission of a telegram intended to warn one Ross that Tally's brothers-in-law were out to kill him.[58] The brothers-in-law did not know of this assistance when they perpetrated the crime. Nonetheless, Tally was convicted as an accomplice.

Other forms of complicity, specifically those of encouragement or moral support, logically require actual communication to the principal. Shouts of encouragement that go unheard cannot be considered a substantial

[49] See section 2.5.3 above.

[50] *Tadić* (Appeals Chamber Judgment) [229]; *Simić* (Appeals Chamber Judgment) [85]; *Mrkšić, Šljivančanin* (Appeals Chamber Judgment) [81].

[51] *Taylor* (Appeals Chamber Judgment) [401].

[52] See *Krstić* (Trial Chamber Judgment) IT-98-33-T (2 August 2001) [601]; *Mrkšić, Šljivančanin* (Appeals Chamber Judgment) [81].

[53] Boas et al. *Forms of Responsibility* 317.

[54] *Mrkšić, Šljivančanin* (Appeals Chamber Judgment) [81].

[55] *Krstić* (Appeals Chamber Judgment) IT-98-33-A (19 April 2004) [135]–[138]; *Blagojević, Jokić* (Appeals Chamber Judgment) IT-02-60-A (9 May 2007) [132].

[56] See Eser, 'Individual Criminal Responsibility' 799–801.

[57] Fletcher, *Rethinking Criminal Law* 678.

[58] *State* v. *Tally* (1894) 15 So 722.

contribution, or indeed any contribution at all.[59] Such conduct does not influence the perpetrator in any way. Extending aiding and abetting liability to include failed attempts at complicity links the complicit actor to conduct to which his actions bear no relation. In Fletcher's words, '[t]hat the accessory actually contributes to the commission of the crime is part of what it means to be an accessory'.[60]

One notable aspect of the criterion of substantial effect at the ad hoc tribunals is its breadth.[61] The tribunals have repeatedly emphasized what substantial effect does *not* require—a cause-effect or condition precedent relationship[62]—but have not spent as much time setting out what it does require. Any form of support, even tacit approval arising on the basis of mere presence, seems to fulfil the nexus requirement.[63] As a basic matter of interpretation, *substantial* effect must mean something more than simply an effect, or a remote effect. Moreover, given the potential breadth of the objective requirement of aiding and abetting,[64] the nexus requirement ought to play a limiting role in excluding more minor contributions.[65] Some forms of encouragement, including many cases of the approving spectator, should probably be insufficient for accomplice liability.[66]

There is also a temporal aspect to the nexus requirement. It is often emphasized in the jurisprudence of the ad hoc tribunals that the assistance may be rendered before, during, or after the principal has committed the crime.[67] Liability for assistance rendered before or during the crime is uncomplicated. In the *Čelebići* case, the Appeals Chamber adopted the Trial Chamber's holding that the act of assistance may occur at a time and place removed from the commission of the crime so long as it is 'found to have contributed to, or have had an effect on', its commission.[68] Evidently, in cases of *ex post*

[59] Fletcher, *Rethinking Criminal Law* 680.

[60] Ibid.

[61] Werle, 'Individual Criminal Responsibility' 968.

[62] See *Blaškić* (Appeals Chamber Judgment) [48]. The denial of a 'causal effect' seems to turn on an attenuated understanding of possible types of causal contribution. See section 2.5.3 above.

[63] See *Brđanin* (Appeals Chamber Judgment) [273].

[64] See *Tadić* (Trial Chamber Judgment) IT-94-1-T (7 May 1997) [689]: 'The Trial Chamber finds that aiding and abetting includes all acts of assistance by words or acts that lend encouragement or support, as long as the requisite intent is present.'

[65] See Eser, 'Individual Criminal Responsibility' 800–1.

[66] As Smith illustrates, it can be difficult to tell whether instances of encouragement make the indirect causal contribution that complicity rules ought to demand. Ordinarily, this will entail a detailed evidentiary inquiry into the effect of the encouragement on the principal. See Smith, *A Treatise on Complicity* 85–7; section 2.5.3 above.

[67] See *Mrkšić, Šljivančanin* (Appeals Chamber Judgment) [81]; *Blagojević, Jokić* (Appeals Chamber Judgment) [127]; *Simić* (Appeals Chamber Judgment) [85].

[68] *Čelebići* (Appeals Chamber Judgment) IT-96-21-A (20 February 2001) [352].

facto assistance, the legwork will be in proving the substantial effect of the assistance.

The cases of *Strugar* and *Blagojević* illustrate this point. In *Strugar*, the Trial Chamber rejected the prosecution's argument that the defendant's failure to properly investigate and punish the unlawful conduct of his subordinates could constitute *ex post facto* assistance having a substantial effect on the commission of those crimes.[69] In *Blagojević*, one issue was whether the reburial of victims of the genocide at Srebrenica carried out with the defendant's assistance could constitute *ex post facto* aiding and abetting in the commission of that crime. Answering affirmatively, the Trial Chamber found that such assistance could be *ex post facto* aiding and abetting. However, it found that liability could only arise in such a case where there was a prior agreement between the principal and *ex post facto* assister that the accomplice would provide assistance.[70] This was not the case in *Blagojević*.

These cases demonstrate the limited reach of *ex post facto* aiding and abetting. The phrasing often adopted by the tribunals should not be read to suggest that international criminal law recognizes complicity liability on the basis of an individual's conduct as an accessory after the fact. As discussed in Chapter 2, despite linguistic similarities, the doctrine of accessory after the fact should not be regarded as a form of complicity.[71] As Blackstone put it, the crime of accessory after the fact was 'always an offence of a different species of guilt…'.[72] It is not that the subsequent assister contributes to the commission of the crime, but that she receives, relieves, or comforts the wrongdoer in the knowledge of its commission.[73] This distinction is generally adhered to in national legal systems.[74]

For this reason, care should be taken in simply asserting that the assistance rendered by an aider or abettor may occur before, during, or after the commission of the crime. The requirement of a substantial contribution to perpetration is essential. This requirement is manifest in the ad hoc tribunals' demand that 'prior agreement exists between the principal and person who subsequently aids and abets in the commission of the crime'.[75] To put it in practical terms, if the principal and aider agree that the principal will murder a civilian and the aider will dispose of the body, criminal liability for aiding

[69] *Strugar* (Trial Chamber Judgment) IT-01-42-T (31 January 2005) [355].

[70] *Blagojević, Jokić* (Trial Chamber Judgment) IT-02-60-T (17 January 2005) [730]–[731]. The line between cases of this kind and joint criminal enterprise liability is not altogether clear.

[71] Smith, *A Treatise on Complicity* 7. See section 2.2 above.

[72] 4 Bl Comm 40.

[73] Ibid 37.

[74] William Schabas, *The UN International Criminal Tribunals—The Former Yugoslavia, Rwanda and Sierra Leone* (CUP 2006) 305.

[75] *Blagojević, Jokić* (Trial Chamber Judgment) [731].

and abetting murder may arise. If the principal kills a civilian, and another party, with no prior knowledge of the murder, agrees to dispose of the body, no accomplice liability arises. The other party may be liable for some other crime, perhaps obstruction of justice, but is not in a legal sense complicit in the murder.

4.3.3. The Fault Element

With a broad conduct element and underdeveloped nexus element for aiding and abetting, much of the burden in delimiting liability is shifted to the fault required of the accomplice. At the ad hoc tribunals, the fault requirement has been formulated in different terms.[76] The classic formulation is that the aider and abettor must know that his conduct assists in the commission of the crime of the principal perpetrator and be aware of the essential elements of the crime ultimately committed.[77] It is not required that his purpose was to provide assistance.[78] A common formulation is that of the Trial Chamber in *Kunarac*: the aider and abettor must 'take the conscious decision to act in the knowledge that he thereby supports the commission of the crime'.[79]

The standard of knowledge preferred by the ad hoc tribunals is consistent with customary international law.[80] For instance, in the *Zyklon B* case before the British Military Tribunal in Hamburg, Bruno Tesch and Karl Weinbacher were convicted of war crimes on the basis of their provision to the SS of poison gas that was used at Auschwitz.[81] As summarized by the Judge Advocate, what needed to be demonstrated was 'that the accused knew that the gas was to be used for the purpose of killing human beings'.[82] In the *Jaluit Atoll* case before the United States Military Commission in the Marshall Islands, Ensign Tasaki, a member of the Japanese Imperial Army, handed over custody of three prisoners of war to their eventual executioners. He was convicted on the basis that he arranged their release in the knowledge that they would be killed.[83] And before the Special Court for Sierra Leone,

[76] Boas et al. *Forms of Responsibility* 319–20.

[77] *Blaškić* (Appeals Chamber Judgment) [49]; *Orić* (Appeals Chamber Judgment) [43].

[78] See *Blaškić* (Appeals Chamber Judgment) [49].

[79] *Kunarac, Kovač, Vuković* (Trial Chamber Judgment) IT-96-23-T & IT-96-23/1-T (22 February 2001) [392]. See Boas et al. *Forms of Responsibility* 321.

[80] For an overview, see *Taylor* (Appeals Chamber Judgment) [413]–[437]; *Presbytarian Church of Sudan* et al. v. *Talisman Energy, Inc* (No 09-1262) (Brief of Amici Curiae of International Law Scholars). See also Van Sliedregt, *Individual Criminal Responsibility* 128–30; Chimène Keitner, 'Conceptualizing Complicity in Alien Tort Cases' (2008) 60 Hastings Law Journal 61, 88–94.

[81] *Zyklon B—Trial of Bruno Tesch and Two Others* (8 March 1946) (1947) I LRTWC 93.

[82] Ibid 101.

[83] *The Jaluit Atoll Case* (13 December 1945) (1947) 1 LRTWC 71, 73 (United States Military Commission, Marshall Islands).

Charles Taylor was convicted on the basis that he knew that his support to the Revolutionary United Front would assist them in their commission of international crimes.[84]

Interestingly, the Rome Statute takes a different approach. Article 25(3)(c) requires that the assistance be given 'for the purpose of facilitating the commission' of the crime.[85] The provision of a specific fault element ousts the applicability of the default rule in Article 30.[86] Textually, at least, aiding and abetting under the Rome Statute thus requires a demonstration of purpose.[87]

This stricter fault element will be of less relevance to cases of abetment as the accomplice's purpose will usually be easily inferred from the nature of the speech.[88] In cases of physical assistance, it may be decisive. Eser gives the example of a person asked by a soldier to disclose the whereabouts of a civilian, who is then killed. If the person assisted out of fear rather than out of an intention to assist in the unlawful killing of a civilian, he may not be liable under Article 25(3)(c), even though he is aware that he would be helping the perpetrator.[89] This logic might absolve the independent shopkeeper who, purely in pursuit of profit, knowingly provides the means for the commission of crime.[90] As argued in Part A, a standard of purpose sets the threshold for accomplice liability too high. Moreover, it does not reflect customary international law.[91]

Returning to the customary standard of knowledge, three additional issues arise. First, complicity rules need to specify exactly what the accomplice must know. In the central case, the ad hoc tribunals have held the fault element to be fulfilled where the aider or abettor is 'aware of the essential elements of the crime which was ultimately committed by the principal'.[92] This echoes the old common law formulation of Lord Goddard in *Johnson* v. *Youden*.[93] In addition, the tribunals have held the fault element to be fulfilled where the accomplice is not certain which of a number of crimes is to be committed, but 'is aware that one of those crimes will probably be

[84] *Taylor* (Trial Chamber Judgment) [6949].

[85] Though see Art 25(3)(d)(ii) Rome Statute.

[86] Art 30 Rome Statute.

[87] Schabas, *A Commentary on the Rome Statute* 435.

[88] Ibid 436.

[89] Eser, 'Individual Criminal Responsibility' 801.

[90] Of course, whether the shopkeeper is absolved will depend on how strictly the court interprets the requirement of purpose in Art 25(3)(b).

[91] For a discussion of the relationship between the Rome Statute and customary international law on this question, see Keitner, 'Conceptualizing Complicity in Alien Tort Cases' (2008) 60 Hastings Law Journal 61, 81–94.

[92] See *Haradinaj* et al. (Appeals Chamber Judgment) [58]; *Orić* (Appeals Chamber Judgment) [43]; *Mrkšić, Šljivančanin* (Appeals Chamber Judgment) [159]; *Simić* (Appeals Chamber Judgment) [86].

[93] *Johnson* v. *Youden* [1950] 1 KB 544, 546.

committed'.[94] So imagine a soldier delivers a prisoner of war to a detention centre manned by paramilitaries in the knowledge that the paramilitaries routinely mistreat, torture, and/or kill detainees. The soldier may not know if the detainee will, in that particular instance, be tortured before being killed, tortured and released, mistreated and released, or immediately killed. If the soldier knew that one of these crimes would be committed and, in fact, one of them is committed, he should be seen to fulfil the *mens rea* requirement of aiding and abetting liability.

The second issue is more far-reaching. James Stewart argues that despite orthodox avowals that knowledge is the requisite fault element, what is really applied in practice is a standard of recklessness.[95] The conceptual foundation of Stewart's argument is his claim that we cannot *know* what will happen in the future.[96] Because we cannot *know* what will happen in the future, the accomplices are necessarily inculpated on the basis of their awareness of a probability that the principal's wrong will occur. For Stewart, because 'awareness of a probability is constitutive of culpable risk-taking' the standard applied must be recklessness rather than knowledge.[97]

As noted in Part A, this argument is true only in a narrow sense: there may indeed be *conceptual* difficulties with using the term knowledge to refer to beliefs about future events. However, in both law and ordinary language, the idea of knowledge as to future events is entirely intelligible. In terms of law, Shute explains that the legal standard of knowledge may be 'less demanding than our normal conceptual understandings would lead us to expect'.[98] In ordinary language, we regularly use phrases like 'you knew that would happen' or 'I knew he'd turn up'. We're really asserting a reasonably certain belief as to what will happen in the ordinary course of events.[99]

But Stewart is not only making a claim as to the conceptual intelligibility of a standard of knowledge for accomplices; he also argues that the standard actually applied by international courts as a matter of doctrine is one of recklessness. In other words, the legal category of knowledge has bled into a standard that looks more like the culpable risk-taking entailed by recklessness.[100]

94 See *Haradinaj* et al. (Appeals Chamber Judgment) [58]; *Mrkšić, Šljivančanin* (Appeals Chamber Judgment) [159]; *Simić* (Appeals Chamber Judgment) [86].

95 Stewart, 'The End of Modes of Liability' 192. 96 Ibid 194. 97 Ibid 192.

98 Shute, 'Knowledge and Belief in Criminal Law' in Shute and Simester, *Criminal Law Theory* 171, 192.

99 For a much more detailed discussion, see Shute, 'Knowledge and Belief in Criminal Law' in Shute and Simester, *Criminal Law Theory* 171.

100 Stewart, 'The End of Modes of Liability' 192.

On this count, Stewart's argument finds some support in the case law. Take for instance, the commonly repeated refrain from the ad hoc tribunals noted above: 'In this regard, where an accused is aware that one of a number of crimes will *probably* be committed, and one of those crimes is in fact committed, he has intended to facilitate the commission of that crime, and is guilty as an aider and abettor.'[101] Likewise, in its recapitulation of the fault element for aiding and abetting in *Taylor*, the Trial Chamber of the SCSL held that it must be shown beyond reasonable doubt that the accused 'knew that his acts or omissions would assist the commission of the crime, or that he was aware of the *substantial likelihood* that his acts would assist the commission of the crime'.[102] In other words, despite consistent averments that knowledge is required, that standard is taken to encompass what looks like a form of recklessness.[103]

The danger here is obvious. Shute argues that '(o)ur non-legal understandings of the nature of belief draw a clear distinction between a "belief that-it-might-be-that p" and a "belief that p"'.[104] Moreover, where 'p' is the commission of an *intentional* offence, and the consequence of that belief is the inculpation of the assisting party, the line between the two becomes critical. At stake is the principle of culpability: such a scheme holds reckless contributors responsible for the intentional wrongdoing of their principals.[105] International criminal law should limit responsibility to situations where it can be shown that the accomplice was at least aware that she was facilitating the principal's crime.[106] In practice, that will mean a reiteration of a test closer to practical certainty than substantial likelihood.

The principled concern with the dilution of the legal category of knowledge is less pronounced in instances where the putative accomplice is certain that an international crime will be committed but is not sure which one of the imagined set of crimes it will be. This is the example noted above where the soldier hands over a prisoner of war to paramilitaries in the knowledge

[101] See *Haradinaj* et al. (Appeals Chamber Judgment) [58]; *Mrkšić, Šljivančanin* (Appeals Chamber Judgment) [159]; *Simić* (Appeals Chamber Judgment) [86] (emphasis added).

[102] *Taylor* (Trial Chamber Judgment) [6904]. See also *Taylor* (Appeals Chamber Judgment) [438].

[103] Ibid 193.

[104] Shute, 'Knowledge and Belief in Criminal Law' in Shute and Simester, *Criminal Law Theory* 171, 195.

[105] On the same problem in the doctrine of command responsibility, see Damaška, 'The Shadow Side of Command Responsibility' 463–4. For a broader discussion, see Kadish, 'Reckless Complicity' 369.

[106] Of course, starting from a blank state it would be possible to set up a detailed scheme of liability responding to negligent complicity, reckless complicity, knowing complicity, and purposive complicity.

that they routinely mistreat, torture, and/or kill detainees, but is unsure which will occur. Here, although we may think of the accomplice as reckless as to the commission of the *particular* crime that does occur,[107] her practical certainty that she is assisting the commission of an international crime puts her beyond a moral threshold sufficient to justify inculpation on the basis of accomplice liability. Such situations, in addition to instances of wilful blindness,[108] should be seen to fit within the legal category of knowledge.

The third and final issue concerns the fault element of complicity for specific intent crimes. The case law of the tribunals is clear that knowledge of the principal's specific intent is sufficient.[109] So for persecutions, for instance, assistance must be provided with awareness of the discriminatory grounds of the perpetrator's conduct.[110] For genocide, the assistance must be provided with awareness of the perpetrator's intent to destroy, in whole or in part, a national, ethnical, racial, or religious group, as such.[111] Some scholars, however, argue that accomplices should share the specific intent of the principal. In respect of genocide, for instance, Mettraux argues that a standard of knowledge is not only incorrect as a matter of law but also, in the undue pursuit of convictions, risks depriving genocide of its specificity and identity as the most serious crime in international law.[112] On his interpretation, accomplices should also hold the intent to destroy the protected group.

Mettraux's argument is not persuasive.[113] Imagine a developer wishes to build a power station in a region heavily populated by a particular racial minority. He knows that a paramilitary group is planning to commit genocide against the group so decides to provide them with funds and logistical support. The developer bears no genocidal intent towards the racial minority; that is to say, in providing the support he does not 'seek to produce' the destruction of the group.[114] In fact, his own intent is directed to forcible displacement of the group, rather than its destruction.[115] The developer knows,

[107] See Ashworth and Horder, *Principles of Criminal Law* 436.

[108] See section 2.5.4.4 above.

[109] See *Krstić* (Appeals Chamber Judgment) [140]; *Blagojević, Jokić* (Appeals Chamber Judgment) [127]; *Ntakirutimana, Ntakirutimana* (Appeals Chamber Judgment) [364].

[110] See generally *Tadić* (Appeals Chamber Judgment) [305]; Ken Roberts, 'The Law of Persecution Before the International Criminal Tribunal for the Former Yugoslavia' (2002) 15 Leiden J Intl L 623.

[111] For a discussion of the intent required for genocide, see Alexander Greenawalt, 'Rethinking Genocidal Intent: The Case for a Knowledge-Based Interpretation' (1999) 99 Colum L Rev 2259; Kai Ambos, 'What Does "Intent to Destroy" in Genocide Mean?' (2009) 91 Intl Rev of the Red Cross 833.

[112] Guénaël Mettraux, *International Crimes and the* Ad Hoc *Tribunals* (OUP 2005) 212.

[113] See Werle, 'Individual Criminal Responsibility' 969.

[114] *Akayesu* (Trial Chamber Judgment) [498].

[115] As in *Krstić*. See *Krstić* (Appeals Chamber Judgment) [133]–[134].

however, of the group's genocidal plans.[116] Assuming genocide is committed, on Mettraux's interpretation he would not be guilty of aiding and abetting genocide.

Such an outcome would be wrong. In essence, complicity liability is about helping or influencing the commission of wrongdoing by another party. As Werle puts it, 'it is not the person assisting who defines the crime committed; it is the perpetrator'.[117] More fundamentally, the culpability of someone who provides assistance to a perpetrator with knowledge of her genocidal intent is not far below that of someone who provides assistance while sharing that intent. This is reflected in case law—knowledge is sufficient to inculpate the accomplice.[118]

4.3.4. Specific Direction

A full account of complicity in international criminal law cannot fail to pay attention to the recent controversy over the requirement of specific direction in the case law of the ICTY. In *Perišić*, the defendant, former Chief of Staff of the Yugoslav Army, was convicted by the Trial Chamber of aiding and abetting the crimes of the VRS on the basis of his provision of weapons, ammunition, fuel, and other types of support.[119] At the time of that support, he was aware of the essential elements of those crimes and that he was thereby providing practical assistance to their commission.[120] The Trial Chamber did not require, however, that his support 'be specifically directed towards assisting' the crimes of the VRS,[121] a requirement the Appeals Chamber held to be relevant in situations of assistance by a geographically or otherwise remote accomplice.[122] On this basis, the Appeals Chamber overturned his convictions.[123]

The decision of the Appeals Chamber in *Perišić* thrust the obscure world of aiding and abetting liability at the ICTY onto the pages of the international press,[124] inflaming internal and external tensions in the process.[125] There are three related issues here. First, is the requirement of specific direction

[116] See *Krstić* (Appeals Chamber Judgment) [137].
[117] Werle, 'Individual Criminal Liability' 969–70.
[118] See *Krstić* (Appeals Chamber Judgment) [140].
[119] *Perišić* (Trial Chamber Judgment) [1650]. [120] Ibid [15]. [121] Ibid [16].
[122] Ibid [38]–[39]. [123] *Perišić* (Appeals Chamber Judgment) [43].
[124] See Kenneth Roth, 'A Tribunal's Legal Stumble' *The New York Times* (New York, 9 July 2013).
[125] Internally, see Marko Milanović, 'Danish Judge Blasts ICTY President' (*EJIL:Talk!*, 13 June 2013) <http://www.ejiltalk.org/danish-judge-blasts-icty-president/> accessed 21 December 2014; externally, see Guy de Launey, 'Momcilo Perisic Hague Acquittal Leaves Little Sense of Justice' *BBC News* (Belgrade, 28 February 2013).

consistent with the prior jurisprudence of the ICTY? Second, is it consistent with customary international law? And third, does it make sense as a matter of criminal law theory and policy?

On the first question, it makes sense to start with the Appeals Chamber's own reasoning. Its first move was to refer back to *Tadić*, where it was held that an 'aider and abettor carries out acts *specifically directed* to assist, encourage or lend moral support to the perpetration' of the principal crimes.[126] It then correctly noted that a number of subsequent ICTY and ICTR decisions have repeated this language verbatim.[127] Taking this holding from *Tadić* as 'settled precedent', the court then reasoned that other decisions that fail to refer to specific direction either did not purport to be an exhaustive review of aiding and abetting liability or did not evince an intention to depart from the settled jurisprudence.[128]

One problem with this reasoning is that it had never been accepted that the stock language from *Tadić* repeated in various judgments added anything to the orthodox test of aiding and abetting.[129] It certainly was not at issue in *Tadić* itself.[130] This point is raised in the partially dissenting opinion of Judge Liu in *Perišić*.[131] Moreover, in *Mrkšić* the Appeals Chamber had explicitly rejected the argument that specific direction is required for aiding and abetting.[132]

The reason that the stock language from *Tadić* was not thought to add anything to the test of aiding and abetting is simple: specific direction as part of the conduct element does not make much sense. On the Appeals Chamber's own understanding, an act would be specifically directed where (i) the recipient organization (the VRS in this case) was one whose sole and exclusive purpose was to commit crimes, or (ii) where the putative accomplice endorsed the policy of assisting the principal's crimes.[133] The first option rests on a binary classification—exclusively criminal groups against *all other groups*—that bears very little relation to the reality that almost all

[126] *Tadić* (Appeals Chamber Judgment) [229] (emphasis added).
[127] *Perišić* (Appeals Chamber Judgment) [28].
[128] *Perišić* (Appeals Chamber Judgment) [30]–[36].
[129] James Stewart, 'The ICTY Loses its Way on Complicity—Part 1' (*Opinio Juris*, 3 April 2013) <http://opiniojuris.org/2013/04/03/guest-post-the-icty-loses-its-way-on-complicity-part-1/> accessed 22 December 2014.
[130] See Manuel Ventura, 'Farewell "Specific Direction": Aiding and Abetting War Crimes and Crimes against Humanity in *Perišić*, *Taylor*, *Šainović* et al. and US Alien Tort Statute Jurisprudence' in Stuart Casey-Maslen (ed.) *The War Report 2013* (OUP 20 November 2014) 10.
[131] *Perišić* (Appeals Chamber Judgment) (Partially Dissenting Opinion of Judge Liu).
[132] *Mrkšić, Šljivančanin* (Appeals Chamber Judgment) [159]. See also *Lukić, Lukić* (Appeals Chamber Judgment) IT-98-31/1-A (4 December 2012) [424].
[133] *Perišić* (Appeals Chamber Judgment) [52].

organizations carry out a mix of lawful and unlawful actions. The second option—the reference to *endorses*—hints at what is really going on: the raising of the fault element of aiding and abetting liability in international criminal law.[134]

More precisely, the introduction of specific direction attempts to resolve in the conduct element two questions arising at other points of any complicity enquiry.[135] First, complicity rules need to specify a certain relationship between the accomplice's acts and the principal's wrong to give them any meaningful content.[136] In international criminal law, this is the requirement of substantial effect or substantial contribution.[137] Second, although the Appeals Chamber asserts that 'specific direction is an analytically distinct element of *actus reus*',[138] it is really saying something about the mental state with which Perišić provided his assistance.[139] It seeks to re-resolve the knowledge/purpose debate with a standard that looks more like the latter.

This point was not lost on the Appeals Chamber. The Joint Separate Opinion of Judges Meron and Agius explicitly notes that 'whether an individual commits acts directed at assisting the commission of a crime relates in certain ways to that individual's state of mind',[140] and that if they were setting out the elements afresh, they would consider including specific direction as an element of *mens rea*.[141] Where their opinion misleads is in its assertion that 'whether an individual specifically aimed to assist relevant crimes logically fits within our current *mens rea* requirement'.[142]

As explained above, at the ICTY and in customary international law the fault element of complicity is knowledge, albeit one that is sometimes reduced to a form of recklessness in practice.[143] Specific direction, properly understood as a disguised increase in the fault element, is thus inconsistent with both bodies of law.[144]

[134] See Stewart, 'The ICTY Loses its Way on Complicity—Part 1'.

[135] Ibid. See also *Taylor* (Appeals Chamber Judgment) [480].

[136] See section 2.5.3 above. [137] See section 4.3.2 below.

[138] *Perišić* (Appeals Chamber Judgment) [48].

[139] See James Stewart 'The ICTY Loses its Way on Complicity—Part 2' (*Opinio Juris*, 3 April 2013) <http://opiniojuris.org/2013/04/03/guest-post-the-icty-loses-its-way-on-complicity-part-2/> accessed 22 December 2014.

[140] *Perišić* (Appeals Chamber Judgment) (Joint Separate Opinion of Judges Meron and Agius) [2].

[141] Ibid [4]. [142] Ibid [3]. [143] See section 4.3.3 above.

[144] To be sure, inconsistency with customary international law does not itself mean that the ICTY was wrong to adopt the standard. As Heller explains, the demand that the ad hoc tribunals apply custom is informed by the *nullen crimen sine lege* principle; that demand is absent where the tribunals *narrow* rather than expand individual criminal liability. See Kevin Heller, 'The SCSL's Incoherent—and Selective—Analysis of Custom' (*Opinio Juris*, 27 September 2013) <http://opiniojuris.org/2013/09/27/scsls-incoherent-selective-analysis-custom/> accessed 22 December 2014.

Two leading cases since *Perišić* have confirmed this. In *Taylor*, the Appeals Chamber of the Special Court for Sierra Leone explicitly rejected the argument that specific direction forms part of the *actus reus* of aiding and abetting liability in customary international law.[145] At the same time, in response to defence counsel's initial submission that specific direction was analogous to a purpose standard in the fault element of aiding and abetting, the Appeals Chamber reaffirmed the customary standard of knowing participation.[146]

In *Šainović*, the Appeals Chamber of the ICTY was again faced with the issue of specific direction. Despite the (tenuous) possibility of distinguishing the facts of Lazarević's appeal in *Šainović* from those in *Perišić* on the basis that the former's proximity to the principal crimes rendered a showing of specific direction unnecessary,[147] the Appeals Chamber chose to address the issue.[148] Recognizing divergence between *Perišić*, on one hand, and *Mrkšić* and *Lukić*, on the other, the Appeals Chamber undertook a comprehensive review of specific direction in the jurisprudence of the ad hoc tribunals and customary international law. The outcome of this review was the unambiguous rejection of specific direction and consequent reaffirmation of the orthodox tripartite test for aiding and abetting: (a) practical assistance, encouragement, or moral support, (b) which has a substantial effect on the perpetration of the crime, (c) provided with knowledge that it assists in the commission of the principal crime.[149]

Šainović should be the last word on the question at the ICTY, though that is not entirely certain. Following *Perišić*, but before *Šainović*, in May 2013 a Trial Chamber of the ICTY acquitted the defendants in *Stanišić and Simatović* of, amongst other modes of liability, aiding and abetting numerous crimes committed against civilian populations in large parts of Bosnia-Herzegovina and Croatia.[150] Part of the reason for the acquittal was the Chamber's finding that it was reasonable to conclude that the assistance provided 'was not specifically directed towards the commission of the crimes of murder, deportation, forcible transfer, or persecution'.[151] The Prosecutor has appealed.[152] Although there is a risk that the composition of the Appeals

[145] *Taylor* (Appeals Chamber Judgment) [481].

[146] *Taylor* (Appeals Chamber Judgment) [467]; [483]. For a longer discussion, see Ventura, 'Farewell "Specific Direction"' 15–21.

[147] See *Šainović* et al. (Dissenting Opinion of Judge Tuzmukhamedov) [43]; Ventura, 'Farewell "Specific Direction"' 23.

[148] *Šainović* et al. (Appeals Chamber Judgment) IT-05-87-A (23 January 2014) [1615]–[1651].

[149] Ibid [1649].

[150] *Stanišić and Simatović* (Trial Chamber Judgment) IT-03-69-T (30 May 2013).

[151] Ibid [2360].

[152] *Stanišić and Simatović* (Prosecution Appeal Brief) IT-03-69-A (25 September 2013).

Chamber in *Stanišić and Simatović* will bear on its resolution, the rejection of specific direction in *Šainović* should be affirmed.

It is clear, then, that specific direction, whether seen as a part of the conduct element or the fault element, is inconsistent with the jurisprudence of the ad hoc tribunals and customary international law. It is also inconsistent with the general claim of this work that as a matter of principle and policy, knowledge should be sufficient for complicity. Before concluding, however, it is worth pausing on the concern that has driven the entire affair, for beneath the doctrinal missteps there is a real issue.

The issue is the potential over-inculpation of contributors to military or armed groups pursuing, for the most part, lawful objectives—funders, arms-suppliers, and so on. Although it has been picked up in the judgments, a focus on geographical remoteness is a misstep; the proximity with which we deliver assistance does not itself affect our culpability. Rather, what's lying behind these cases is the question of how legal doctrines of complicity, premised to some degree on individualized connections between accomplice and principal, can deal with large-scale provisions of aid to groups or collections of actors carrying out a mix of lawful and unlawful activities.[153]

This concern can be seen in Judge Moloto's questions to the prosecution during closing arguments in *Perišić* as well as in his dissent in the Trial Chamber.[154] In the former, Judge Moloto raised (with scepticism) the potential criminal responsibility of commanders of various NATO armies for continuing to contribute to the war effort in Afghanistan while being aware of the crimes committed at Guantánamo Bay, at Bagram Airfield, and in Kabul. In the latter, he was drawn by the reality of significant military aid between states, often aimed at supporting legitimate interests such as the deterrence of war and promotion of peace and security. This concern also features in ongoing debates about the arming of rebel groups. To take the specific example of Syria, there is strong evidence that some of the rebels have committed international crimes.[155] It seems probable that in the ongoing course of hostilities, more crimes will be committed. Yet, the debate about providing arms and other assistance persists.

[153] See Jens Ohlin, 'Why did the ICTY Acquit Stanišić and Simatović?' (*Lieber Code*, 1 June 2013) <http://www.liebercode.org/2013/06/why-did-icty-acquit-stanisic-and.html> accessed 22 December 2014.

[154] *Perišić* (Trial Chamber Judgment) (Dissenting Opinion of Judge Moloto) [8]–[34]; *Perišić* (Prosecution Closing Statement) (28 March 2011) 14657–61.

[155] See UNHRC, 'Report of the Independent International Commission of Inquiry on the Syrian Arab Republic' (4 June 2013) UN Doc A/HRC/23/58; Human Rights Watch, 'Open Letter to the Leaders of the Syrian Opposition' (20 March, 2012).

Whenever we consider large-scale assistance to a group or collection of actors who carry out a mix of lawful and unlawful activities, difficult questions arise for complicity. The ICTY's solution—smuggling what looks like a purpose standard into the *actus reus*—threatens to leave aiding and abetting under-inclusive, potentially allowing knowing accomplices to escape liability. One way to mitigate concerns of over-inculpation would be to place renewed emphasis on the nexus and fault elements.[156] For the nexus element, the tribunals have not properly spelled out the requirements of 'substantial assistance' or 'substantial contribution';[157] for the fault element, the slide towards recklessness should be averted.

Beyond that, there is no easy answer. As the probability that some of that aid will be used to commit international crimes increases, so the burden should fall on the potentially complicit party to either refrain from providing aid or do more to ensure that its assistance does not *substantially contribute* to the commission of international crimes. The generic idea of 'arming the rebels' obscures a raft of choices therein: who exactly is armed, with what, on what conditions, with what kinds of training. In the (rare) instance where arming a group is strictly required to avert a humanitarian catastrophe, even though we *know* that the group will commit international crimes, there is the possible application of the doctrine of necessity.[158]

Longer term, the conditions under which putative accomplices are willing to assist may affect the conduct of potential perpetrators—the assisters' refusal to provide aid on the basis of their own liability informing the assisted party's own desire to comply with international law. That there may seem to be good strategic, policy, or even humanitarian reasons for supporting one side to a conflict in a particular case should not render inapplicable ordinary doctrines of complicity.[159]

[156] James Stewart, '"Specific Direction" is Indefensible: A Response to Heller on Complicity' (*Opinio Juris*, 12 June 2013) <http://opiniojuris.org/2013/06/12/specific-direction-is-indefensible-a-response-to-heller-on-complicity/> accessed 22 December 2014.

[157] For a much wider discussion, see James Stewart, 'Overdetermined Atrocities' (2012) 10 J Intl Crim Just 1189; Uwe Murmann, 'Problems of Causation with Regard to (Potential) Actions of Multiple Protagonists' (2014) 12 J Intl Crim Just 283.

[158] See Stewart, '"Specific Direction" is Indefensible'; *Gillick* v. *West Norfolk and Wisbech Area Health Authority and the Department of Health and Social Security* [1986] AC 112. Cf *Erdemović* (Appeals Chamber Judgment) IT-96-22-A (7 October 1997).

[159] How international law should respond in situations where assistance might both (i) constitute complicity in an international crime, and (ii) be, on balance, the *right* thing to do, clearly requires further thought. For a fascinating discussion in this direction, see Chiara Lepora and Robert Goodin, *On Complicity and Compromise* (OUP 2013).

4.4. The Structure of Complicity in International Criminal Law

4.4.1. Differentiation in the Attribution of Responsibility

As argued in Chapter 2, complicity is a particular way of contributing to wrongdoing. In law, accomplices ought to be held responsible for their own complicit contribution to the principal's wrong and not for the principal's wrong itself. The corollary of this point is a preference for non-imputational complicity rules: those who help or influence a principal perpetrator should be held responsible in those terms—instigating war crimes, aiding crimes against humanity, or abetting genocide—and punished for their own contribution to the principal's wrong.[160] Liability of this kind is still derivative in that the complicit actor's conduct is linked to the principal offence. But it is not imputational.

In evaluating the structure of the rules, Chapter 2 also argued that it is insufficient to look only to legal doctrine—that is, whether the system recognizes different forms of complicity as a matter of doctrine. Rather, it is important to ask how the system attributes responsibility to the accomplice.[161]

Under Article 6 of the Nuremberg Charter, accomplices were responsible for all acts committed by the principal; under Article 2 of Allied Control Council Law No 10, accessories and abettors were deemed to have committed the principal's crime.[162] At the ad hoc tribunals, there is evidently doctrinal differentiation among different participants: we can specify, as a matter of legal doctrine, the elements of rules prohibiting instigation and aiding and abetting. But there is no differentiation in the attribution of responsibility. The provisions on criminal responsibility in the statutes of the tribunals specify that any person who instigated or aided and abetted a crime within the jurisdiction of the tribunal 'shall be individually responsible for the crime'.[163] In practice, this is how the tribunals have proceeded. Stewart argues that in 95 per cent of cases involving convictions for aiding and abetting, instigating, ordering, or planning, the disposition makes no mention

[160] See section 2.4.1 above. [161] See section 2.4.2 above.

[162] Art 6 Nuremberg Charter; Art II(2) Allied Control Council Law No. 10, Punishment of Persons Guilty of War Crimes, Crimes against Peace and Humanity (20 December 1945) 3 Official Gazette Control Council for Germany 50–5 (1946).

[163] Art 7(1) ICTY Statute, Art 6(1) ICTR Statute.

of the particular doctrine in play.[164] Rather, responsibility is attributed to the defendant *for* the underlying crime he aided, abetted, or instigated.[165]

In this way, the approach of the ad hoc tribunals to complicity is similar to that in England and Wales. There is clearly doctrinal differentiation—we can look to the law reports and textbooks to find out exactly what it means to aid, abet, or instigate. Moreover, it is often implicitly, and sometimes explicitly, assumed by judges that there is a gradation in culpability in different modes of participation.[166] But this doctrinal differentiation does not give rise to normative differentiation at the level of responsibility. In other words, the principal's wrong is imputed to the accomplice.

This problem is likely to continue at the ICC. Article 25(3) of the Rome Statute sets out a number of modes of liability, including commission, ordering, solicitation, and aiding and abetting. On the face of it, Article 25(3)(a) appears to be an attempt to grade the culpability of different participants—that is to say, it establishes a normative hierarchy among participants.[167] This question of normative hierarchy has provoked disagreement within the court and is discussed in section 4.4.2 below.[168]

Of more interest at this point is the related question of whether the doctrinal differentiation among participants in wrongdoing carries over into differentiation in the attribution of responsibility. It does not. Article 25(3) provides that any person who fulfils one of the specified modes 'shall be criminally responsible and liable for punishment for a crime within the jurisdiction of the Court'.[169] That phrasing is worth emphasizing: accomplices 'shall be criminally responsible and liable for punishment for a crime within the jurisdiction of the Court'. In other words, instigation under Article 25(3)(b), and aiding, abetting or otherwise assisting under Article 25(3)(c), are ways that an individual may be responsible for genocide, war crimes, or crimes against humanity. Whether we call these modes of participation, modes of

[164] Stewart, 'The End of Modes of Liability' n 114. Cf *Mrkšić* et al. (Trial Chamber Judgment) [712]; *Taylor* (Trial Chamber Judgment).

[165] Ibid. Van Sliedregt, *Individual Criminal Responsibility* 80–1. See also *Taylor* (Appeals Chamber Judgment) [366].

[166] See *Tadić* (Appeals Chamber Judgment) [192].

[167] Kai Ambos, 'The First Judgment of the International Criminal Court (*Prosecutor* v. *Lubanga*): A Comprehensive Analysis of the Legal Issues' (2012) 12 Intl Crim L Rev 114, 146–7; Werle, 'Individual Criminal Responsibility' 957.

[168] See *Lubanga* (Trial Chamber Judgment) ICC-01/04-01/06 (14 March 2012) [996]–[998]; *Katanga* (Trial Chamber Judgment) ICC-01/04-01/07 (7 March 2014) [1386]; *Lubanga* (Separate Opinion of Judge Fulford) [7]–[9]; *Chui* (Concurring Opinion of Judge Van den Wyngaert) ICC-01/04-02/12 (18 December 2012) [22]–[30]; section 4.4.2 below.

[169] Art 25(3) Rome Statute.

liability, or modes of attribution,[170] the outcome is the same: participants are responsible for the underlying crime.[171]

This conclusion follows from the text as well as from the structure of criminal responsibility embraced by the Rome Statute.[172] In this structure, committing a crime is just another way that one might become criminally responsible for it.[173] This appears to deny that there is anything special about commission. However, when committers are held responsible for the principal crime, either (i) their acts of killing, inflicting, or forcibly transferring constituted the crime,[174] or (ii) assuming a normative model of perpetration, they were responsible for its commission.[175]

Why, however, should instigators or aiders be 'criminally responsible and liable for punishment for' the crime committed by the perpetrator? Solicitors, inducers, and aiders and abettors ought not be responsible for crimes that they did not commit. Instead, informed by the principles of culpability and fair labelling, they ought to be held responsible for soliciting genocide or aiding war crimes, as the case may be. This would be the case in a properly differentiated system of criminal responsibility.[176] The model of criminal responsibility employed by the Rome Statute is commendable in its attempt to distinguish the different ways we might participate in crime. It is not commendable in rendering those different participants responsible for the underlying crime.

4.4.2. Differentiation at Sentencing

As explained in Chapter 2, in understanding how legal systems address participation in wrongdoing it is helpful to distinguish doctrinal differentiation, differentiation in the attribution of responsibility, and differentiation in sentencing. Evidently, there is doctrinal differentiation in international criminal law, though this does not give rise to differentiation in the attribution of responsibility. What about differentiation in sentencing?

It is difficult to draw any conclusions as to differentiation in sentencing from the International Military Tribunal. Likewise, Heller shows that no

[170] Stewart, 'The End of Modes of Liability' n 2.

[171] See Ambos, 'Article 25' 745: 'This approach confirms the general tendency in comparative criminal law to reject a pure unitarian concept of perpetration (*Einheitstätermodell*) and to distinguish, *at least on the sentencing level*, between different forms of participation.' (emphasis added).

[172] See Van Sliedregt, *Individual Criminal Responsibility* 85.

[173] Art 25(3) Rome Statute.

[174] See Lepora and Goodin, *On Complicity and Compromise* 34.

[175] Van Sliedregt, *Individual Criminal Responsibility* 72; Vogel, 'Twelve Models' 155.

[176] See Van Sliedregt, *Individual Criminal Responsibility* 70 using 'pure' to describe such a model.

coherent sentencing practices were developed across the 12 trials constituting the Nuremberg Military Tribunals.[177]

At the ad hoc tribunals, Trial Chambers are required to 'take into account such factors as the gravity of the offence and the individual circumstances of the convicted person'.[178] In the case law, the gravity of the offence has been taken to include the form and degree of the accused's participation in the crime.[179] In *Vasiljević*, the Appeals Chamber stated that 'aiding and abetting is a form of responsibility which generally warrants a lower sentence than is appropriate to responsibility as a co-perpetrator'.[180] In terms of outcomes, aiders and abettors are generally given a lower sentence than orderers, perpetrators, or participants in a JCE.[181] At the ICTY, the median sentence for aiding and abetting in all cases up to June 2010 was 15 years, compared to 18 for perpetrators.[182] Interestingly, the median sentence of instigators was 25 years, though the sample size was only three cases.[183]

The cases establish a discretionary mitigation principle for aiders and abettors at the ICTY.[184] There are insufficient data to draw any firm conclusions about the doctrine of instigation but a tendency towards the German model where instigators do not receive a discount vis-à-vis the principal may be assumed.[185] This is evidently an area where further research is needed.[186]

Beyond the case law of the ad hoc tribunals, the position is confused. The idea that aiding and abetting generally warrants a lower sentence was picked up by the Trial Chamber of the SCSL in *Taylor*,[187] though it is not entirely clear that the principle was given much weight in the final determination of sentence.[188] The Appeals Chamber, although affirming the final sentence, held that neither the Statute of the SCSL nor customary international law provides for a hierarchy among different forms of criminal participation.[189] Rather, in its

[177] Heller, *The Nuremberg Military Tribunals* 330.

[178] Art 24(2) ICTY Statute, Art 23(2) ICTR Statute. See also Rule 101 ICTR/ICTY Rules of Procedure and Evidence (22 May 2013) IT/32/Rev 49.

[179] See *Čelebići* (Appeals Chamber Judgment) [731]; *Kupreškić* et al. (Trial Chamber Judgment) IT-95-16-T (14 January 2000) [852]. See also Barbora Holá, Alette Smeulers, and Catrien Bijleveld, 'International Sentencing Facts and Figures—Sentencing Practice at the ICTY and ICTR' (2011) 9 J Intl Crim Just 411, 415.

[180] *Vasiljević* (Appeals Chamber Judgment) IT-98-32-A (25 February 2004) [182]. See also *Krstić* (Appeals Chamber Judgment) [240]; Werle, 'Individual Criminal Responsibility' 955.

[181] Holá, Smeulers, and Bijleveld, 'International Sentencing' 417. [182] Ibid 429.

[183] Ibid. [184] Van Sliedregt, *Individual Criminal Responsibility* 79.

[185] See StGB § 26.

[186] See generally Silvia D'Ascoli, *Sentencing in International Criminal Law: The UN ad hoc Tribunals and Future Perspectives for the ICC* (Hart 2011).

[187] *Taylor* (Sentencing Judgment) SCSL-03-01-T (30 May 2012) [21].

[188] See Kevin Heller, 'The *Taylor* Sentencing Judgment: A Critical Analysis' (2013) 11 J Intl Crim Just 835.

[189] *Taylor* (Appeals Chamber Judgment) 670.

view, the so-called totality principle—that the sentence must reflect the totality of the defendant's culpable conduct—exhausts the criteria for determining the proper sentence.[190]

It is too soon to draw any firm conclusions about the ICC.[191] Article 78(1) of the Rome Statute borrows language from the statutes of the ad hoc tribunals in providing that in determining sentence, the court should 'take into account such factors as the gravity of the crime and the individual circumstances of the convicted person'.[192] As set out in Rule 145(1)(c) of the court's Rules of Procedure and Evidence, this includes 'the degree of participation of the convicted person'.[193]

More generally, though, it is here where the dispute mentioned in section 4.4.1 as to a normative hierarchy amongst modes of liability becomes important. Early indications from the Trial Chamber in *Lubanga* seemed to recognize a systematic and normative gradation of responsibility in Article 25(3).[194] More recently, however, the Trial Chamber in *Katanga* held that the modes only identify different kinds of illegal behaviour and do not, as a matter of principle, establish a hierarchy of blameworthiness.[195] Crucially, in the court's view, this means that there is no necessary correlation between the mode of liability and the punishment imposed.[196]

As a matter of law, then, it is not entirely clear where we stand. As a matter of principle, modes of liability in international criminal law should be seen as more than a phenomenological description of participation in wrongdoing.[197] The principles of culpability and fair labelling demand that we trace out, as clearly as possible, the contribution of individual participants to the principal wrong in the attribution of responsibility and at sentencing. In respect of the latter, although of course the totality of the defendant's culpability will be the guiding criterion, it is helpful to sketch some general presumptions as to the relationship between different modes of responsibility. In addition to

190 Ibid.

191 For a general discussion of sentencing at the ICC, see D'Ascoli, *Sentencing in International Criminal Law* 263–85.

192 Art 78(1) Rome Statute.

193 ICC Rules of Procedure and Evidence. See Schabas, *A Commentary on the Rome Statute* 902. See also the discussion in *Taylor* (Appeals Chamber Judgment) [646]–[671].

194 *Lubanga* (Trial Chamber Judgment) ICC-01/04-01/06 (14 March 2012) [996]–[998]. See Werle, 'Individual Criminal Responsibility' 957. As noted in section 4.4.1 above, this normative hierarchy does not result in proper differentiation in the attribution of responsibility.

195 *Katanga* (Trial Chamber Judgment) ICC-01/04-01/07 (7 March 2014) [1386]. See also *Chui* (Concurring Opinion of Judge Van den Wyngaert) [23]–[25].

196 *Katanga* (Trial Chamber Judgment) ICC-01/04-01/07 (7 March 2014) [1386].

197 Werle, 'Individual Criminal Responsibility' 957.

capturing normatively significant differences among modes, this would serve the fundamental goal of consistent and coherent sentencing.[198]

As to the putative mitigation for assistors and ordinary abettors, a presumptive discount vis-à-vis the principal, along the lines established at the ICTY, makes sense. This reflects a general intuition that aiders and abettors are less intimately connected to bringing the wrong into existence,[199] and makes sense of international criminal law's attempt, through the adoption of a normative model of principalship, to capture the most responsible as principals.[200] As to the potential parity of instigators, the provision by the instigator of a *reason*[201] for the principal to act suggests a closer connection to the wrong. Both presumptions remain exactly that—a device to structure the court's reasoning.[202]

4.5. Assessing the Rules within the Analytical Framework

The doctrines of instigation and aiding and abetting form a significant part of the wider story of international law's regulation of complicity. As part of that wider story, this work places these rules of complicity into a single analytical framework. The first axis of analysis concerns the forms of complicity prohibited. Here, international criminal law's approach is comprehensive.[203] This point is illustrated by reference to the establishment of the rules. In some legal regimes, rules of complicity develop organically from an initial absence to a prohibition of a certain kind of complicit conduct.[204] As will be seen, as a matter of the primary obligations of states, international law prohibits states from allowing their territory to be used in the commission of acts of aggression by other states. This is a complicity rule, but it is not one that was derived from a general prohibition on complicity. Rather, a specific kind of complicit conduct in a specific wrong is prohibited.

Complicity in international criminal law started from the opposite position. As part of the general provisions on international criminal responsibility,

198 See *Čelebići* (Appeals Chamber Judgment) [756].

199 See Ashworth, *Principles of Criminal Law* 406.

200 See Van Sliedregt, *Individual Criminal Responsibility* 72; Vogel, 'Twelve Models' 155.

201 Hart and Honoré, *Causation in the Law* 54.

202 For a wider discussion, see Vest, 'Problems of Participation' 305–9.

203 Of course, the set of international crimes onto which these complicity rules graft is itself narrow.

204 See Vogel, 'Twelve Models' 160–1.

a prohibition on complicity is established. This prohibition takes the form of general doctrines—instigation and aiding and abetting. Together, these doctrines capture the ways in which we might be complicit in another's acts, denoting both the provision of help and psychological influence.

An important point springs from this approach: the range of conduct that might give rise to complicity liability is immensely broad. Any action that aids, abets, or instigates another's commission of crime is potentially implicated. The breadth of the conduct element demands the development of a nexus requirement, the second axis of the framework. Without such a requirement, complicity liability is likely to inculpate actors who make very minor contributions to wrongdoing. At present, the case law sets out a test of 'substantial assistance', though there is little evidence that it is being applied diligently.

The final issue concerns the fault required of accomplices. Here, international criminal law prescribes a standard of knowledge, although at times this is reduced to a form of recklessness. Best captured in the judgment of ICTY Trial Chamber in *Kunarac*, the accomplice must 'take the conscious decision to act in the knowledge that he thereby supports the commission of the crime'.[205] It should be reiterated that the Rome Statute follows this approach for instigators but introduces a purpose standard for those who aid, abet, or otherwise assist the principal.[206] They must act with 'the purpose of facilitating the commission' of such a crime. Given that many acts of psychological influence will fall under Article 25(3)(b), and thus entail a standard of knowledge, the purpose standard will apply mostly to material acts of assistance, or, in Kadish's terminology, the provision of help to the principal.[207] In principle, cases of knowing assistance should not be excluded from the ambit of complicity.

Part of the value of mapping these rules onto a single analytical framework is to illustrate how the different elements of any complicity rule work together. Complicity liability tends to be overbroad when, in the absence of a substantiality requirement, assistance knowingly provided is sufficient to inculpate the accomplice. A complicity rule conditioned by a standard of purpose and a substantiality requirement is likely to exculpate participants who ought to be responsible.[208] In international criminal law, these issues

[205] *Kunarac, Kovač, Vuković* (Trial Chamber Judgment) IT-96-23-T & IT-96-23/1-T (22 February 2001) [392]. See Boas et al. *Forms of Responsibility* 321.

[206] Arts 25(3)(b), 25(3)(c), 30 Rome Statute.

[207] Kadish, 'Complicity, Cause and Blame' 342.

[208] In this respect, given the textual standard of purpose in Art 25(3)(c) of the Rome Statute, the ICC may wish to apply a nexus requirement short of substantial assistance. See Ambos, 'Article 25' 756–7.

must be located within a structural scheme that holds accomplices responsible for the underlying crime committed by the principal.

4.6. Complicity in Genocide—A Coda for Non-Imputational Complicity

4.6.1. Introduction

In defining the crime of genocide in the statutes of the ICTY and ICTR, the Security Council borrowed the definition set out in Article II of the Genocide Convention.[209] In addition, it lifted unchanged Article III.[210] For this reason, the statutes of both tribunals provide a definition of genocide and specify that, in addition to genocide, the following acts are also punishable: conspiracy, incitement, attempt, and complicity.[211] The reference to complicity in genocide is interesting, for it might be taken to suggest that complicity is a substantive crime in its own right. The question, then, is how this reference to complicity in genocide is reconciled with the statutes' provisions on individual criminal responsibility, which include aiding and abetting as a mode of participation in the substantive crimes within the tribunals' jurisdiction.[212]

4.6.2. Case Law

This question has provoked a great deal of academic discussion.[213] As a matter of positive law, the judgment of the ICTR Trial Chamber in *Akayesu* is a starting point. On its interpretation, complicity in genocide is a substantive crime marked by different *mens rea* and *actus reus* requirements from aiding and abetting as a mode of participation in genocide.[214] Doubt was cast on this position by decisions of the ICTR in *Semanza* and the ICTY in *Stakić*.[215]

[209] UNSC Res 827; UNSC Res 955. [210] Genocide Convention.

[211] Art 4(3) ICTY Statute, Art 2(3) ICTR Statute.

[212] This issue does not arise under the Rome Statute: see Arts 6, 25.

[213] See Chile Eboe-Osuji, '"Complicity in Genocide" versus "Aiding and Abetting Genocide": Construing the Difference in the ICTR and ICTY Statutes' (2005) 3 J Intl Crim Just 56; Grant Dawson and Rachel Boynton, 'Reconciling Complicity in Genocide and Aiding and Abetting Genocide in the Jurisprudence of the United Nations Ad Hoc Tribunals' (2008) 21 Harv Human Rights J 241; Flavia Giustiniani, 'The Responsibility of Accomplices in the Case-Law of the Ad Hoc Tribunals' (2009) 20 Crim L Forum 417, 435–41; Daniel Greenfield, 'The Crime of Complicity in Genocide: How the International Criminal Tribunals for Rwanda and Yugoslavia Got It Wrong, and Why It Matters' (2008) 98 J Crim L & Criminology 921.

[214] *Akayesu* (Trial Chamber Judgment) 545–8.

[215] *Semanza* (Trial Chamber Judgment) [394]; *Stakić* (Trial Chamber Judgment) IT-97-24-T (31 July 2003) [531].

These decisions may be read to suggest that there is 'no material distinction' between complicity in genocide and aiding and abetting genocide.[216] In *Krstić*, the Appeals Chamber of the ICTY specifically noted the variant approaches. At first, it seemed to suggest that Article 7(1), the Statute's provision on individual criminal responsibility, was the proper route for litigating potentially complicit conduct. However, the Appeals Chamber proceeded to maintain that 'complicity in genocide' might be distinct from aiding and abetting liability on the basis that it 'may encompass broader conduct than that of aiding and abetting'.[217]

In *Karemera*, the accused were charged with (i) genocide committed by means of a joint criminal enterprise and, in the alternative, (ii) complicity in genocide committed by means of a joint criminal enterprise.[218] In other words, on the prosecutor's construction complicity in genocide was a substantive crime that was perpetrated by the defendants through the mode of JCE. This was firmly rejected by the ICTY Trial Chamber:

> Whereas the genocide is the crime, joint criminal enterprise and complicity in genocide are two modes of liability, two methods by which the crime of genocide can be committed and individuals held responsible for this crime. It is therefore impossible to plead that complicity in genocide has been committed by means of a joint criminal enterprise. Complicity can only be pleaded as a form of liability for the crime of genocide.[219]

It is a stretch to suggest that a single Trial Chamber decision has settled the matter. One of the three judges, Judge Short, issued a separate opinion disagreeing with the majority's reasoning.[220] Short pointed out that the authority on which the majority purported to rely to establish that complicity in genocide is only a mode of liability is far less categorical and consistent than the majority assumed.[221] His own solution attempted to split the difference: 'In my view, complicity in genocide has the indicia of a criminal offence, whilst encompassing a particular mode of liability.'[222] As things stand, the position is unclear.[223]

[216] *Semanza* (Trial Chamber Judgment) [394].

[217] *Krstić* (Appeals Chamber Judgment) [139].

[218] *Karemera, Ngirumpatse, Nzirorera* (Trial Chamber Decision on Defence Motions Challenging the Pleading of a Joint Criminal Enterprise in a Count of Complicity in Genocide in the Amended Indictment) ICTR-98-44-T (23 May 2006) [1].

[219] Ibid [8].

[220] *Karemera* et al. (Separate Opinion of Judge Short on Trial Chamber Decision on Defence Motions Challenging the Pleading of a Joint Criminal Enterprise in a Count of Complicity in Genocide in the Amended Indictment) [7]–[8].

[221] Ibid. [222] Ibid [8].

[223] See also *Blagojević, Jokić* (Trial Chamber Judgment) [777]; *Brđanin* (Trial Chamber Judgment) [725].

4.6.3. Academic Discussion and Analysis

Chile Eboe-Osuji, now a judge at the ICC, provides one of the earlier academic attempts to resolve the issue. Eboe-Osuji's starting point is that the drafters used two terms that essentially mean the same thing but that the rule of effective construction—*ut res magis valeat quam pereat*—demands that judges make 'every interpretative effort' to reasonably give effect to the text of the Statutes without overlap or redundancy.[224] On his interpretation, there are a number of constructions that may be adopted on the basis of such an interpretive effort. One of these is *Akayesu's* preference for different *mens rea* (and *actus reus*) standards.[225] This Eboe-Osuji rejects on the basis that distinguishing complicity in genocide and aiding and abetting by reference to fine-grained elemental distinctions is strained and hard to justify.[226] His preferred solution focuses on the purpose of each provision within the context of the statute as a whole. The provision on individual criminal responsibility prescribes that those who aid and abet genocide are responsible for genocide itself. Complicity in genocide appears within the definitional section of substantive crimes. This substantive crime should be interpreted to capture (i) accessories after the fact and (ii) a 'residue of culpable genocide-related conducts that do not rise to the level of individual responsibility described in Article 6(1)'.[227]

Eboe-Osuji's approach is the most interesting attempt to resolve the apparent contradiction. Others have been put forward. Some writers seek to maintain a fine-grained elemental distinction between complicity as a crime and aiding and abetting as a mode rejected by Eboe-Osuji.[228] Dawson and Boynton adopt what they call *a heads of responsibility approach*. On this view, complicity in genocide is hybrid of a substantive crime and mode of liability.[229] As a substantive crime, it may be committed through any of the modes of liability under Article 6(1), including aiding and abetting. The authors concede that this would mean that one could aid and abet complicity to commit genocide, but suggest this is a minor issue within their doctrinal scheme as a whole.[230]

All attempts, judicial and academic, to distinguish complicity and aiding and abetting are marked by a similar sense of strain. This is because the

[224] Eboe-Osuji, 'Complicity in Genocide' 59.

[225] *Akayesu* (Trial Chamber Judgment) [545]–[548].

[226] Eboe-Osuji, 'Complicity in Genocide' 67.

[227] Ibid 79 (emphasis omitted).

[228] See Greenfield, 'The Crime of Complicity in Genocide'.

[229] Dawson and Boynton, 'Reconciling Complicity in Genocide' 278. See also *Karemera* (Separate Opinion of Judge Short) [8].

[230] Dawson and Boynton, 'Reconciling Complicity in Genocide' 278.

two concepts express the same idea: assisting or encouraging another person to perpetrate a crime is wrong. If this starting point is correct, how can the inclusion of complicity in genocide as a substantive crime be explained? The answer is simple and, indeed, implicitly illustrated by the strained attempts at reconciliation: the comprehensive and verbatim lifting of Articles II and III of the Genocide Convention resulted in the inclusion of a redundant provision in both statutes.

It is highly unlikely that having decided on the general approach to criminal liability represented in Articles 6(1) and 7(1), including the provision of complicity liability through the doctrines of aiding and abetting and instigation, the drafters decided to carve out a special substantive crime of complicity in genocide. It would follow that such a crime could be committed through all other modes, including aiding and abetting and instigation. The better explanation is that a perceived desire to avoid a loophole led to the inadvertent inclusion of a redundant provision.[231] This point is widely understood and is implicitly accepted by the Appeals Chamber in *Krstić*:

> Because the Statute must be interpreted with the utmost respect to the language used by the legislator, the Appeals Chamber may not conclude that the consequent overlap between Article 7(1) and Article 4(3)(e) is a result of an inadvertence on the part of the legislator where another explanation, consonant with the language used by the Statute, is possible.[232]

In other words, we know that it was inadvertence, but we must try to explain it away. In a similar vein, Eboe-Osuji presents his attempt to explain the contradiction with the qualification that it follows from his understanding that it *must* be explained. He concedes that his solution does not follow 'from a definitional or elemental conception of "complicity"'.[233]

The attempts to explain it either are interpretively strained beyond breaking point or do not resolve the redundancy.[234] Even if some solution could be reached that carves out a specific substantive crime of complicity in genocide, it would still fail to cohere with the general structure of criminal liability set out in the statutes of the tribunals and in international criminal law more generally. A better approach would be to abandon the search for a substantive crime of complicity in genocide and continue to develop a coherent

[231] See Schabas, *The UN International Criminal Tribunals* 183; Marko Milanović, 'State Responsibility for Genocide: A Follow Up' (2007) 18 Eur J Intl L 669, 680.

[232] *Krstić* (Appeals Chamber Judgment) [139].

[233] Eboe-Osuji, 'Complicity in Genocide' 79.

[234] See Boas et al. *Forms of Responsibility* 301; Payam Akhavan, 'The Crime of Genocide in the ICTR Jurisprudence' (2005) 3 J Intl Crim Just 989, 994.

conception of complicity liability through aiding and abetting. The rule of effective construction is not unlimited.

In the context of this work, this argument is somewhat paradoxical. After all, the work's normative argument is that non-imputational rules of complicity are a more principled way to hold responsible those who influence or assist others to commit wrongdoing. On this basis, it might be thought that complicity in genocide ought to be considered a substantive crime in its own right. However, the incoherence of such a crime within the general structure of liability would cause more harm than good. Moreover, this issue does not arise under the Rome Statute, and it is not inconceivable that the ICC could interpret Article 25 in a way that realizes the broader normative claim—that the doctrinal differentiation amongst participants in crime in Article 25 is carried through into differentiation in the attribution of responsibility.

4.7. Conclusion

Complicity in international criminal law is primarily accounted for by the doctrines of instigation and aiding and abetting. The distinction drawn between serious forms of influence over the perpetrator and less serious encouragement is to be supported. In content, the rules are marked by the breadth of the conduct they prohibit, a standard of knowledge in the fault element, and an explicit but underdeveloped substantiality criterion in assessing the relationship between the accomplice's actions and the principal's crime. Structurally, despite doctrinal differentiation among participants in wrongdoing, there is no differentiation in the attribution of responsibility. In holding accomplices responsible for their principal's crime, international criminal law fails to respect the principles of culpability and fair labelling.

5

Omissions and Complicity in International Criminal Law

5.1. Introduction

Other than the case of the approving spectator, the discussion of complicity in Chapter 4 assumed that the conduct at issue is an action—the provision of weapons, the guarding of a detainee, the shout of encouragement. Chapter 5 considers how international criminal law deals with complicit omissions.[1] It does so in two ways. First, it is now recognized that an omission is another way that the conduct element of aiding and abetting liability may be fulfilled. As a matter of fact, some omissions do aid or abet a principal's commission of crime. Normatively, some of those failures to act are sufficiently culpable to place the actor on an equivalent footing to those who help or influence by positive action. Second, failure by a superior to prevent crimes carried out by her subordinates gives rise to liability under the doctrine of command responsibility. At least where the superior had actual knowledge of the crimes, the rule may be regarded as a very specific iteration of complicity by omission. Where the superior ought to have known that her subordinates were committing or about to commit the crimes, the doctrine of command responsibility may be thought of as a species of negligent complicity.

5.2. Aiding and Abetting By Omission

5.2.1. Introduction

The case law of the ad hoc tribunals establishes that a failure to fulfil a legal duty may give rise to international criminal liability for aiding and abetting

[1] On the distinction between acts and omissions, see generally Fletcher, *Rethinking Criminal Law* 421–39; Kadish, 'Act and Omission, *Mens Rea*, and Complicity' 65–89.

by omission. Some earlier formulations of the conduct element of aiding and abetting seem to limit its scope to acts.[2] In *Blaškić*, the Appeals Chamber of the ICTY explicitly raised the possibility that an omission could found aiding and abetting liability but did not rule on it.[3] The absence of unambiguous examples of aiding and abetting by omission was noted by the ICTR Trial Chamber in *Mpambara*,[4] and led some commentators to conclude that there is no proper support for aiding and abetting by omission as a form of responsibility in international criminal law.[5]

Such a conclusion is no longer tenable after *Mrkšić* at the ICTY. Beyond its affirmation of legal principle, *Mrkšić* provides an example of the potential factual basis of omissions liability in international criminal law, an analysis of the essential criterion of duty, and a foundation for the development and critique of the law. The defendants, Veselin Šljivančanin, Mile Mrkšić, and Miroslav Radić were charged with crimes committed in November 1991 against Croats and others who had sought refuge in Vukovar hospital after the fall of the city.[6] The victims were evacuated from the hospital to Ovčara farm, where they were tortured and eventually executed.[7] In the main, the crimes were physically perpetrated by Territorial Defence (TO) forces and paramilitaries rather than by soldiers of the Yugoslav People's Army (JNA). The case concerned the relationship between the defendants, all officers in the JNA, and the crimes committed at Ovčara.

Šljivančanin was a major in the JNA. His superior, Colonel Mrkšić, put him in charge of evacuating the hospital in which the victims had sought refuge.[8] Under Šljivančanin's orders, the victims were transported from the hospital to Ovčara farm via the local JNA barracks. A number of TO forces and paramilitaries gathered at the farm. In the course of the day, acts of torture and cruel treatment were perpetrated against the victims, predominantly by the TO forces and paramilitaries. Military police within the official structure of the JNA were present at Ovčara, ostensibly to ensure the security of the prisoners. On Mrkšić's orders, they withdrew in the early evening.[9] The withdrawal left the prisoners under the control of the TO forces and paramilitaries. Shortly after the withdrawal, the TO forces and paramilitaries murdered the prisoners.[10]

[2] See *Vasiljević* (Appeals Chamber Judgment) [102]: 'The aider and abettor carries out acts specifically directed to assist, encourage or lend moral support to the perpetration of a certain specific crime... and this support has a substantial effect upon the perpetration of the crime.'

[3] *Blaškić* (Appeals Chamber Judgment) [47].

[4] *Mpambara* (Trial Chamber Judgment) ICTR-01-65-T (11 September 2006) [23].

[5] See Boas et al. *Forms of Responsibility* 314–15.

[6] *Mrkšić* et al. (Trial Chamber Judgment) [1]. [7] Ibid [539]. [8] Ibid [400].

[9] Ibid [293]. [10] Ibid [613].

5.2.2. The ICTY Trial Chamber in *Mrkšić*

It is helpful to split the substantive crimes into (a) murder as a violation of the laws and customs of war and (b) torture and cruel treatment as violations of the laws and customs of war. The charges of crimes against humanity were dismissed on the basis of the absence of the required jurisdictional requirements under Article 5 of the Statute.[11] The indictment charged the defendants with a number of modes of responsibility under Article 7(1) of the Statute. On the charge of joint criminal enterprise, the Trial Chamber found that the evidence did not support individual responsibility. Likewise, the defendants were not found to have planned, ordered, or instigated the crimes.[12] Only aiding and abetting liability remained.

Mrkšić was convicted of aiding and abetting murder on the basis that his order for the JNA soldiers to withdraw from the farm rendered substantial practical assistance to the TO forces and paramilitaries who executed the prisoners. The Trial Chamber was satisfied that when he gave the order he was aware the TO forces and paramilitaries presented a grave threat to the prisoners of war.[13] On the charges of torture and cruel treatment, the evidence demonstrated that Mrkšić knew that violence was being committed against the prisoners and that the TO forces and paramilitaries had a propensity towards extreme violence.[14] He had readily available means to ensure that the violence abated, and yet failed to act. This failure was found to have rendered practical assistance to the perpetrators of cruel treatment and torture.[15]

Šljivančanin was convicted by the Trial Chamber of aiding and abetting *torture* by omission. His initial involvement in the transfer of prisoners to Ovčara was not the basis of this conviction—participation therein was not allied with anticipation of the crimes subsequently committed.[16] Rather, it was that having later become aware of the mistreatment of the prisoners, he was under a duty to prevent the further commission of the crimes and made no effort to do so.[17]

The Trial Chamber found three sources of such a duty: (i) the laws and customs of war, in particular Article 13 of the Third Geneva Convention; (ii) Šljivančanin's remit as chief security officer of the relevant division of

[11] Ibid [711]. [12] Ibid [608], [614]–[618]. [13] Ibid [621]. [14] Ibid [627].
[15] Ibid [623]–[633].
[16] Ibid [660]. The basis of this finding was that there had not yet been a final decision by Mrkšić as to how the prisoners would eventually be secured. At the time, JNA military police were present at the farm.
[17] Ibid [667].

the JNA; and (iii) the specific responsibility for the security of the prisoners entrusted to him by Mrkšić, his superior.[18] The Trial Chamber set out a number of measures he could have taken to fulfil this duty.[19] In failing to do so, it was found that he must have been aware that he was facilitating the commission of torture and cruel treatment.

The Trial Chamber did not convict Šljivančanin of aiding and abetting *murder* by omission. In this regard, the events should be divided into pre- and post-withdrawal of the JNA forces. At the time of Šljivančanin's visit to the farm in the afternoon—before the withdrawal—it was found that he could reasonably have believed that the TO forces and paramilitaries would not have killed the prisoners.[20] This was because of the ongoing presence of the JNA forces. As noted above, after Mrkšić gave the order to withdraw, the prisoners were murdered. In the Trial Chamber's view, Šljivančanin's responsibility for providing for the security of the prisoners ended with the withdrawal of the last JNA troops. On this basis, although he may have had the requisite *mens rea*, he was no longer under a duty to act.[21]

5.2.3. The ICTY Appeals Chamber in *Mrkšić*

The prosecution appealed Šljivančanin's acquittal for aiding and abetting murder by omission. As to the events before the withdrawal of the JNA soldiers, the Appeals Chamber upheld the Trial Chamber's finding: 'it was [not] unreasonable for the Trial Chamber to find that it was unable to conclude that, at the time of his visit to Ovčara, Šljivančanin was aware that the prisoners of war would probably be murdered...'.[22] As to the events after the withdrawal, the Appeals Chamber first held that Šljivančanin must have known of Mrkšić's order to withdraw and therefore that it was likely that the prisoners would be killed.[23] This finding left the vexing issue of whether Šljivančanin owed a duty to secure the welfare of the prisoners after the order to withdraw had been given.

In this regard, the prosecution argued that Šljivančanin was under a continuing legal duty under international humanitarian law.[24] In focusing on the putative duty imposed by international humanitarian law, the prosecution appeared to concede (i) that no duty arose on the basis of Šljivančanin's position as chief security official, and (ii) that his specially

[18] Ibid [668]. [19] Ibid [670]. [20] Ibid [672]. [21] Ibid [673].
[22] *Mrkšić, Šljivančanin* (Appeals Chamber Judgment) [60]. [23] Ibid [62].
[24] Ibid [64].

delegated authority from Mrkšić had been terminated on Mrkšić's order to withdraw.[25]

The Appeals Chamber first ruled on the applicability of the Third Geneva Convention and Common Article 3 to the conflict.[26] Article 13 of GCIII provides that '[a]ny unlawful act or omission by the Detaining Power causing death or seriously endangering the health of a prisoner of war in its custody is prohibited, and will be regarded as a serious breach of the present Convention'.[27] Although this provision is directed to the Detaining Power, the Appeals Chamber found that members of armed forces also acquire these international obligations with respect to prisoners of war.[28] These moves culminated in its finding that:

> Geneva Convention III invests all agents of a Detaining Power into whose custody prisoners of war have come with the obligation to protect them by reason of their position as agents of that Detaining Power. No more specific investment of responsibility in an agent with regard to prisoners of war is necessary. The Appeals Chamber considers that all state agents who find themselves with custody of prisoners of war owe them a duty of protection regardless of whether the investment of responsibility was made through explicit delegation such as through legislative enactment or a superior order, or as a result of the state agent finding himself with *de facto* custody over prisoners of war such as where a prisoner of war surrenders to that agent.[29]

Šljivančanin was thus under an obligation to protect the prisoners of war held at Ovčara farm and not to transfer custody of the prisoners without assuring himself that they would not be harmed by the recipients. He remained an officer of the JNA and agent of the detaining power even after the order to withdraw was given.[30] On the basis that he had the requisite *mens rea* and that his failure to protect the prisoners substantially contributed to the principal crimes, Šljivančanin was convicted of aiding and abetting murder by omission.[31]

[25] Ibid [64]. [26] Ibid [70].

[27] Art 13 Convention (III) Relative to the Treatment of Prisoners of War (adopted 12 August 1949, entered into force 21 October 1950) 75 UNTS 135 (GCIII).

[28] *Mrkšić, Šljivančanin* (Appeals Chamber Judgment) [72]. [29] Ibid [73].

[30] Ibid [75].

[31] Ibid [103]. Šljivančanin's conviction for aiding and abetting murder by omission was subsequently vacated by the Appeals Chamber in a review judgment of 8 December 2010. As noted above, Šljivančanin's conviction was based on the inference that Mrkšić must have informed him of his order to withdraw JNA soldiers securing the prisoners from Ovčara. New testimony by Miodrag Panić, a former JNA officer, made this inference untenable. See *Šljivančanin* (Appeals Chamber Review Judgment) IT-95-13/1-R.1 (8 December 2010).

5.2.4. Analysis

Mrkšić demonstrates how cases of complicit omission arise in times of war. The general principle that an omission may fulfil the conduct element of aiding and abetting liability should be supported. As a matter of fact, sometimes a failure to act does assist the commission of crime; think of the cleaner who intentionally fails to lock the bank so as to facilitate a robbery.[32] As a normative matter, sometimes such failures are sufficiently reprehensible as to warrant the imposition of complicity liability. The key, of course, is the existence of a duty of protection owed towards the victims.[33]

The case gets to the core of the issue concerning the kinds of duty that may found international criminal liability for complicity by omission. As noted, the prosecution initially pointed to three potential sources of Šljivančanin's duty to act: his duty under the laws and customs of war; his duty in his capacity as chief of the security organ; and his duty under Mrkšić's delegated authority.[34] The Trial Chamber appeared to recognize all three.[35] During the appeal, the prosecution subsequently appeared to concede that Šljivančanin's capacity as chief of the security organ founded no duty towards the prisoners and that any delegated duty from Colonel Mrkšić had terminated. This led the Appeals Chamber to focus on the laws and customs of war as the source of the legal duty to act. In the case at hand, Article 13 of GCIII was interpreted to impose a duty on 'each agent in charge of the protection or custody of the prisoners of war to ensure that their transfer to another agent will not diminish the protection the prisoners are entitled to'.[36]

One possible implication of the Appeals Chamber's reasoning is that omissions liability *must* be founded on a duty arising under the laws and customs of war. This approach may be seen in certain judgments of the ad hoc tribunals.[37] However, references to other sources of duty may be found. In *Orić*, the Trial Chamber suggested that a duty to act may be located in the defendant's position of authority or in his antecedent conduct by which the victim was exposed to danger.[38] In *Rutaganira*, the Trial Chamber of the ICTR referred not only to domestic criminal law but also to the state's obligations

[32] Ashworth, *Principles of Criminal Law* 410–11.

[33] See Section 2.5.2.2 above.

[34] *Mrkšić, Šljivančanin* (Appeals Chamber Judgment) [64].

[35] *Mrkšić* et al. (Trial Chamber Judgment) [669].

[36] *Mrkšić, Šljivančanin* (Appeals Chamber Judgment) [71].

[37] See *Vasiljević* (Trial Chamber Judgment) IT-98-32-T (29 November 2002) [62]. For discussion, see Lars Berster, '"Duty to Act" and "Commission by Omission" in International Criminal Law' (2010) 10 Intl Crim L Rev 619, 621–2.

[38] *Orić* (Trial Chamber Judgment) [304].

under international human rights law as potential sources.[39] In *Bagambiki*, the defendant was bound by a legal duty under Rwandan domestic law—the Law on the Organization and Function of the Prefecture—to ensure the protection of those within his prefecture.[40] This duty was not *criminal* in nature. For this reason, the Trial Chamber found that the breach could not give rise to international criminal liability.[41] It recognized, however, that a domestic criminal law duty could give rise to liability.[42]

The question of which duties count for the purposes of omissions liability in international criminal law is a difficult one. To take a step back, in ordinary domestic criminal law cases of omission, the role of the duty is two-fold. First, it reflects a normative judgment of the legal system that a particular failure to act is so culpable that the eventuating harm should be attributed to the individual: the father ought not to watch his child drown, Miller ought not to watch his cigarette burn, and Pittwood ought not to leave his railway post unattended.[43] Second, the duty fulfils doctrinal requirements of legal causation—identifying a specific person whose culpable relationship with an eventuating harm is such that she may be held responsible for it. One lesson here is that neither of the two roles of duty in criminal omissions cases has anything to do with criminal law per se. The source of the duty in each case varies—it may be statutory, contractual, or based on an undertaking, it may arise on the basis of a particular relationship with the victim or it may stem from the defendant's prior creation of risk of the subsequent harm. A second lesson is that the duty is constituted as a criminal law duty by the court's determination that it is to be so.[44]

In this instance, what is true in national legal orders should also be true on the international plane.[45] Take the duty arising under the laws and customs of war in *Mrkšić*. As the Appeals Chamber concedes, the duties set out in the Third Geneva Convention bind the high contracting parties thereto.[46] The duty itself did not bind Šljivančanin. To put it another way, Šljivančanin is not being held responsible for breaching Article 13 of GCIII. Instead, we should recognize that the duty that bound Šljivančanin was constituted and

[39] *Rutaganira* (Trial Chamber Judgment) ICTR-95-1C-T (14 March 2005) [78], [82]. See Berster, 'Duty to Act' 621–4.

[40] *Ntagerura, Bagambiki, Imanishimwe* (Trial Chamber Judgment) ICTR-99-46-T (25 February 2004) [660].

[41] Ibid.

[42] Ibid [659].

[43] See section 2.5.2.2 above. In respect of Germany, see StGB § 13; Bohlander, *Principles of German Criminal Law* 40–8.

[44] See Fletcher, 'Criminal Omissions' 706.

[45] See Duttwiler, 'Liability for Omission' 56.

[46] *Mrkšić, Šljivančanin* (Appeals Chamber Judgment) [72].

imposed by the court itself. Of course, Article 13 of GCIII is central to its reasoning process. Article 13 prohibits any act or omission by a Detaining Power that causes the death of, or seriously endangers the health of, any prisoner of war within its custody.[47] From this, the court reasoned that any agent of the Detaining Power into whose custody the prisoners have come is required to protect them by virtue of their position as agent.[48] Failing to protect a prisoner in your custody is one of the ways that the conduct element of aiding and abetting may be fulfilled.

On the basis of the same reasoning, to suggest that only the laws and customs of war could ground an international court's constitution and imposition of liability for aiding and abetting by omission would exclude from the ambit of international criminal law a range of complicit omissions for which responsibility should arise. An example might illustrate this point. A civil war is ongoing. Operatives from one of the parties to the conflict regularly ambush and murder civilians as they traipse across an exposed mountain pass. This happens every second or third night for a month. In response, the government employs two civilians to man a checkpoint on each side of the mountain pass. The two undertake to prevent any civilians from entering the pass whenever sources inform them that the operatives are in the area. The system works and civilian deaths plummet, allowing them to cross undisturbed on the nights when the group are not operating and preventing them from crossing on nights when they are. After receiving the relevant information one night, one of the men deliberately omits to warn civilians at the checkpoint that the group is waiting on the pass. The civilians pass through the checkpoint and are murdered in violation of the laws and customs of war.

It would be difficult to argue that the checkpoint operator breached any duty to act imposed by international law.[49] But to give that answer is really to ask the wrong question. Rather than asking whether the omission violated a duty imposed by international law, we should be searching for those individuals with a culpable relationship to the perpetration of the wrong proscribed by international criminal law.[50] That is the essence of complicity liability. In this case, there is little doubt that the checkpoint operator's omission aided the commission of the war crime; indeed, it is difficult to distinguish from positive conduct that might have facilitated the principal wrong. Likewise, he acted with a guilty mind. The duty arising on the basis of his undertaking to

[47] Art 13 GCIII. [48] *Mrkšić, Šljivančanin* (Appeals Chamber Judgment) [73].

[49] For a different example see Duttwiler, 'Liability for Omission' 55–6.

[50] Cf Berster, 'Duty to Act' 631.

prevent such harms from occurring brings him into the category of culpable participant and ought to ground individual criminal responsibility.

This reasoning ought to be adopted at the ICC. Omissions liability in general was a matter under negotiation in the drafting process of the Rome Statute.[51] Despite the inclusion of a general provision on omissions in the draft statute,[52] it was cut from the final text, primarily owing to strong objections from France.[53] The upshot of this exclusion has divided academic commentators. On the one hand, Eser is emphatic that 'the abstinence from explicit regulation cannot be interpreted in any other way than the rejection of individual criminal responsibility for commission by omission...'.[54] Ambos agrees, though is a little more tentative.[55] On the other hand, Werle argues that the Statute should be interpreted to cover omissions, primarily on the basis that omissions liability may be seen as a general principle of law.[56] This too is Duttwiler's position.[57]

Early indications from the court suggest an implicit assumption that the Statute includes omissions liability.[58] On assessment, the deletion of a general provision on omissions from the final text should not be seen to bar the court from developing a theory of omissions liability. First, the Rome Statute refers to conduct rather than acts—the former being a term often seen to encompass acts and omissions.[59] Omissions liability would thus not be inconsistent with the terms of the Statute. Second, the case law on omissions liability at the ad hoc tribunals, including liability for aiding and abetting by omission, may be a source of applicable law under Article 21(1)(b) of the Statute.[60] Third, Article 21(1)(c) of the Statute empowers the court to apply general principles of law derived from national legal systems.[61] In a comprehensive survey, Duttwiler demonstrates widespread recognition that omissions in the face of a duty to prevent harm are at times sufficiently culpable so as to be treated in the same way as actions.[62] This widespread recognition reflects a principled assessment of the wrongfulness of some omissions.

[51] Duttwiler, 'Liability for Omission' 57–8.

[52] See Art 28(1), Report of the Preparatory Committee for the Establishment of an International Criminal Court—Draft Statute for the International Criminal Court (14 April 1998) UN Doc A/Conf.183/2/Add.1.

[53] Per Saland, 'International Criminal Law Principles' in Roy Lee (ed.) *The International Criminal Court: The Making of the Rome Statute—Issues, Negotiations, Results* (Kluwer Law International 1999) 189, 212.

[54] Eser, 'Individual Criminal Responsibility' 819.

[55] Ambos, 'Article 25' 770.

[56] Werle, 'Individual Criminal Responsibility' 966.

[57] Duttwiler, 'Liability for Omission' 60.

[58] See *Lubanga* (Decision on the Confirmation of Charges) [351]–[354].

[59] See Duttwiler 'Liability for Omission' 59.

[60] Art 21(1)(b) Rome Statute.

[61] Art 21(1)(c) Rome Statute.

[62] Duttwiler, 'Liability for Omission' 26–56.

Legal systems must make judgments on which failures to act are culpable and which conduct constitutes complicity. In international criminal law, these are questions that cannot be answered unequivocally by reference to the statutes of the tribunals or the Rome Statute. In Berster's view, the use of non-criminal duties in this endeavour exceeds the judicial competence of a court not empowered to make law.[63] A better view is that determining the ambit of aiding and abetting liability is not necessarily illegitimate judicial law-making. Once we recognize that certain omissions help or encourage other actors to commit a wrong, the subsequent step is to ask which of these omissions are sufficiently culpable as to justify the imposition of accomplice liability.[64]

On this basis, some tentative sources of duty may be put forward.[65] These are not necessarily exhaustive. First, certain professional or statutory obligations ought to be recognized. Duttwiler gives the example of a doctor who, after the outbreak of a genocidal programme, deliberately refuses to treat members of the persecuted minority, thereby letting them die.[66] Second, an individual's prior dangerous act should give rise to a duty to avert the specific kind of harm threatened by that act.[67] Say, for instance, a soldier is transporting landmines and absentmindedly fails to tie down the box containing the mines. The mines fall off the truck. On her way to retrieve the mines, the soldier sees a group of civilians approaching and intentionally omits to warn them. A civilian is blown up. Here, the soldier should be liable for wilful killing as a war crime on the basis of her failure to fulfil her duty to prevent the harm from occurring. The basis of that duty is her prior dangerous act.

Third, and perhaps most importantly, a duty to prevent harm may arise on the basis of a voluntary undertaking. The source of duties of this kind is sometimes described as contractual, but, taking Fletcher's position, the idea of an undertaking provides a more coherent basis for understanding why liability should be imposed.[68] The undertaking to prevent harm explains the liability imposed on the lifeguard who fails to save a drowning swimmer, the railway operator who fails to close the boom, and the lookout who fails to warn civilians about the gang operating along the mountain pass. The duty not only marks out what action ought to have been taken but also plays an essentially causal role, linking the omission to the harm that resulted.

[63] Berster, 'Duty to Act' 631. [64] See StGB § 13.

[65] See Kadish, 'Act and Omission, *Mens Rea*, and Complicity' 71 on the virtues of a 'case-by-case evolution of common law duties'. See also Bohlander, *Principles of German Criminal Law* 40–8 for an explanation of the German position.

[66] Duttwiler, 'Liability for Omission' 55–6. [67] See *Miller* [1983] 2 AC 161.

[68] Fletcher, *Rethinking Criminal Law* 615.

5.2.5. Omissions and the Other Elements of Aiding and Abetting Liability

The ad hoc tribunals have repeatedly held that the basic elements of aiding and abetting apply notwithstanding whether this form of liability is charged as an omission or an act, rejecting the argument that a more stringent nexus should arise between the omission and the principal crime.[69] Both acts and omissions must have a substantial effect on the commission of the crime.[70] What this means in the context of omissions is difficult to specify in the abstract.[71]

Besides the requisite *mens rea*, any assessment of complicit omissions is asking: (i) should the defendant have acted to prevent the harm, and (ii) could the defendant have acted to prevent the harm? The former question shifts much of the evaluative burden onto the search for a duty to act. The latter question is one of capacity, a condition required by the principle of fairness.[72] In this regard, Šljivančanin argued in *Mrkšić* that a number of other officers had the material ability—and were better placed—to act to prevent the mistreatment of prisoners.[73] For the Appeals Chamber this did not matter, holding that the fact that the accused's omission had a more limited effect on the commission of the crime than the conduct of others did not mean that the omission could not have rendered substantial assistance.[74] What the Appeals Chamber is really saying is that Šljivančanin should have acted and could have acted—that others might have acted detracts from neither of these claims.

This argument is tenable where we have narrowly circumscribed duties arising to protect against narrowly specified kinds of harm. The lifeguard at a swimming pool is the classic example. But where the scope of the duty is broad and it binds a wide-ranging class of subjects we might want the nexus element to play an increased role. Imagine their contract of employment imposes on all soldiers in the army a duty to prevent acts of torture from occurring during conflict. Twenty thousand soldiers are stationed on an army base and it is known a small unit is torturing prisoners. None of the soldiers acts. Are all twenty thousand liable to conviction for aiding and abetting torture by omission?

[69] *Mrkšić, Šljivančanin* (Appeals Chamber Judgment) [81], [146]. See also *Perišić* (Trial Chamber Judgment) IT-04-81-T (6 September 2011) [134].

[70] *Mrkšić, Šljivančanin* (Appeals Chamber Judgment) [200].

[71] See Eser, 'Individual Criminal Responsibility' 801.

[72] Ashworth, 'Criminal Liability for Omission' 449.

[73] *Mrkšić, Šljivančanin* (Appeals Chamber Judgment) [197].

[74] Ibid. See also *Blagojević, Jokić* (Appeals Chamber Judgment) [134].

One response might emphasize that capacity to act to prevent the harm from occurring is an essential element of omissions liability. This is true as far as it goes. But even if proper emphasis is placed on capacity, it still seems that some sort of proximity requirement should be imposed for criminal liability. Of course, each of the soldiers who knew about the torture ought to have taken some steps to avert the harm, even if that was just reporting it up the chain of command. A failure in this regard could rightly give rise to direct responsibility for such a failure. But the jump to criminal accomplice liability is bigger, and in cases of broad-ranging duties we should be concerned with identifying those most responsible within the class—perhaps the nearby commander rather than the peripheral private. This is how the idea of substantial assistance may be given bite for omissions.

In addition to the pressure that the inclusion of omissions puts on the nexus requirement, it also puts increased focus on the fault required of the accomplice. Consider the paradigmatic case of aiding and abetting by omission where the cleaner intentionally omits to lock the entrance to a bank in order to assist in a bank robbery.[75] Imagine the omission was careless instead and the bank was robbed. If the legal system uses non-imputational complicity rules then a differentiated wrong of reckless complicity might be recognized. In an imputational system, however, recklessness or carelessness should not be the basis of attributing an intentional crime to the accomplice.

In *Mrkšić*, the Appeals Chamber rejected the argument that 'mere knowledge' was insufficient to fulfil the fault element of aiding and abetting by omission.[76] Instead, it reiterated the orthodox framing 'that (i) the aider and abettor must know that his omission assists in the commission of the crime of the principal perpetrator; and (ii) he must be aware of the essential elements of the crime which was ultimately committed by the principal'.[77] In the very same paragraph, however, the Appeals Chamber appears to dilute the standard to one of probability.[78] The criticisms made in the previous chapter apply with equal force in the context of omissions.[79]

This point has implications for the assessment of the doctrine of command responsibility, a matter taken up in the section that follows. It is also relevant to the obligation on states to ensure that their territory is not used to launch hostile attacks against other states. As will be seen, international law imposes wide-ranging preventive duties on states, ordinarily conditioned by a requirement of due diligence. In most cases, failure to exercise due diligence

[75] See Ashworth, *Principles of Criminal Law* 410–11.

[76] *Mrkšić, Šljivančanin* (Appeals Chamber Judgment) [159]. [77] Ibid. [78] Ibid.

[79] See section 4.3.3 above.

to prevent an attack will only be a direct breach of the diligence obligation, rather than complicity in the attack itself. However, an intentional omission in the knowledge of a specific attack is a form of complicity and should give rise to responsibility in those terms.[80]

5.2.6. Conclusion

There is little difficulty in seeing that some omissions assist or encourage the perpetration of crimes by other actors. The imposition of liability for complicit omissions turns on the recognition of a duty to protect against the occurrence of the particular harm as well as the accomplice's capacity to have done so. The recognition of aiding and abetting by omission is underpinned by the normative judgment that certain failures to act are as culpable as action itself.

5.3. Command Responsibility

5.3.1. Introduction

The previous section addressed one way that international criminal law responds to complicit omissions. This section addresses the doctrine of command responsibility in international law and its relationship with complicity. Commanders and other superiors may be criminally responsible under any of the ordinary modes of participation in international criminal law—ordering, instigating, aiding and abetting, and so on.[81] International criminal law also sets out a special doctrine that responds to the culpable omissions of superiors. This is command responsibility.

The prosecution of General Yamashita by the US Military Tribunal in Manila is generally seen as its modern foundation.[82] Yamashita was a commander in the Imperial Japanese Army. On 3 September 1945, he surrendered to the United States Armed Forces, after which he was charged with failing to discharge his duty to control soldiers under his command, thereby permitting them to commit atrocities, including starvation, executions, rape, and torture.[83]

[80] See section 2.5.2.2 above; section 7.3.5.1 below.
[81] Damaška, 'The Shadow Side of Command Responsibility' 455.
[82] Guénaël Mettraux, *The Law of Command Responsibility* (OUP 2009) 5.
[83] *Trial of General Tomoyuki Yamashita* (4 February 1946) (1948) IV LRTWC 1, 3–4.

The tribunal convicted Yamashita and sentenced him to death by hanging, which was carried out on 23 February 1946. The critical passage in the judgment, given by the President of the Tribunal, is as follows:

> It is absurd, however, to consider a commander a murderer or rapist because one of his soldiers commits a murder or a rape. Nevertheless, where murder and rape and vicious, revengeful actions are widespread offences, and there is no effective attempt by a commander to discover and control the criminal acts, such a commander may be held responsible, even criminally liable, for the lawless acts of his troops, depending upon their nature and the circumstances surrounding them.[84]

Despite concerns as to its source and doubts about its fairness,[85] command responsibility is deeply embedded in customary international law.[86] It is sufficient for present purposes to sketch the elements of the doctrine.[87] At the ad hoc tribunals, command responsibility comprises three elements:

1. the existence of a superior-subordinate relationship;
2. the superior knew or had reason to know that the criminal act was about to be or had been committed; and
3. the superior failed to take the necessary and reasonable measures to prevent the criminal act or punish the perpetrator thereof.[88]

Article 28 of the Rome Statute sets out a more detailed standard than the statutes of the ad hoc tribunals, including the elements of the rule and making separate provision for non-military superiors.

There are a number of ongoing issues relating to the scope of command responsibility, both under the statutes of the tribunals and in customary international law. These are not addressed in detail here. A more relevant question concerns the structure of command responsibility. There are two

[84] *Yamashita* 35.

[85] See generally *In re Yamashita* 327 US 1 (1946) (Dissenting Opinion of Justice Murphy); Mettraux, *The Law of Command Responsibility* 5–11; Damaška, 'The Shadow Side of Command Responsibility'; Jenny Martinez, 'Understanding *Mens Rea in* Command Responsibility' (2007) 5 J Intl Crim Just 638; Darryl Robinson, 'How Command Responsibility Got So Complicated: A Culpability Contradiction, Its Obfuscation, and a Simple Solution' (2012) 13 Melb J Intl L 1.

[86] For discussion of the customary status, see *Čelebići* (Trial Chamber Judgment) IT-96-21-T (16 November 1998) [330]–[343].

[87] For doctrinal analysis, see Mettraux, *The Law of Command Responsibility*; Chantal Meloni, *Command Responsibility in International Criminal Law* (TMC Asser 2010); Schabas, *A Commentary on the Rome Statute* 454–65; Roberta Arnold and Otto Triffterer, 'Article 28—Responsibility of Commanders and Other Superiors' in Triffterer (ed.) *Commentary on the Rome Statute* 795–843.

[88] *Čelebići* (Trial Chamber Judgment) [346].

basic schools of thought.[89] On one interpretation, command responsibility is a mode of liability, such that the commander is held responsible *for* the wrongdoing of his subordinate. This view renders command responsibility akin to a rule of imputational complicity. In imputational systems, just as one's acts of instigation or assistance give rise to criminal responsibility for the acts of a principal perpetrator, so the failure to prevent or punish the crimes of one's subordinates gives rise to criminal responsibility for those acts. On the second interpretation, liability is imposed for a separate offence of omission—the failure to prevent or punish the crimes committed by the subordinate.

5.3.2. Diverging Interpretations

Both approaches are evident in the origins of the doctrine and early instances of codification, though there is a tendency towards command responsibility as a mode of liability.[90] At the ICTY there are divergent holdings on this question, sometimes in the same judgment. In *Halilović*, the Trial Chamber stated:

> [W]hether command responsibility is a mode of liability for the crimes of subordinates or responsibility of a commander for dereliction of duty has not been considered at length in the jurisprudence of the Tribunal. However, the consistent jurisprudence of the Tribunal has found that a commander is responsible for the crimes of his subordinates under Article 7(3).[91]

The finding that the commander *is responsible for* the crimes of his subordinates mirrors the language used by the ICTY Trial Chamber in *Čelebići*.[92] Later on in *Halilović*, however, the Trial Chamber suggests that the commander does not 'share' responsibility with his subordinates but is responsible in 'proportion' to the gravity of the offences.[93] Meloni suggests that this marks a shift in interpretation of command responsibility at the ICTY.[94] So in *Orić*, the Trial Chamber held that the 'superior cannot be considered as if he had committed the crime himself, but merely for his neglect of duty with regard to crimes committed by subordinates'.[95] The Appeals Chamber

[89] Chantal Meloni, 'Command Responsibility: Mode of Liability for the Crimes of Subordinates or Separate Offence of the Superior?' (2007) 5 J Intl Crim Just 619, 620. See also Darryl Robinson, 'How Command Responsibility Got So Complicated' 8.

[90] See Meloni, 'Command Responsibility: Mode of Liability?' 621–4; Robinson, 'How Command Responsibility Got So Complicated' 33–4.

[91] *Halilović* (Trial Chamber Judgment) IT-01-48-T (16 November 2005) [53].

[92] *Čelebići* (Trial Chamber Judgment) [331].

[93] *Halilović* (Trial Chamber Judgment) [54].

[94] Meloni, 'Command Responsibility: Mode of Liability?' 625–6.

[95] *Orić* (Trial Chamber Judgment) [293].

did not express a view on the matter, though Judge Shahabudeen reiterated his long-held view that the commander is responsible only for his omission.[96]

This dispute has grounded an emerging academic interpretation of the ICTY case law that attempts to plot a middle course between command responsibility (i) as a mode of liability and (ii) as a substantive offence of omission. This interpretation emphasizes the so-called *sui generis* nature of command responsibility.[97] The commander is neither responsible solely for a separate offence of omission nor for the crimes committed by his subordinates. Rather, he is responsible for his own omission 'with regard to',[98] 'in respect of',[99] or 'because of'[100] the crimes committed by his subordinates.[101] This approach is evident in the sentencing of Naser Orić. Here, the Trial Chamber emphasized that the defendant was actually convicted of the 'failure to prevent and punish' the crimes of his subordinates, and that his own failure and the gravity of the crimes committed by his subordinate were primary considerations in imposing sentence.[102]

There is an interesting parallel between this approach and non-imputational complicity rules. In a sense, non-imputational complicity rules may be seen as a middle ground between an entirely inchoate approach to help or influence in the commission of crime, under which liability is fixed at the moment the help or influence is given without regard to whether the principal offence is committed, and imputational rules that render the accomplice responsible for the principal's acts. Non-imputational complicity rules hold the accomplice responsible for her own acts of help or influence in respect of the principal's crime—so assisting murder or abetting robbery. Likewise, under the emerging approach to command responsibility, the superior is responsible for his own acts of omission but his responsibility for that omission is assessed with respect to the gravity of the principal crime.

96 *Orić* (Appeals Chamber Judgment) (Declaration of Judge Shahabudeen) [18]–[26]. See also *Hadžihasanović, Alagić, Kubura* (Appeals Chamber Decision on Interlocutory Appeal Challenging Jurisdiction in Relation to Command Responsibility) (Partially Dissenting Judgment of Judge Shahabudeen) IT-01-47-AR72 (16 July 2003). See also *Krnojelac* (Appeals Chamber Judgment) IT-97-25-A (17 September 2003) [171].

97 *Halilović* (Trial Chamber Judgment) [78]; *Orić* (Trial Chamber Judgment) [293]. See also Mettraux, *The Law of Command Responsibility* 80–1; Meloni, 'Command Responsibility: Mode of Liability?' 631.

98 *Orić* (Trial Chamber Judgment) [293].

99 *Čelebići* (Appeals Chamber Judgment) [225].

100 *Halilović* (Trial Chamber Judgment) [54].

101 See Mettraux, *The Law of Command Responsibility* 81; Robinson, 'How Command Responsibility Got So Complicated' 36–9.

102 *Orić* (Trial Chamber Judgment) [724].

The issue of determining the nature of command responsibility arises in respect of Article 28 of the Rome Statute. Again, there are different approaches, evident in both academic commentary and in state parties' implementing legislation.[103] In England and Wales, after setting out the text of Article 28, the International Criminal Court Act provides that a 'person responsible under this section for an offence is regarded as aiding, abetting, counselling or procuring the commission of the offence'.[104] This links command responsibility to the Accessories and Abettors Act of 1861, under which accomplices are indicted, tried, and punished as principals.[105] On the other hand, Canada's Crimes against Humanity and War Crimes Act contemplates a separate indictable offence of omission.[106]

In the academic commentary, Ambos argues that Article 28 is a separate crime of omission. On his reading, the superior is liable only for his own failure to act and not for the crimes committed by his subordinate.[107] Schabas is less categorical, though does argue that command responsibility is 'a distinct crime whose gravamen is the failure to supervise or punish'.[108] Werle, on the other hand, argues that Article 28 is a subsidiary mode of participation in crime within the general scheme set out by the Statute.[109] On this basis, the commander is liable for the crimes committed by his subordinates although, in keeping with the graded model of participation set out in Article 25, he is potentially liable to a lesser degree than direct or indirect perpetrators.[110]

As a matter of interpretation, Werle is probably correct. The language of Article 28 strongly suggests that command responsibility is not a separate crime of omission. In the first place, the introductory phrase positions command responsibility as a doctrine '[i]n addition to other *grounds of criminal responsibility* under this Statute for crimes within the jurisdiction of the Court…'.[111] Second, the language specifically states that military commanders or other superiors 'shall be criminally responsible *for* crimes within the jurisdiction of the Court committed by their' subordinates.[112] This language

[103] Robert Cryer, 'General Principles of Liability in International Criminal Law' in Dominic McGoldrick, Peter Rowe, and Eric Donnelly (eds.) *The Permanent International Criminal Court: Legal and Policy Issues* (Hart 2004) 233, 258.

[104] International Criminal Court Act 2001, s 65(4). In respect of Scotland, see the International Criminal Court (Scotland) Act 2001, s 5.

[105] Accessories and Abettors Act, s 8.

[106] Crimes against Humanity and War Crimes Act 2000, s5 (Canada). See Cryer, 'General Principles of Liability' 258.

[107] Kai Ambos, 'Superior Responsibility' in Cassese et al. (eds.) *The Rome Statute* 805, 832–3.

[108] Schabas, *A Commentary on the Rome Statute* 457.

[109] Gerhard Werle, *Principles of International Criminal Law* (TMC Asser 2009) 189.

[110] Ibid. On the Rome Statute's culpability scheme, see section 4.4.1 and 4.4.2 above.

[111] Art 28 Rome Statute (emphasis added).

[112] Ibid (emphasis added).

is clear.[113] Although the ICC has not directly addressed the debate concerning the nature of command responsibility, a natural interpretation of its decision in *Bemba* confirms that command responsibility is a mode of responsibility rather than a separate offence of omission:

> The Chamber notes that article 28 of the Statute reflects a different form of criminal responsibility than that found under article 25(3)(a) of the Statute in the sense that a superior may be held responsible for the prohibited conduct of his subordinates for failing to fulfil his duty to prevent or repress their unlawful conduct or submit the matter to the competent authorities.[114]

5.3.3. Analysis

While the nature of command responsibility at the ad hoc tribunals remains controversial and subject to fragmented decisions, under the Rome Statute such a failure to act will likely be a mode of participation in the crimes of the principal. Given the drafting of the Rome Statute, the superior will thus be responsible *for* the perpetrator's crimes.[115] Understanding command responsibility as a separate offence or even a so-called 'sui generis' doctrine of responsibility, as has been suggested at the ad hoc tribunals, raises fewer principled concerns in terms of the foundational principle of culpability in criminal law.[116] Although responsibility in this form may still be classified as derivative—there is no liability without the perpetration of the underlying crime[117]—it is not imputational. The commander's own failure is the subject of prosecution with the seriousness of the underlying crime bearing on the gravity of the commander's sentence.[118]

Principled concerns arise when the commander is held responsible *for* the acts of the subordinate. In assessing these principled concerns, it does not make sense to talk of a unitary doctrine of command responsibility.[119] Under the Rome Statute, command responsibility involves three different duties that may be coupled with three different mental states.[120] The three duties are

[113] See Robert Cryer, 'Command Responsibility at the ICC and ICTY: Two Minds on the Mental Element' (*EJIL:Talk!*, 20 July 2009) <http://www.ejiltalk.org/command-responsibility-at-the-icc-and-icty-in-two-minds-on-the-mental-element/> accessed 22 December 2014. Cf *Halilović* (Trial Chamber Judgment) [54].

[114] *Bemba* (Decision on the Confirmation of Charges) ICC-01/05-01/08 (15 June 2009) [405]. See Robinson, 'How Command Responsibility Got So Complicated' 53–4.

[115] See section 4.4.1 above.

[116] Robinson, 'How Command Responsibility Got So Complicated' 30–1.

[117] Mettraux, *The Law of Command Responsibility* 79–80.

[118] *Orić* (Trial Chamber Judgment) [727].

[119] Meloni, *Command Responsibility* 145.

[120] For a more detailed analysis of the elements, see Meloni, *Command Responsibility* 139–207.

duties to prevent, repress, and submit the matter to competent authorities for investigation and prosecution. These duties are discrete and arise at different stages of the commission of crimes by the subordinate.[121] The duty to prevent arises prior to the commission of crimes.[122] The duty to repress comprises two separate elements: an obligation to stop ongoing crimes and an obligation to punish forces after the commission of crimes.[123] The duty to submit requires that the commander take steps to ensure that the perpetrators are brought to justice.[124]

For both civilian and military superiors, actual knowledge of the crimes committed will give rise to liability. Such actual knowledge must be demonstrated by direct or circumstantial evidence.[125] In addition, for military commanders, liability may also arise where, owing to the circumstances at the time, they should have known that the forces were committing or about to commit crimes.[126] This standard involves an active duty to take measures to obtain knowledge about the conduct of troops under their command.[127] Under the Rome Statute at least, for civilian superiors the standard is higher, requiring a conscious disregard of information that clearly indicated that crimes were being committed. This is a standard of gross recklessness or wilful blindness.[128]

For the purposes of a more general analysis, the duty to prevent may be grouped with the first element of the duty to repress—the obligation to stop ongoing crimes. Likewise, the second element of the duty to repress—the obligation to punish perpetrators—may be grouped with the duty to submit the matter for investigation and prosecution. In addition, focus will be placed on the standard binding military superiors set out in the Rome Statute rather than that binding civilians. For analytical purposes, this leaves four kinds of violation:

A. failure to prevent or stop the commission of crimes with actual knowledge of their commission;
B. failure to prevent or stop the commission of crimes where the commander should have known of their commission;

[121] *Bemba* (Decision on the Confirmation of Charges) [436]. [122] Ibid [437].
[123] Ibid [439]. [124] Ibid [442]. [125] Ibid [430].
[126] Art 28(1)(a) Rome Statute; Art 7(3) ICTY Statute; *Čelebići* (Trial Chamber Judgment) [346]. The Rome Statute standard of 'should have known' may entail a small difference from the standard of 'had reason to know' at the tribunals. See Martinez, 'Understanding *Mens Rea* in Command Responsibility' 642; Robinson, 'How Command Responsibility Got So Complicated' 8.
[127] *Bemba* (Decision on the Confirmation of Charges) [433].
[128] See Schabas, *A Commentary on the Rome Statute* 463.

C. failure to punish perpetrators or submit crimes for investigation with actual knowledge of their commission; and
D. failure to punish perpetrators or submit crimes for investigation where the commander should have known of their commission.[129]

One complication is that categories A through D specify quite different kinds of wrongdoing.[130] This point may be illustrated by reference to complicity. Category A—knowing failure to prevent the commission of crimes in breach of a duty to do so—may be considered aiding and abetting by omission.[131] Indeed, Category A adds little to an ordinary conception of complicity.[132] It establishes a general rule that such a failure helps or encourages the conduct of the subordinate.

Likewise, Category B—failure to prevent the crime where the superior should have known about its commission—may also be seen as helping or encouraging the conduct of the subordinate. As in Category A, there is a causal relationship between the omission and the harm.[133] However, in contrast to the intentionality of his wrongdoing in Category A, it is only required that the superior in Category B should have known about his subordinate's wrongdoing. A standard of 'should have known' encompasses a range of mental states.[134] At one end of the spectrum there is a 'scheming superior who condones the delinquency of his underlings and engineers his own ignorance' of their plans.[135] In such situations, concern about the reduced mental element are somewhat diminished. Wilful blindness and intentional wrongdoing are not too far apart.[136]

But a standard of 'should have known' is one encompassing a species of negligence.[137] In essence, category B establishes a rule of negligent complicity. The violation of the principle of culpability is obvious. Given the structure of Article 28, and the fact that the crimes within the jurisdiction of the court require intention, under category B the commander is held liable for an intentional offence on the basis of his own negligence in failing to prevent

[129] This analytical structure is equivalent to the two-fold obligation of prevent and punish. See Mettraux, *The Law of Command Responsibility* 229–34; Meloni, *Command Responsibility* 196–204.

[130] Cryer, 'General Principles of Liability' 258–9.

[131] Meloni, *Command Responsibility* 198.

[132] Damaška, 'The Shadow Side of Command Responsibility' 462; 'Robinson, 'How Command Responsibility Got So Complicated' 8.

[133] See *Bemba* (Decision on the Confirmation of Charges) [423].

[134] Damaška, 'The Shadow Side of Command Responsibility' 462.

[135] Ibid.

[136] Ibid.

[137] Meloni, 'Command Responsibility: Mode of Liability?' 634; Damaška, 'The Shadow Side of Command Responsibility' 463; *Bemba* (Decision on the Confirmation of Charges) 429.

its commission.[138] As Damaška puts it, '*Sub silentio*, as it were, a negligent omission has been transformed into intentional criminality of the most serious nature…'.[139] In this way, command responsibility establishes a 'special form of incrimination' particular to international law, said to be justified by the ability of commanders to prevent wrongdoing.[140]

Thus in the form envisaged by the Rome Statute, the doctrines of command responsibility denoted by categories A and B are subject to criticism. Category A is best thought of as a form of complicity by omission, and on these terms is open to the normative argument against complicity rules that hold accomplices responsible for the acts of their principals. This principled objection is magnified in respect of category B. Here, not only does negligent omission give rise to responsibility for another's acts, but also gives rise to responsibility for intentional crimes where the superior did not act intentionally.

Categories C and D—intentional and negligent failures to punish the crimes of subordinates—are subject to the same objections but are also problematic in an additional way. A failure to punish can have no causal effect on the preceding commission of crimes.[141] In other words, it can make no contribution to that crime. Of course, such a failure may encourage the subsequent commission of crimes by subordinates and thereby give rise to aiding and abetting liability for those crimes.[142] But subsequent failures can in no way assist or encourage the initial crimes. The imposition of criminal responsibility in the absence of a causal connection to the crime is rarely justifiable.[143] Here, superiors are being held responsible for crimes in which they did not participate at all.

Robinson denies that this problem of non-contributory command responsibility under categories C and D arises under the Rome Statute. In a recent article, he argues that the Rome Statute does not, as a matter of textual interpretation, provide for the responsibility of commanders in the absence of a

[138] Meloni, 'Command Responsibility: Mode of Liability?' 635–6.

[139] Damaška, 'The Shadow Side of Command Responsibility' 463–4.

[140] Robert Cryer, *Prosecuting International Crimes: Selectivity and the International Criminal Law Regime* (CUP 2005) 316. For recent work on possible justifications for a standard of *mens rea* lower than knowledge for command responsibility, see Martinez, 'Understanding *Mens Rea in* Command Responsibility' 660–4.

[141] *Bemba* (Decision on the Confirmation of Charges) [424]. See also Meloni, 'Command Responsibility: Mode of Liability?' 636.

[142] Damaška, 'The Shadow Side of Command Responsibility' 467; Robinson, 'How Command Responsibility Got So Complicated' 16–17.

[143] Ilias Bantekas, 'On Stretching the Boundaries of Responsible Command' (2009) 7 J Intl Crim Just 1197, 1199; Robinson, 'How Command Responsibility Got So Complicated' 12–13.

causal contribution to subordinate's crimes.[144] This is because of the language of Article 28:

(a) A military commander or person effectively acting as a military commander shall be criminally responsible for crimes within the jurisdiction of the Court committed by forces under his or her effective command and control, or effective authority and control as the case may be, *as a result of his or her failure to exercise control properly over such forces*, where:
   (i) That military commander or person either knew or, owing to the circumstances at the time, should have known that the forces were committing or about to commit such crimes; and
   (ii) That military commander or person failed to take all necessary and reasonable measures within his or her power to prevent or repress their commission or to submit the matter to the competent authorities for investigation and prosecution.[145]

This is a complicated question of interpretation that need not be resolved at this point. Robinson's position does draw support from the text, not only from the italicized clause above, but also from the grammar of Article 28(a)(i). On the other hand, other than in respect of the subsequent commission of crimes, Robinson's interpretation would render criminal responsibility based on the well-established customary law obligation of commanders to punish the crimes of their subordinates a dead letter.[146] When responsibility is based on a failure to punish a crime, it makes no sense to additionally require that the crime itself occurred as a result of the commander's failure to exercise control.[147] This is the view of the ICC Pre-Trial Chamber in *Bemba*: 'the element of causality only relates to the commander's duty to *prevent* the commission of future crimes.'[148]

5.3.4. Command Responsibility and Complicity: Conclusion

The doctrine of command responsibility comprises quite different forms of responsibility. The gravest conduct encompassed therein—knowing failure to prevent the commission of crimes—may be considered a form of complicity by omission. It may be justified in those terms, though it will be subject to the normative argument against holding accomplices responsible for their principal's acts. Failure to prevent crimes when the commander

[144] Robinson, 'How Command Responsibility Got So Complicated' 56–7.
[145] Art 28(a) Rome Statute (emphasis added).
[146] Cf Robinson, 'How Command Responsibility Got So Complicated' 27–9.
[147] *Orić* (Trial Chamber Judgment) [338].
[148] *Bemba* (Decision on the Confirmation of Charges) [424] (emphasis added).

should have known about their commission is a form of negligent complicity by omission. Negligence should not give rise to responsibility *for* intentional crimes. Command responsibility founded on a failure to punish wrongdoing gives rise to responsibility for crimes to which the superior bears no causal relation.

These principled objections disappear if command responsibility were recognized to give rise to responsibility for a separate crime defined by the superior's own acts or to *properly differentiated* responsibility as an accessorial party. In either case, the superior would be held responsible for her own omission, the gravity of which may be assessed by reference to the underlying crime. Those who negligently fail to prevent their subordinates from committing crimes would be responsible for exactly that, as would those who either intentionally or negligently fail to punish those crimes. Intentional failure to prevent the crimes of a subordinate could be cleaved from the doctrine of command responsibility and assessed as a form of complicit omission.

5.4. Conclusion to Part B

The central means by which international law prohibits individual complicity are the doctrines instigation and aiding and abetting. The forms of complicit conduct encompassed by these doctrines are comprehensive, and include complicit omissions. In general, the rules are marked by a (sometimes diluted) standard of knowledge in the fault element and an underused nexus requirement connecting the accomplice to the principal's wrong. These are the hallmarks of individual complicity in international law.

International criminal law embraces a doctrinally differentiated model of participation in crime—in respect of complicity, instigation and aiding and abetting have their own doctrinal requirements. However, in the post-Second World War cases, at the ad hoc tribunals, and under the Rome Statute, the language of the provisions on international responsibility render each of those nominally differentiated participants responsible *for* the underlying crime. That is to say, someone who instigates or aids and abets genocide is responsible for the crime of genocide, the crime committed by the principal. This approach is open to objection on the basis of the principles of culpability and fair labelling. In terms of punishment, international courts have a degree of discretion to take into account varying degrees of participation at sentencing.

In Part C, this structure of complicity will be contrasted with the dominant approach to *state* complicity in international law. The rule reflected in

Article 16 ARSIWA prohibits states from aiding or assisting other states in the commission of an internationally wrongful act.[149] Under this rule, the assisting state is held responsible for its own acts of assistance.[150] That is to say, the conduct of the principal state is not imputed to the accomplice state. This model of complicity is to be preferred on principled grounds.

[149] Art 16 ARSIWA. [150] ARSIWA Commentary on Art 16 [10].

PART C

STATE COMPLICITY IN INTERNATIONAL LAW

6

State Complicity—A Framework

6.1. State Complicity in State Wrongdoing

Historically, international law failed to adequately regulate state complicity in the wrongdoing of other states. In his Hague Lectures of 1939, Ago argued that:

> [I]t appears inconceivable in international law to have any form of complicity, participation, or incitement to a delict. The law of nations, in its current structure, does not allow for such forms of a consideration shared by several subjects with respect to a single delict; these constructs are characteristic of the nature and development of domestic criminal law.[1]

One way to understand the traditional absence of a general prohibition on state complicity is within the competing constructs of bilateralism and community interest.[2] In this context, bilateralism engenders an understanding of international law defined by correlative rights and obligations owed by subjects to each other.[3] The participation of third states—that is to say, the complicity of third states—in the breach of obligations owed by one state to another might be said to be difficult to account for within a bilateralist framework.[4] There is something to this view. These difficulties are heightened at the stage of dispute settlement before an international tribunal, where the *Monetary Gold* principle may limit the admissibility of claims for

[1] Roberto Ago, 'Le Délit International' (1939) 68 (II) Recueil des Cours 419, 523 (translated). See also Aust, *Complicity and the Law of State Responsibility* 12.

[2] Aust, *Complicity and the Law of State Responsibility* 11–49. See also Bruno Simma, 'From Bilateralism to Community Interest in International Law' (1994) 250 Recueil des Cours 217, 229–55.

[3] Simma, *From Bilateralism to Community Interest* 231–2.

[4] See Aust, *Complicity and the Law of State Responsibility* 12–15. Aust seeks to look beyond an analysis based on bilateralism and community interest in accounting for the development of complicity in the law of state responsibility.

responsibility.[5] The non-prohibition of complicity epitomizes what Bruno Simma has called the 'value-poverty of bilateralist international law'.[6] It is insufficient that states concern themselves only with the wrongs they commit themselves.[7]

But even within a traditional bilateralist framework, ideas of complicity and its kindred forms of responsibility played a role.[8] One example is the law of neutrality. Neutrality regulates the relationship between neutral states and belligerents through the core principles of non-participation and non-discrimination.[9] The principle of non-participation gives rise to a number of duties that are related to forms of complicity.[10] For instance, Article 6 of the Hague Convention concerning the Rights and Duties of Neutral Powers in Naval War provides that '[t]he supply, in any manner, directly or indirectly, by a neutral Power to a belligerent Power, of war-ships, ammunition, or war material of any kind whatever, is forbidden'.[11] Neutrality also prescribes extensive rules on the use of neutral powers' territory by belligerents.[12] The point is not that the breach of the rule of non-participation gives rise to a form of derivative responsibility in respect of a subsequent wrong of the belligerent. Rather, the law of neutrality entails an instance where obligations arise on a third state in respect of their relationship with other states.

The law of neutrality was inevitably affected by the rise of the Charter system of collective security and the prohibition on the use of force in international law.[13] Interestingly, the Charter system sets out a rule much closer in rationale to that of a prohibition on complicity. Article 2(5) of the Charter requires that '[A]ll Members . . . refrain from giving assistance to any state against which the United Nations is taking preventive or enforcement action'.[14] Complicity entails participation in wrongdoing. The decision of the Security Council to take preventive or enforcement action both triggers

[5] *Case of the Monetary Gold Removed from Rome in 1943 (Italy* v. *France, United Kingdom and United States of America)* (Preliminary Question) [1954] ICJ Rep 19. See also *East Timor (Portugal* v. *Australia)* [1995] ICJ Rep 90; section 7.3.8 below.

[6] Simma, *From Bilateralism to Community Interest* 233.

[7] Lowe, 'Responsibility for the Conduct of Other States' 13.

[8] See Aust, *Complicity and the Law of State Responsibility* 15–23.

[9] Yoram Dinstein, *War, Aggression and Self-Defence* (5th edn. CUP 2011) 25.

[10] See Lowe, 'Responsibility for the Conduct of Other States' 13.

[11] Art 6 Convention concerning the Rights and Duties of Neutral Powers in Naval War (adopted 18 October 1907, entered into force 26 January 1910) 36 Stat 2415.

[12] See Dinstein, *War, Aggression and Self-Defence* 26–7.

[13] See *Legality of the Threat or Use of Nuclear Weapons* (Advisory Opinion) [1996] ICJ Rep 226 [89]; Dinstein, *War, Aggression and Self-Defence* 176–80.

[14] Art 2(5) Charter of the United Nations (adopted 26 June 1945, entered into force 25 October 1945) 1 UNTS XVI.

member states' obligations of non-assistance and, in some instances, entails a (political, at least) determination of wrongful conduct by the aggressor state.[15]

Leaving aside the law of neutrality and changes brought by the Charter system, Ago's general point about the traditional absence of complicity rules is accurate. International law traditionally contained no general prohibition on state complicity in the internationally wrongful act of another state—there was no international analogue to common domestic doctrines of accomplice or accessorial liability.[16] Short of joint perpetration, as a general rule, participants in another state's commission of an internationally wrongful act were not implicated by international law's assignment of responsibility.

6.2. State Participation in the Acts of Non-State Actors—A Conceptual Difficulty

Participating in the wrongful acts of other *states* is not the only way that states contribute to harmful conduct. Non-state actors commit acts inimical to the rights and interests of both states and individuals. States sometimes participate in those acts. With a sufficient degree of dependence, direction, or control, the conduct of the non-state actor becomes attributable to the state.[17] As argued below, the requisite connection between the state and non-state actor for attribution is marked by a search for an agency relationship.[18] In the absence of *lex specialis*, a complicit relationship is insufficient for attribution.

Short of such an agency relationship, the question is whether international law imposes complicity obligations on states in respect of the conduct of non-state actors. Here, there is a conceptual difficulty for complicity. The essential logic of complicity is to tie the accomplice, through its complicit acts, to the wrongdoing committed by another actor.[19] Where international law is silent as to the wrongfulness of the acts committed by the other actor, it is difficult to see what wrong the putative accomplice can be complicit in.[20] This problem flows from the essential derivative nature of complicity.[21]

[15] See Dinstein, *War, Aggression and Self-Defence* 176. See also Aust, *Complicity and the Law of State Responsibility* 158–62 for discussion of United Nations resolutions relating to non-assistance.

[16] See Quigley, 'Complicity in International Law' 77.

[17] Arts 4, 8 ARSIWA.

[18] See section 8.2 below; Becker, *Terrorism and the State* 43–79; Chinkin, *Third Parties in International Law* 142.

[19] Kadish, 'Complicity, Cause and Blame' 337.

[20] De Frouville, 'Attribution of Conduct' 276.

[21] See section 1.2 above. See also Becker, *Terrorism and the State* 19.

This conceptual difficulty is but one implication of the traditional normative structure of the international legal system.[22] Historically, international law was addressed to states, and indeed states remain the primary bearers of rights and obligations in international law.[23] The absence of regulation of the conduct of non-state actors simply denied the possibility of state complicity in relation to that conduct, for there was no wrong to which the state might be linked by the complicity rule.

This is not to say that international law is silent on state participation—short of attribution—in harms caused by another actor. In a number of areas, international law does impose what might be called obligations of non-participation, as opposed to complicity obligations, in the actions of another actor. For instance, as elements of the principle of the non-use of force, the General Assembly's Declaration on Friendly Relations, adopted unanimously in 1970, provides:

> Every State has the duty to refrain from organizing or encouraging the organization of irregular forces or armed bands, including mercenaries, for incursion into the territory of another State.
>
> Every State has the duty to refrain from organizing, instigating, assisting or participating in acts of civil strife or terrorist acts in another State or acquiescing in organized activities within its territory directed towards the commission of such acts, when the acts referred to in the present paragraph involve a threat or use of force.[24]

These provisions, which reflect customary international law,[25] might be seen as analogous to traditional duties of neutrality. Just as the violation of the duty of neutrality does not give rise to a form of derivative responsibility in relation to some wrongful act of the belligerent state, so the participation by the state does not give rise to derivative responsibility in relation to some wrongful act of the armed band. In both cases, the state's responsibility for its wrongful participation is not linked to any wrong of a principal actor.[26] Instead, a number of classic modes of complicity are used to constitute a direct and independent obligation of non-participation binding the state.[27]

[22] De Frouville, 'Attribution of Conduct' 276.

[23] Robert Jennings and Arthur Watts, *Oppenheim's International Law—Volume 1: Peace* (9th edn. Longman 1996) 16; Crawford, *Brownlie's Principles of Public International Law* 115.

[24] UNGA Res 2625 (XXV) (24 October 1970) (Declaration on Friendly Relations).

[25] *Armed Activities on the Territory of the Congo (Democratic Republic of Congo* v. *Uganda)* (Merits) [2005] ICJ Rep 168 [162].

[26] For a general discussion, see Ian Brownlie, 'International Law and the Activities of Armed Bands' (1958) 7 ICLQ 712; Thomas Franck, 'Who Killed Article 2(4)? Or: Changing Norms Governing the Use of Force by States' (1970) 64 Am J Intl L 809.

[27] In respect of state participation in terrorism, see UNSC Res 1373 (28 September 2001) UN Doc S/RES/1373; UNGA Res 40/61 (9 December 1985) UN Doc A/RES/40/61; UNGA Res

In addition, many instances of state participation in the harms caused by non-state actors are swept up by broader positive obligations imposed on states to protect against harms to other states or individuals.[28] The obligation on states to protect against harm is ordinarily conditioned by a due diligence rule, and thus may give rise to state responsibility where the state did not actually participate in the commission of the harm.[29]

Obligations of this kind are often traced to international law's regulation of the treatment of non-nationals.[30] In the *Spanish Zone of Morocco* arbitration, Max Huber held that:

> ...the State is not responsible for the revolutionary events themselves...it may nevertheless be responsible for what the authorities do or do not do to mitigate the consequences as far as possible. Responsibility for the action or inaction of the public authorities is quite different from the responsibility for acts that may be imputed to persons outside the control of the authorities or openly hostile to them.[31]

The obligation to protect against harms to aliens, as a primary rule of international law, is well established.[32] The nature of the obligation is revealed in diplomatic correspondence between the Italian and United States governments after the destruction of property belonging to a US citizen in Italy in 1925:[33] '[Italy] holds itself obligated, not absolutely to prevent certain occurrences from taking place, but to exercise in order to obviate them ordinary vigilance for the protection of foreigners and citizens alike...'[34] Lillich and Paxman explain that the Department of State accepted this position and informed its Embassy in Italy that a claim ought to be pursued only if it

44/29 (4 December 1989) UN Doc A/RES/44/29; UNGA Res 49/60 (9 December 1994) UN Doc A/RES/49/60; UNGA Res 51/210 (17 December 1996) UN Doc A/RES 51/210; UNGA Res 53/108 (26 January 1999) UN Doc A/RES/53/108. See also Eric Rosand, 'Security Council Resolution 1373, the Counter-Terrorism Committee and the Fight Against Terrorism' (2003) 97 Am J Intl L 333; Andrea Bianchi, 'Enforcing International Law Norms against Terrorism: Achievements and Prospects' in Andrea Bianchi (ed.) *Enforcing International Law Norms against Terrorism* (Hart 2004) 491; Pierre-Marie Dupuy, 'State Sponsors of Terrorism: Issues of International Responsibility' in Bianchi (ed.) *Enforcing International Law Norms against Terrorism* 3; Ben Saul, *Defining Terrorism in International Law* (OUP 2006).

[28] See generally Pisillo-Mazzeschi, 'Due Diligence'; Barnidge, *The Due Diligence Principle under International Law.*

[29] See Monica Hakimi, 'State Bystander Responsibility' (2010) Eur J Intl L 341; Olivier Corten and Pierre Klein, 'The Limits of Complicity as a Ground of Responsibility: Lessons Learned from the *Corfu Channel* Case' in Bannelier et al. (eds.) *The ICJ and the Evolution of International Law* 315.

[30] See Richard Lillich and John Paxman, 'State Responsibility for Injuries to Aliens Occasioned by Terrorist Activities' (1977) 26 Am Univ L Rev 217.

[31] *Spanish Zone of Morocco Case (United Kingdom/Spain)* (1923) 2 RIAA 615, 641–2.

[32] See Becker, *Terrorism and the State* 24–42; Lillich and Paxman, 'State Responsibility' 222–31.

[33] Lillich and Paxman, 'State Responsibility' 226.

[34] Hackworth, *Digest of International Law* 5 (1943) 659.

could be shown that 'the authorities had knowledge, or should have had knowledge of the impending attack and failed to take proper precautions to thwart it…'.[35]

The obligation to protect against harm to aliens may be thought of as a specific iteration of a more general principle flowing from the territorial sovereignty of the state. In the *Island of Palmas* arbitration, Huber expressed the principle in exactly these terms:

> Territorial sovereignty, as has already been said, involves the exclusive right to display the activities of a State. This right has as corollary a duty: the obligation to protect within the territory the right of other States, in particular their right to integrity and inviolability in peace and in war, together with the rights which each State may claim for its nationals in foreign territory.[36]

In the *Corfu Channel* case, Albania's responsibility was engaged on the basis of its failure to warn the UK of the existence of a minefield in Albanian territorial waters—every state was under an 'obligation not to allow knowingly its territory to be used for acts contrary to the rights of other states'.[37] A due diligence obligation to protect against certain harms is central to international environmental law[38] and international human rights law.[39] In the *Bosnian Genocide* case, Serbia's international responsibility was engaged for failing to prevent the genocide at Srebrenica.[40] The obligation is one of conduct, not result, and requires the state to exercise due diligence in taking all means reasonably available to prevent the harm from occurring.[41]

It is clear, then, that obligations of due diligence to prevent harm arise in many areas of international law. In many instances where the state has participated in the commission of harm, it will have breached the broader obligation to prevent that harm from occurring.[42] So if Turkey intentionally provides information to a non-state actor in Turkey that facilitates the latter's

[35] Lillich and Paxman, 'State Responsibility' 227 citing Hackworth 660–1.

[36] *Island of Palmas (Netherlands/USA)* (1928) 2 RIAA 829, 839.

[37] *Corfu Channel (United Kingdom* v. *Albania)* (Merits) [1949] ICJ Rep 4, 22. See also *United States Diplomatic and Consular Staff in Tehran (United States of America* v. *Iran)* (Merits) [1980] ICJ Rep 3; Luigi Condorelli, 'The Imputability to States of Acts of International Terrorism' (1989) 19 Isr YB Human Rights 233, 240–1.

[38] See *Trail Smelter (United States of America/Canada)* 3 RIAA 1911; Karine Bannelier, 'Foundational Judgment or Constructive Myth? The Court's Decision as a Precursor to International Environmental Law' in Bannelier et al. (eds.) *The ICJ and the Evolution of International Law* 242.

[39] See generally UNHRC, 'General Comment 31' (29 March 2004) UN Doc CCPR/C/21/Rev.1/Add.13 (2004) [6]-[8]; *Velasquez Rodriguez* (29 July 1988) Inter-AmCtHR (Ser C) No 4 (1988) [161]–[167]; *Ireland* v. *United Kingdom* (App 5310/71) (1978) 2 EHRR 25 [239].

[40] *Bosnian Genocide* [438].

[41] *Bosnian Genocide* [430].

[42] See Corten and Klein, 'The Limits of Complicity' 332–3; Lillich and Paxman, 'State Responsibility' 237.

killing of a journalist, it will be responsible for failing to protect the right to life under Article 2 of the European Convention on Human Rights.[43] If Serbia intentionally provides logistical support to a non-state actor that facilitates the commission of genocide by that actor, its responsibility for failing to prevent genocide would certainly be engaged.[44]

6.3. The Role of Complicity?

If these obligations of prevention are so capacious as to encompass many situations in which a state participates in the conduct of another actor, why should a study of international law pay attention to the idea of state complicity?[45] There are three reasons. First, as a matter of positive law, international law—treaty and custom—does impose certain complicity obligations on states. States and other actors articulate the responsibility of other states in terms of their *complicity* rather than simply their failure to exercise due diligence in preventing harms.

Second, it is not yet the case that all forms of state participation in the wrongful actions of another state or non-state actor will breach a due diligence obligation to protect against harm to other states or individuals.[46] Despite the development of due diligence obligations of this kind, they largely retain their territorial character.[47] Imagine that State A, with full knowledge of the circumstances, provides a credit guarantee for one of its

[43] Cf *Kiliç* v. *Turkey* (App 22492/93) (2000) 33 EHRR 1357.

[44] See *Bosnian Genocide* [382]:

> If a State is held responsible for [complicity in genocide] then there is no point in asking whether it complied with its obligation of prevention in respect of the same acts, because logic dictates that a State cannot have satisfied an obligation to prevent genocide in which it actively participated.

[45] See Corten and Klein, 'The Limits of Complicity' 332–3.

[46] Daniele Amoroso, 'Moving Towards Complicity as a Criterion of Attribution of Private Conducts: Imputation to States of Corporate Abuses in the US Case Law' (2011) 24 Leiden J Intl L 989, 992. Cf Corten and Klein, 'The Limits of Complicity' 332–3.

[47] See *Island of Palmas*; Vladyslav Lanovoy, 'Responsibility for Complicity in an Internationally Wrongful Act: Revisiting a Structural Norm' (SHARES Conference—Foundations of Shared Responsibility in International Law, Amsterdam, 17, 18 November 2011) 1, 7; Heathcote, 'State Omissions and Due Diligence' 297–9. Obligations of this kind may also arise where the state exercises effective control or jurisdiction over territory. See *Legal Consequences for States of the Continued Presence of South Africa in Namibia (South West Africa) notwithstanding Security Council Resolution 276 (1970)* (Advisory Opinion) [1971] ICJ Rep 16 [118]; Condorelli, 'Imputability to States' 240–1.

companies' participation in a project carried out in and by State B.[48] The project constitutes an internationally wrongful act by State B, such as a violation of its obligations to protect cultural property.[49] It is not clear that the responsibility of the assisting state would be engaged under an existing obligation to protect against harm to cultural property. In the absence of a complicity rule, State A's contribution to an internationally wrongful act would not engage its responsibility.

The third reason for paying attention to complicity goes beyond the confines of positive law. The absence of complicity rules in international law marks a lack of sophistication in the legal system.[50] In Chapter 2, it was argued that complicity is a particular way of contributing to wrongdoing. This is why the language of complicity is compelling:[51] it articulates and condemns a common way that states and individuals participate in the principal wrongs of others. It is not a judgment that the individual or state committed the wrong, itself or through its agents.[52] Neither is it a judgment that the individual or state simply failed to take reasonable measures to protect against the harm.[53] Rather, it responds to complicity as a way of contributing to wrongdoing—'making a difference to the difference that principals make'.[54]

6.4. The Structure of Part C

Part C of the work (comprising this chapter and Chapters 7–9) is concerned with the complicity obligations that international law imposes on states. Chapter 7 addresses a specific rule and a general rule prohibiting state complicity in the wrongful acts of other *states*. It positions these rules within the analytical framework of the work and evaluates them against the normative claim set out in Chapter 2. International law now prohibits states from aiding or assisting another state in the commission of an internationally

[48] See Lowe, 'Responsibility for the Conduct of Other States' 6. [49] Ibid.

[50] Ibid 13. [51] Aust, *Complicity and the Law of State Responsibility* 418.

[52] See Ago, 'Seventh Report on State Responsibility' [57].

[53] On this point, see Antonio Cassese, 'A Judicial Massacre' *The Guardian* (London, 27 February 2007) describing the ICJ's finding that Serbia was responsible for failing to take reasonable measures to prevent genocide from occurring, but not responsible for genocide or complicity in genocide, as a 'consolation prize'. See also contemporaneous newspaper headlines, e.g. Beti Bilandzic and Nedim Dervisbegovic, 'Serbs Relieved, Bosnia Dismayed by Genocide Ruling' *Reuters* (Sarajevo, 26 February 2007); 'Court Clears Serbia of Genocide' *BBC News* (London, 26 February 2007).

[54] Gardner, 'Complicity and Causality' 128.

wrongful act. This is an international analogue to municipal doctrines of accomplice liability.

Chapters 8 and 9 assess two ways that international law has dealt with the conceptual difficulty noted above concerning state participation in the harms caused by *non-state actors*. To recap, the conceptual difficulty is that in a system where norms are addressed to states, there is no international legal wrong committed by the non-state actor.[55] Although state participation in that conduct may be (and sometimes is) prohibited directly, the conceptual possibility for derivative responsibility based on complicity is foreclosed. There is simply no wrong in which the participating state might be complicit.

International law has responded in two quite different ways to this difficulty. Chapter 8 considers the claim that complicity has penetrated the rules of attribution in international law. The idea here is not quite like the operation of a complicity rule, as defined in Chapter 2, where the complicit party is linked to the wrongdoing of another actor. Rather, the attributional idea posits that a *complicit relationship* is sufficient to transform the conduct of the non-state actor into state conduct. It is not that the state is held derivatively responsible in relation to another actor's wrongdoing; rather, the conduct of that other actor becomes state conduct on the basis of its acts of support or assistance. Claims of this kind are open to principled objection and should be rejected.

Chapter 9 considers a second way that the conceptual difficulty noted above has been addressed. The conceptual difficulty is premised on the absence of legal regulation of the conduct of non-state actors. Of course, international law no longer imposes obligations only on states: individuals and other non-state actors have rights and obligations in international law. Once it is recognized that a non-state actor can violate international law, it becomes possible that a state might be complicit in that wrongdoing. Chapter 9 considers the prohibition on state complicity in genocide and raises the possibility that a non-state analogue to the general prohibition on state complicity in the wrongdoing of other states will emerge.

Together, these chapters (Part C) analyse the different ways that international law deals with state complicity. The story is one of an increasing recognition of complicity as a particular way that states contribute to wrongdoing. In respect of state participation in the wrongs committed by other states, a general complicity rule supplements existing specific rules. In respect of state participation in harms caused by non-state actors, the

[55] See De Frouville, 'Attribution of Conduct' 712.

obligations now imposed by international law on non-state actors have opened up the possibility of accounting for that participation as a form of complicity. Even if Ago was correct in 1939, it is not the case now that 'any form of complicity, participation, or incitement to a delict' is inconceivable in international law.

7

State Complicity in the Internationally Wrongful Act of Another State

7.1. Introduction

States sometimes go to war alone. More often, they do so with the support of other states.[1] Given that international peace and security is at the heart of the Charter system,[2] it is no surprise that one of the clearest manifestations of a prohibition on state complicity arises in respect of the wrong of aggression. Here, international law prohibits a specific form of state complicity in a specific wrongful act by the principal state.

There are other instances of state practice condemning state participation in other international wrongs.[3] The International Law Commission relied on this practice to derive its claim that international law assigns 'international responsibility to a State which deliberately participates in the internationally wrongful conduct of another through the provision of aid or assistance…'.[4] This is the rule reflected in Article 16 ARSIWA. Despite its shortcomings, Article 16 is a radical leap in the morality of international law.[5]

Article 16 represents a move from the specific to the general. It prohibits general forms of complicity—aid or assistance—in the commission of *any* international wrong by the recipient state, so long as the act committed by the principal state would be wrongful if committed by the accomplice state.[6] That international law is moving from specific rules to a general rule in the

[1] See Georg Nolte and Helmut Aust, 'Equivocal Helpers—Complicit States, Mixed Messages and International Law' (2009) 58 ICLQ 1.

[2] Art 1(1) UN Charter; Declaration on Friendly Relations.

[3] For an overview of state practice and *opinio juris* in respect of other potential state complicity rules, see generally Aust, *Complicity and the Law of State Responsibility* 97–191; Quigley, 'Complicity in International Law' 81–107.

[4] ARSIWA Commentary on Art 16 [7].

[5] Lowe, 'Responsibility for the Conduct of Other States' 12.

[6] Art 16 ARSIWA.

context of complicity is no surprise. In fact, it mirrors the historical evolution of complicity rules in the municipal criminal context. Vogel explains that:

> In modern criminal codes, [rules on participation] are laid down in the general part, they apply—in principle—to any specific offence and are spelt out in an abstract, general and not casuistic way which may be called the 'general part' model. In contrast, a 'special part' model provides for specific participation rules in specific offences. Historically speaking, the law on participation in the offence started from specific and casuistic rules in the special part—e.g. as annex to the murder prohibition in ancient criminal law—and developed into the abstract, general rules in the general part which are now the international standard.[7]

The rule reflected in Article 16 should be understood to entrench a general complicity rule in the law of state responsibility, at least with respect to state participation in wrongdoing committed by other states. This chapter places the specific rule prohibiting complicity in aggression and the general rule reflected in Article 16 into the analytical framework proposed in Chapter 2 and evaluates them against the normative claim of the work.

7.2. State Complicity in Aggression—A Specific Complicity Rule

7.2.1. Introduction

The prohibition on aggression outlaws the use by states of armed force against the sovereignty, territorial integrity, or political independence of other states.[8] The rule pursues the principal aim of the Charter system—the maintenance of international peace and security—and thereby reflects a fundamental value of the international legal system.[9] In perpetrating acts of aggression, states often act with the assistance of other states. In practice, such assistance takes a variety of forms. There is not, however, a general rule prohibiting complicity in aggression, the content of which is fleshed out from first principles to cover these various forms of assistance. Rather, practice establishes the prohibition of a specific kind of complicity: the placing of territory at the disposal of an aggressor state. There are, in addition, some indications of the existence of a wider rule in this context.

[7] Vogel, 'Twelve Models' 160.

[8] Art 1 Definition of Aggression.

[9] Art 1(1) UN Charter. See also *Armed Activities* [148].

7.2.2. Placing Territory at the Disposal of an Aggressor State

7.2.2.1. International Practice

The essence of the prohibition on state complicity in aggression is found in the provision by one state of its territory to an aggressor state; that is, a state perpetrating an act of aggression against a third state. Article 3(f) of the Definition of Aggression, adopted by the General Assembly in Resolution 3314 of 1974 following the work of the Assembly's Special Committee on the Question of Defining Aggression, provides the textual basis of the rule:

> Any of the following acts, regardless of a declaration of war, shall, subject to and in accordance with the provisions of article 2, qualify as an act of aggression:
>
> . . .
>
> (f). The action of a State in allowing its territory, which it has placed at the disposal of another State, to be used by that other State for perpetrating an act of aggression against a third State.[10]

State practice confirms the existence of this specific rule, much of which is cited in the commentary to ARSIWA as support for the rule reflected in Article 16.[11] For example, in 1958 the Federal Republic of Germany was accused by the Union of Soviet Socialist Republics of being complicit in an armed attack by the United States on Lebanon. The basis of the allegation was that US aircraft had used German airfields during the intervention. The ILC explains that the FRG 'seems to have accepted that the act of a State in placing its own territory at the disposal of another State in order to facilitate the commission of an unlawful use of force by that other State was itself an internationally wrongful act'.[12] This interpretation of the FRG's position is accurate and is demonstrated by the following note sent by the FRG to the USSR:

> There can be no doubt that the allies of the German Federal Republic were not guilty of any aggression in the Near and Middle East…The Government of the German Federal Republic has never approved nor favored an act of aggression. Neither has it ever placed the territory of the Federal Republic at the disposal of another for such an act.[13]

Quigley explains that similar protests from the USSR followed in 1958 in respect of Italy's granting of air and sea rights to the US in the course of its

[10] Art 3(f) Definition of Aggression.

[11] ARSIWA Commentary on Art 16.

[12] Ibid [8].

[13] Helmut Alexy, 'Völkerrechtliche Praxis der Bundesrepublik Deutschland im Jahre 1958' *Zeitschrift für ausländisches öffentliches Recht und Völkerrecht*, 20 (1959–60) 636, 663–4 quoted in Quigley, 'Complicity in International Law' 83.

intervention in Lebanon, and Israel's granting the UK and US permission to fly over its territory in the course of Britain's intervention in Jordan.[14] Guinea and Mali charged the United Kingdom with complicity in aggression for allowing Ascension Island to be used by Belgian and US forces for intervention in the Democratic Republic of the Congo.[15] In addition, it appears that the United Kingdom itself accepts that such a prohibition exists. Following an attack by Egypt on a village in Saudi Arabia in 1965, Britain protested not only Egypt's aggression but also Yemen's alleged complicity in the attack.[16]

The attacks on Libyan targets carried out by the United States on 14 and 15 April 1986, provide a range of state practice in support of the specific rule. France and Spain denied the US over-flight rights on the basis of concerns over the operation's legality.[17] The United Kingdom agreed to a request by the US for use of its air bases.[18] In response to this support, both the Libyan Arab Jamahiriya[19] and the United Arab Emirates (as a member of the Security Council at the time) condemned the UK's involvement in the attacks. The UAE made the following statement:

> We hold the United States—a permanent member of the Council—responsible for that act of aggression and for its consequences; we also hold the United Kingdom responsible, since it authorized the use of bases on its territory for the purpose of launching a military act of aggression against Libya.[20]

In response to these accusations, the United Kingdom defended the attack by the US as lawful rather than deny that responsibility arises in law for conduct of this kind.[21] A proposed Security Council resolution was vetoed but the General Assembly called on all states 'to refrain from extending any assistance or facilities for perpetrating acts of aggression against the Libyan Arab Jamahiriya'.[22]

The Iraq war of 2003 provides an array of state practice concerning the provision of territory to an aggressor state, though it is difficult to draw any strong conclusions from it.[23] Some states, notably Switzerland, Turkey, and

[14] Quigley, 'Complicity in International Law' 83–4.

[15] UN Doc S/PV.1171 [8], [53]. See Aust, *Complicity and the Law of State Responsibility* 110–11.

[16] Quigley, 'Complicity in International Law' 84.

[17] See Chinkin, *Third Parties in International Law* 296.

[18] Statement of Prime Minister Thatcher HC Deb 15 April 1986 vol. 95, cols. 729–39.

[19] UN Doc S/PV.2674 p 11–12.

[20] UN Doc S/PV.2674 p 6.

[21] HC Deb 15 April 1986 vol. 95, cols. 729–39. See Aust, *Complicity and the Law of State Responsibility* 112.

[22] UNGA Res 41/38 (20 November 1986) UN Doc A/RES/41/38 [3]; ARSIWA Commentary on Art 16 [8].

[23] See Nolte and Aust, 'Equivocal Helpers' 1–5.

Norway, refused to permit the use of their airspace, though Aust argues that considerations other than a legal concept of complicity may have informed their positions.[24] The conduct of other states, including Germany, was ambiguous,[25] and, as is often the case, can best be explained by reference to the interplay between legal judgment and political need.[26]

Although drawn from international criminal law, some support for the prohibition on complicity in aggression may also be inferred from the text of the definition of aggression adopted by consensus at the Kampala Review Conference of the Rome Statute of the International Criminal Court. The crime of aggression is defined as the 'planning, preparation, initiation or execution...of an act of aggression...'.[27] It includes within the definition of an 'act of aggression' the conduct specified in Article 3(f) of the General Assembly's 1974 Definition of Aggression.[28] The inclusion of Article 3(f) within the statute of the International Criminal Court may be read as further confirmation of the existence of the rule.

7.2.2.2. The Content of the Rule

Chapter 2 proposed an analytical framework in which complicity rules may be assessed and defended a normative claim as to how they should be structured. This section uses that framework and claim to evaluate the obligation imposed on states by international law not to allow their territory to be used for an act of aggression. Before doing so, it is worth pausing on a simple, yet fundamental, point. Responsibility arises for the complicit state only where the principal state actually perpetrates an act of aggression against a third state—without the principal's wrongful act, there is nothing for the complicit state to be complicit in.[29] This follows from the essential derivative nature of complicity.[30] For this reason, any defence available to the putative aggressor state absolves the complicit state of responsibility for complicity. In the case of the US bombing of Libya in 1986, the United Kingdom argued that the US's actions, and thus its provision of air bases to the US, was justified by the law of self-defence.[31] The wrongfulness of the UK's participation turned on the wrongfulness of the US's actions.

[24] Aust, *Complicity and the Law of State Responsibility* 115–20. [25] Ibid 117.

[26] See generally Nolte and Aust, 'Equivocal Helpers' 22–30.

[27] Resolution RC.Res.6 adopted at the 13th Plenary Meeting, Review Conference of the Rome Statute, Kampala, Uganda (11 June 2010), Annex 1 [1].

[28] Ibid [2]. [29] Quigley, 'Complicity in International Law' 86.

[30] Kadish, 'Complicity, Cause and Blame' 337.

[31] HC Deb 15 April 1986 vol. 95, cols. 729–39. See also ARSIWA Commentary on Art 16 [8]; Christopher Greenwood, 'International Law and the United States' Air Operation against Libya' (1986/1987) 89 W Va L Rev 933.

The three elements of the analytical framework concern the forms of complicity prohibited, the nexus between the accomplice's acts and the principal's wrong, and the fault required of the accomplice. Starting with the forms of complicity prohibited, the first thing to note is the narrowness of the prohibition on complicity in aggression—allowing another state to use its territory for perpetrating an act of aggression. In contrast to the generality of the doctrines of instigation and aiding and abetting in international criminal law, the customary prohibition on state complicity in aggression prohibits a very specific form of assistance. Its specificity should not be taken to signify a lack of importance; indeed, the inclusion of Article 3(f) within the Definition of Aggression indicates a targeted concern at a particularly culpable way in which states help other states to commit aggression.

A second point to note is the curious formulation of Article 3(f)—'[t]he *action* of a State in allowing its territory, which it has *placed* at the disposal of another State…'.[32] This may be read to suggest that positive action on the part of the complicit state is required, possibly excluding liability for complicit omissions. In some cases, the complicit state will be heavily involved in the military operation, providing logistical support for troop movements on its territory, or perhaps air-traffic control for aerial attacks. In other cases, the complicit state's involvement will be minor. Too much should not be made of this conduct element. It requires only that the complicit state *allow* its territory to be used by the aggressor state. A simple grant of permission will suffice.

Within this second point is the concept of territory. In the absence of practice to the contrary, territory in the prohibition on complicity in aggression should be defined under ordinary principles of international law. The concept of territory includes a state's land, airspace, and territorial sea.[33] It would also extend to occupied territory. Beyond these obvious and core instances, this issue may arise in more complicated situations such as vassalage, suzerainty, and lease. The most sensible standard to adopt in these situations is one of effective exercise of jurisdiction by the state over the disputed territory. Brownlie explains that this has been the approach of national courts when interpreting the term territory in various international agreements and treaties.[34] If a state exercises jurisdiction over territory, it is not unreasonable to prohibit it from placing that territory at the disposal of an aggressor state.

[32] Definition of Aggression (emphasis added).

[33] See Ian Brownlie, *Principles of Public International Law* (7th edn. OUP 2008) 105; Antonio Cassese, *International Law* (2nd edn. OUP 2005) 81.

[34] Brownlie, *Principles of Public International Law* 112.

The second element of the analytical framework concerns the nexus between the accomplice's acts and principal's wrong. As argued in Chapter 2, accomplices are best viewed as making an indirect causal contribution to the harm caused by the principal.[35] We do not need to ask if the act would have occurred in any case—that the actor's assistance was not a *sine qua non* does not mean that she did not make a contribution. In assessing that contribution, however, Chapter 2 also argued for a nexus requirement that excludes de minimis contributions—a standard of substantial contribution was suggested as a general rule.[36]

What that means in the context of complicity in aggression is not easy to determine. The need for a substantiality standard in the *criminal law* is driven by the generality and breadth of criminal prohibitions of complicity. Usually, the doctrine encompasses *any* form of complicity in *any* crime. The current rule concerns a *specific* (and serious) kind of complicity—the placing of territory at the disposal of the aggressor state—in a *specific* (and serious) wrong—aggression. For this reason, it makes sense to argue that the placing of territory at the disposal of an aggressor state always fulfils the nexus requirement, no matter where the territorial state lies in relation to the site of conflict.

The third element of the framework concerns the culpability of the complicit actor. In this regard, responsibility of the complicit state will not arise where it did not know about the use of its territory by the aggressor state. This flows from the language of the rule reflected in Article 3(f). If an aggressor state were to launch an aggressive act from the territory of another state without that state's knowledge, it could not be said that the state had 'placed' its territory at the disposal of the aggressor state for perpetrating an act of aggression. In such a case, no responsibility would arise under this rule.[37]

The relationship between the conduct and fault elements raises a difficult question. Would responsibility for complicity in aggression arise where a state, without explicitly placing its territory at the disposal of the aggressor state, acquiesces in that state of affairs? Putting that another way, if State A knows that State B is flying over its territory en route to an act of aggression against State C but does nothing to protest the action, is State A responsible to State C? One argument is that in the absence of state practice to

[35] See section 2.5.3 above; Smith, *A Treatise on Complicity* 89; Gardner, 'Complicity and Causality' 128.

[36] See section 2.5.3 above.

[37] This is not to say that in such a case responsibility would not arise for breach of the duty to ensure that one's territory is not used for acts contrary to the interests of other states, a duty conditioned by a due diligence standard.

the contrary, responsibility should be confined to situations where there is a positive act of consent by the complicit state. Any concern that states would acquiesce in acts of aggression launched from their territory may be mitigated by adopting a broad view of what constitutes positive action. A broad view of the action requirement could include any action by a state prior to, or during, the aggressive act suggesting consent or approval. This might include an indication short of explicit consent that the state would not protest the use of its territory.

The better interpretation is that the rule reflected in Article 3(f) encompasses the possibility of complicity by omission. As argued in Chapter 2, particularly culpable omissions should give rise to responsibility for complicity. As noted above, states are undoubtedly bound by a general obligation, conditioned by a requirement of due diligence, 'to protect within [their] territory the right of other States'.[38] This broader obligation will be breached in many more instances than will constitute a complicit omission, and is an example of direct responsibility; it does not operate so as to link the state to the subsequent wrongful act of the other state.[39] However, in respect of particularly culpable omissions, specifically those where the accomplice state had *knowledge* of the wrongful act and failed to act in breach of such a specific obligation, the omission should also be seen as a form of complicity.[40] In the present case, a state that acquiesces in the use of its territory for an act of aggression should be responsible for complicity in aggression.[41]

7.2.2.3. The Structure of the Rule

Chapter 2 set out the normative claim of this work. Complicity is a particular way of contributing to wrongdoing. In reflecting complicity as a particular way of contributing to wrongdoing, the law should hold accomplices responsible for, and label them in terms of, their own contribution to the principal's wrong rather than for the wrong of their principal. When we are dealing with individual responsibility, the principle of culpability sustains this claim. When we are dealing with state responsibility, this claim is underpinned by the fundamental value of sovereignty.[42]

[38] *Island of Palmas* 839. [39] See Fletcher, *Rethinking Criminal Law* 423.

[40] Here, Ashworth's example of a cleaner working in a bank is helpful. On one hand, the cleaner may fail to exercise due diligence in locking up at the end of the day. If a robbery takes place, we would hold the cleaner responsible directly for breaching his obligation to lock up the bank. On the other hand, if the cleaner, with knowledge of the planned robbery, intentionally failed to lock up at the end of the day, we would also see him as an accomplice to the robbery. See Ashworth, *Principles of Criminal Law* 410–11.

[41] For further discussion of complicit omissions and state responsibility, see section 7.3.5.1 below.

[42] See Nollkaemper and Jacobs, 'Shared Responsibility in International Law' 386.

The customary rule reflected in Article 3(f) prohibits a specific kind of complicity in a specific wrong—allowing one's territory to be used for an aggressive act. The formulation of the rule is interesting: it provides that complicity of this kind itself 'qualif[ies] as an act of aggression'.[43] On the face of it, the complicit state is not perpetrating some discrete wrong of facilitating or assisting aggression, but rather aggression itself. This point was made by Germany in its comments on a previous draft of ARSIWA:

> [T]he action of a State allowing its territory to be used by another State for perpetrating an act of aggression as described in article 3(f) of the Definition of Aggression qualifies as an act of aggression and not as aiding aggression.[44]

Here, care should be taken. The formulation of Article 3(f) might be interpreted as an imputational complicity rule. This is not the case. Although the act of assistance is itself an act of aggression, the complicit state is not responsible *for* the acts of the aggressor state; that is, it is not responsible for the aggressor state's acts of aggression. The responsibility of the complicit state is derivative in one sense—it arises only where the primary acting state actually commits aggression[45]—but it is not derivative *and* imputational. The acts of the aggressor state are not imputed to the complicit state.

Thus on first glance, the central problem of a common law conception of complicity is avoided. As illustrated in Chapter 2, the common-law model of complicity *imputes* to the accomplice the wrong of the principal. This is not the case in this instance—the law holds the complicit state responsible for its own acts. However, imposing the label of aggression on a state that allows another state to commit aggression from its territory is something of a fiction.[46] The logic of complicity is to render an otherwise lawful act wrongful when it assists in the perpetration of a wrong by another actor. In this instance, the principal wrong is the act of aggression by the principal state. The wrongfulness of the complicit state's conduct lies in its facilitation of that act of aggression.

For this reason, the rule reflected in Article 3(f) of the Definition of Aggression may be subject to criticism in terms of the principle of fair labelling. The fact that the assisting state is not actually held responsible for the principal state's acts is important, and goes some way to immunizing

[43] Art 3(f) Definition of Aggression.

[44] International Law Commission, 'State Responsibility—Comments and Observations Received from Governments' (1998) UN Doc A/CN.4/488, Germany, 76.

[45] Quigley, 'Complicity in International Law' 86.

[46] See section 2.4.2 above. For an example of this approach in domestic criminal law, see W Va Code § 61-3-1 (1977) cited in Robinson, 'Imputed Criminal Liability' n 6.

the rule from criticism. However, the accomplice state's indirect causal contribution—its complicity—is not properly described. A better description would be complicity in aggression, or, more precisely, facilitating an act of aggression.

7.2.3. Beyond Territorial Complicity

The rule prohibiting the placing of territory at the disposal of an aggressor state addresses a narrow and specific form of complicity. There is also state practice denoting a wider rule in respect of both aggression and the prohibition on the use of force. The strongest evidence may be found in the provision of military aid that is used to commit aggression, though some practice is more general both at the level of aid provided and in respect of the wrong assisted.[47] As a general principle, the provision of aid, military or otherwise, is lawful in international law, setting a base-line presumption allowing free intercourse among nations.[48] This base-line is circumscribed by allegations of complicity.

Some examples may illustrate the point. In 1951, the General Assembly condemned the People's Republic of China's participation in North Korea's acts of aggression during the Korean Crisis, stating that: '[T]he Central People's Government of the People's Republic of China, by giving direct aid and assistance to those who were already engaged in committing aggression ... has itself engaged in aggression in Korea.'[49] The ILC, again citing practice in support of the general rule in Article 16 ARSIWA, notes that the Islamic Republic of Iran protested the UK's supply of aid to Iraq in the Iran-Iraq war, aid which allegedly facilitated Iraq's aggression.[50] This allegation was denied by the UK. In 1982, after declaring that Israel's occupation of the Golan Heights constituted an act of aggression, the General Assembly called on member states to refrain from supplying aid or assistance

[47] See Quigley, 'Complicity in International Law' 87–95; Aust, *Complicity and the Law of State Responsibility* 129–45; Ago, 'Seventh Report on State Responsibility' [71].

[48] See the response of the United Kingdom Secretary of State for the Colonies to inquiries regarding the use of arms by Yemeni forces against the Crown colony of Aden in 1958, arms supplied to Yemen by a third state—House of Commons Debates, vol. 589, col. 891 (17 June 1958) reprinted in Elihu Lauterpacht, 'The Contemporary Practice of the United Kingdom in the Field of International Law—Survey and Comment' (1958) 7 ICLQ 514, 551. See also Lowe, 'Responsibility for the Conduct of Other States' 6, discussing the requirement of knowledge for state responsibility to arise: 'There is, for example, nothing wrong, in principle, with supplying vehicles to another State.'

[49] UNGA Res 498 (V) (1 February 1951) UN Doc A/RES/498 [1]. See Aust, *Complicity and the Law of State Responsibility* 109.

[50] ARSIWA Commentary on Art 16 [7].

to Israel.[51] The relevant part of the resolution passed by 87 votes to 22, with 31 abstentions.

A broad notion of complicity may also be seen in national and supranational statements and policies that limit the sale of arms.[52] In 1950, Britain, France, and the United States issued a short statement concerning the maintenance of peace and stability in the Middle East. After recognizing that both Israel and the Arab states 'need to maintain a certain level of armed forces for the purposes of assuring their internal security and their legitimate self-defense', the declaration states that:

> The three Governments declare that assurances have been received from all the states in question, to which they permit arms to be supplied from their countries, that the purchasing state does not intend to undertake any act of aggression against any other state. Similar assurances will be requested from any other state in the area to which they permit arms to be supplied in the future.[53]

In a comprehensive survey, Aust details a range of international practice, including domestic legislation on arms exports, concerning the provision of military support to states suspected of violating international law.[54] More recently, ideas of complicity can be seen in the statements of Azerbaijan regarding Russia's support for what Azerbaijan characterizes as Armenia's aggression during the Nagorno-Karabakh war of 1992–1994.[55] Following the break-up of the Soviet Union, and spurred by tensions between ethnic Armenians and Azeris within Nagorno-Karabakh, Armenian forces occupied parts of Azerbaijan. In a statement to the United Nations Economic and Social Council, Azerbaijan's Permanent Representative condemned Russia's supply of large quantities of weapons to Armenia, stating that 'the arms supplies have substantially enhanced the fighting capacity of the Armenian forces, which have carried out warlike actions and occupied Azerbaijani territory'. Continuing, the letter describes such arms transfers to a belligerent as 'violat[ing] the principles and standards of international law...'.[56]

[51] UNGA Res 37/123 (16 December 1982) UN Doc A/RES/37/123 [13]. See also UNGA Res 36/27 (13 November 1981) UN Doc A/RES/36/27 in respect of Israel's destruction of the Osirak reactor in Iraq.

[52] See Aust, *Complicity and the Law of State Responsibility* 129.

[53] Tripartite Declaration of France, Britain, and the United States 25 May 1950.

[54] See Aust, *Complicity and the Law of State Responsibility* 129–45.

[55] The Security Council issued four resolutions regarding the conflict in 1993: UNSC Res 822 (30 April 1993) UN Doc S/RES/822; UNSC Res 853 (29 July 1993) UN Doc S/RES/853; UNSC Res 874 (14 October 1993) UN Doc S/RES/874; UNSC Res 884 (12 November 1993) UN Doc S/RES/884.

[56] Letter dated 21 July 1998 from the Permanent Representative of the Republic of Azerbaijan to the United Nations Office at Geneva, addressed to the secretariat of the Sub-Commission

This practice raises particular interpretive difficulties because it is not entirely clear that the illegality articulated by Azerbaijan relates specifically to a rule of complicity in aggression.[57] It may refer to obligations relating to an ongoing occupation, or to the supply of weapons used to violate human rights norms, or indeed to the general rule of aid or assistance in the commission of an international wrong.

These interpretive difficulties are not confined to assessments of Azerbaijan's practice in the present case. Nonetheless, it seems likely that international law imposes a specific obligation on states prohibiting the knowing provision of military aid to an aggressor state. Lauterpacht, writing in 1958, suggests that a state may not escape responsibility for complicity in aggression where it 'knowingly supplies arms to another [state]'.[58] Quigley to some extent founds his assertion of a general rule of complicity in public international law on practice and *opinio juris* arising in the context of material aid to an aggressor state.[59] And Graefrath, criticizing the broad approach to complicity taken in Article 27, now Article 16, of an earlier draft of ARSIWA, describes 'the supply of weapons to support a State which commits aggression' as one of the typical examples of primary rules of complicity.[60] This rule may be seen as an interstate analogue of the prohibition on the supply by states of arms to non-state actors engaged in acts of civil strife in another state.[61]

7.2.4. Conclusion

Where states seek to use force against non-neighbouring states, the territory of other states is often implicated. To serve the value of international peace, international law prohibits states from placing their territory at the disposal of an aggressor state. Such complicit conduct will constitute an independent act of aggression by the aiding state. It is also likely that states will invoke the language of complicity to condemn the provision of weapons to aggressor states. These rules are constrained by their specificity, especially when contrasted with the wide construction of

on Prevention of Discrimination and Protection of Minorities, Economic and Social Council, E/CN.4/Sub.2/1998/31 (22 July 1998).

[57] For a discussion of difficulties along these lines see Aust, *Complicity and the Law of State Responsibility* 103–7.

[58] Lauterpacht, 'The Contemporary Practice of the United Kingdom—1958' 551.

[59] Quigley, 'Complicity in International Law' 87–90.

[60] Bernhard Graefrath, 'Complicity in the Law of International Responsibility' (1996) Rev Belge de Droit Intl 371, 373.

[61] Art 1 Declaration on Friendly Relations. See *Nicaragua* [228]; *Armed Activities* [162].

complicity in international criminal law. Nonetheless, these rules are an important step in the development of international law's concern with complicity—first the move from a historical absence of complicity rules to a specific and piecemeal approach, and then, as will be seen in section 7.3 below, the move from a specific and piecemeal approach towards a general and principled approach.

7.3. A General Complicity Rule—Article 16 ARSIWA

7.3.1. Introduction

The prohibition on state complicity in aggression is a specific complicity rule—it emerged to prohibit a specific form of participation in a specific international wrong. International law now recognizes a general prohibition on state complicity. After nearly 50 years of work, the International Law Commission's Draft Articles on Responsibility of States for Internationally Wrongful Acts were adopted at the ILC's fifty-third session in 2001, submitted to the General Assembly, and commended by that body to governments in Resolution 56/83.[62] Much ink has been spilled over certain aspects of the Articles, notably concerning the ultimately abandoned notion of state crimes.[63] Chapter IV ARSIWA, which concerns the responsibility of states in connection with the actions of another state, includes Article 16. Article 16 sets out a rule that prohibits states from aiding or assisting another state in the commission of an internationally wrongful act.[64]

This section assesses the place of Article 16 within the conceptual structure of the ILC's Articles as a whole, considers the content of the rule within the analytical framework of this work, and evaluates the structure of the rule. Despite limitations, Article 16 is a great step forward in the way international law deals with state complicity.

[62] UNGA Res 56/83 [3].

[63] See Joseph Weiler, Antonio Cassese, and Marina Spinedi (eds.) *International Crimes of State: A Critical Analysis of the ILC's Draft Article 19 on State Responsibility* (Walter de Gruyter 1989); Derek Bowett, 'Crimes of State and the 1996 Report of the International Law Commission on State Responsibility' (1998) 9 Eur J Intl L 163; Alain Pellet, 'Can a State Commit a Crime? Definitely, Yes!' (1999) 10 Eur J Intl L 425; Nina Jørgensen, *The Responsibility of States for International Crimes* (OUP 2000).

[64] Art 16 ARSIWA.

7.3.2. The Basic Structure of the Articles on State Responsibility

A distinction between primary and secondary rules underpins the Articles on State Responsibility.[65] As is well known, Roberto Ago, the second special rapporteur on the project, provided this conceptual framework in his second report in 1970.[66] His underlying idea was that the law of state responsibility consists of a coherent set of secondary rules that apply in the event of a breach of a primary rule—that is, a substantive obligation binding states. The Articles are a set of default rules and include those determining which acts are state acts, what consequences arise from the breach of an international obligation, and when the wrongfulness of an act may be precluded.[67] Primary rules, then, are rules of international law that determine the scope of acceptable conduct of the subject to whom they are addressed.[68] These were seen not to be a matter of state responsibility and thus not a matter for ARSIWA. As Ago put it: '[I]t is one thing to define a rule and the content of the obligation it imposes, and another to determine whether that obligation has been violated and what should be the consequences of the violation.'[69]

The Articles' foundational premise thus denies a concern with defining primary rules of conduct that create obligations for states. It is fair to say that Ago's decision to confine the project to secondary rules of responsibility contributed to state engagement during the drafting process and, in turn, to the eventual adoption of the Articles by the General Assembly.[70] Nonetheless, the distinction is not without its critics, being termed elusive and unnecessary,[71]

[65] See James Crawford, 'The ILC's Articles on Responsibility of States for Internationally Wrongful Acts: A Retrospect' (2002) 96 Am J Intl L 874, 876 terming the distinction the Articles' 'central organizing device'.

[66] Roberto Ago, 'Second Report on State Responsibility—the Origin of International Responsibility' (1970) UN Doc A/CN.4/233 (1970) II YILC 177. This Report formalized the position taken by Ago as chairman of the sub-committee set up by the ILC in 1963 in proposing a new approach to the codification of the law of state responsibility after the difficulties experienced during the tenure of Special Rapporteur FV García-Amador. See Daniel Bodansky and John Crook, 'Symposium: The ILC's State Responsibility Articles—Introduction and Overview' (2002) 96 Am J Intl L 773, 777–8.

[67] ARSIWA General Commentary [3].

[68] See Crawford, 'A Retrospect' 876–7.

[69] Ago, 'Second Report on State Responsibility' 178. See also ARSIWA General Commentary [2]; Crawford, 'A Retrospect' 876.

[70] Crawford, 'A Retrospect' 877; Bodansky and Crook, 'Introduction and Overview' 780. See generally Alain Pellet, 'The ILC's Articles on State Responsibility for Internationally Wrongful Acts and Related Texts' in Crawford et al. (eds.) *The Law of International Responsibility* 75–94.

[71] Bodansky and Crook, 'Introduction and Overview' 780. See also Christian Tams, 'All's Well that Ends Well—Comments on the ILC's Articles on State Responsibility' (2002) Heidelberg J Intl L 759, 764–5.

and said to lead to a misunderstanding of the operation of the international legal system.[72] These criticisms of the Articles' conceptual structure are not central to the assessment of Article 16; it is Article 16's position within that supposed structure that is of concern.

7.3.3. The Primary Nature of Article 16

Article 16 sets out the following rule:

> A State which aids or assists another State in the commission of an internationally wrongful act by the latter is internationally responsible for doing so if:
> (a) that State does so with knowledge of the circumstances of the internationally wrongful act; and
> (b) the act would be internationally wrongful if committed by that State.[73]

In spite of its inclusion in ARSIWA, Article 16 embodies a primary rule of international law.[74] That is to say, it is a rule that defines the scope of acceptable conduct for states. In fact, it may be thought of as a sort of primary meta-rule, in that it defines the bounds of acceptable state conduct in respect of all other primary rules.[75]

This conclusion flows from ARSIWA's internal logic. Article 2 ARSIWA provides:

> There is an internationally wrongful act of a State when conduct consisting of an action or omission:
> (a) is attributable to the State under international law; and
> (b) constitutes a breach of an international obligation of the State.[76]

If we consider any matter between states in which Article 16 forms the basis of the claim, attribution—part (a) of the test—will be assessed in the ordinary manner. This may implicate one or more provisions in Chapter II of the Articles. Part (b), of course, will be founded on Article 16. In other words, Article 16 is the specified international obligation of the state. On this basis, Article 16 is clearly a primary rule.[77]

[72] Ulf Linderfalk, 'State Responsibility and the Primary-Secondary Rules Terminology—The Role of Language for an Understanding of the International Legal System' (2009) 78 Nordic J Intl L 53, 72. See also Philip Allott, 'State Responsibility and the Unmaking of International Law' (1988) 29 Harv Intl L J 1.

[73] Art 16 ARSIWA.

[74] See Graefrath, 'Complicity in the Law of International Responsibility' 372; André Nollkaemper, 'Internationally Wrongful Acts in Domestic Courts' (2007) 101 Am J Intl L 760, n 100.

[75] See generally Lanovoy, 'Revisiting a Structural Norm' 1.

[76] Art 2 ARSIWA.

[77] See Nollkaemper and Jacobs, 'Shared Responsibility in International Law' 409.

No doubt the drafters were aware of this incongruity.[78] Indeed, a previous iteration of Article 16 was said by the member of the Commission from New Zealand to 'leap the barrier between secondary and primary rules'.[79]

The drafters attempt to explain the incongruity in two ways. First, the commentary notes that the Chapter in which Article 16 falls might be seen to blur the boundary between primary and secondary rules, but that its inclusion is nonetheless justified because responsibility 'is in a sense derivative'.[80] Taking this a step further, it likens the rules in Chapter IV to those in national legal systems dealing with conspiracy, complicity, and inducing breach of contract. Because rules of this kind may appear in the general part of the law of obligations, the inclusion of Articles 16, 17, and 18 ARSIWA is defensible. The final part of this justification is a *non sequitur*. It does not follow from the inclusion of complicity within the general part of the law of obligations that the ILC could prescribe rules that define the boundaries of substantive conduct for states without crossing into the sphere of primary rules.

The second way that the drafters justify the incongruity of Article 16 is, on closer analysis, an argument made more in mitigation than defence. More than once, the commentary emphasizes the exceptional nature of responsibility under Chapter IV.[81] Then, in defining the applicable test, it underlines the limited scope of Article 16. The language used betrays unease with the rule's position within the conceptual framework of the Articles as a whole: 'Article 16 limits the scope of responsibility for aid or assistance in three ways.'[82] This is not quite correct. Rather, Article 16 reflects a rule that *imposes* responsibility for aid and assistance—substantive conduct—and limits the scope of the primary obligation thereby imposed in three ways. The emphasis on its limited nature is an affirmation of the Article's incongruity. It confirms the view that Article 16 is a primary rule of international law.

7.3.4. The Legal Status of Article 16

During the drafting process, state responses to Article 16 and its prior iterations were mixed.[83] Commenting on the draft articles adopted by the Commission in its 48th session, Switzerland argued that Article 27, as it was then, had no basis in positive law, and Germany that its foundation in

[78] ARSIWA General Commentary on Chapter IV [7]: 'A feature of this chapter is that it specifies certain conduct as internationally wrongful.' See also Graefrath, 'Complicity in the Law of International Responsibility' 372.

[79] (1978) I YILC 1, 236.

[80] ARSIWA General Commentary on Chapter IV [7].

[81] Ibid [5], [8].

[82] ARSIWA Commentary on Art 16 [3].

[83] See generally, James Crawford, *State Responsibility: The General Part* (CUP 2013) 400–1.

international law and practice was doubtful.[84] The United Kingdom supported the basic principle.[85] At other stages of the process, responses were likewise mixed, though more states favoured Article 16's inclusion than opposed it.[86]

One preliminary question is whether this incongruity in the nature of Article 16 will affect its reception as a rule of international law in comparison to the other Articles. It is doubtful that this would be so. At this point, it is sufficient to note that the ILC was established by the General Assembly to promote the progressive development of international law and its codification, and that there is nothing within the Commission's broader mandate denying it the ability to define and prescribe primary rules of international law.[87] Indeed, the promotion of substantive rules of conduct has always formed part of its work.[88] In the long term, it is likely that states and international institutions will approach the rule in Article 16 in a manner akin to any other Article.

Indeed, the rule reflected in Article 16 has quickly been accepted as one of customary international law. Considering Serbia's potential complicity in the genocide at Srebrenica under Article III(e) of the Genocide Convention, the ICJ declared that Article 16 reflects a rule of customary international law.[89] In 2003, the Federal Constitutional Court of Germany considered a matter involving the luring by trickery of a Yemeni national to Germany carried out by an agent of the United States. The Yemeni national was then subject to an extradition request by the US. The court held that if a rule of international law existed prohibiting the luring of a national to another state by trickery such that the United States' responsibility was established vis-à-vis Yemen, it may follow that Germany would be responsible to Yemen for assistance under the rule in Article 16.[90] The court also held that Article 16 codifies customary international law.[91]

[84] International Law Commission, 'State Responsibility—Comments and Observations Received from Governments' (1998) 75–6.

[85] Ibid 76.

[86] Nolte and Aust, 'Equivocal Helpers' 8. In support see International Law Commission, 'Observations and Comments from Governments on Chapters I, II, and III of Part I of the Draft Articles on State Responsibility for Internationally Wrongful Acts' (1980) UN Doc A/CN.4/328, Mali, 101; International Law Commission, 'State Responsibility—Comments and Observations Received from Governments' (1999) UN Doc A/CN.4/492, Japan, 11.

[87] UNGA Res 174 (II) (21 November 1947).

[88] See International Law Commission 'Draft Code of Offences against the Peace and Security of Mankind' text adopted at its 48th session (1996) II(2) YILC 30.

[89] *Bosnian Genocide* [420].

[90] *Al-M* (5 November 2003) 2 BVerfG 1506/03.

[91] Ibid [47]. See Nollkaemper, 'Internationally Wrongful Acts in Domestic Courts' 780. The complaint was dismissed on the basis that no rule of international law established the responsibility

In addition, Article 16 has played an increasingly prominent role in international and national responses to state participation in the war on terror.[92] In 2009, the report of the Special Rapporteur on human rights and terrorism reiterated the applicability of Article 16 in the context of rendition, detention, and interrogation,[93] as did an earlier report by the Venice Commission adopted at its plenary session in 2006.[94] A good example of how the rule has influenced domestic practice is the report of the UK Parliament's Joint Committee on Human Rights into allegations of UK complicity in torture. Drawing on Article 16 and the Convention against Torture, the Committee adopted the following definition of state complicity in torture:

> [F]or the purposes of State responsibility for complicity in torture…complicity means simply one State giving assistance to another State in the commission of torture, or acquiescing in such torture, in the knowledge, including constructive knowledge, of the circumstances of the torture which is or has been taking place.[95]

The acceptance of Article 16 as a rule of customary international law might be evidence of what David Caron terms the paradoxical relationship between the form of the Articles and their authority.[96] The paradox is that in their present form the ILC's Articles may come to have a greater influence on international law than would have been the case if they had instead formed the basis of a multilateral treaty.[97] This criticism is particularly valid in respect of Article 16, where the evidence adduced by the Commission for its customary status was not entirely convincing. In the commentary, the ILC refers to a number of specific primary rules prohibiting states from participating in the wrongs of other states—those in respect of aggression, human rights violations, and the evasion of Security Council sanctions—as evidence of a

of the United States vis-à-vis Yemen for the trickery. There was no wrong for Germany to be complicit in.

[92] See Aust, *Complicity and the Law of State Responsibility* 120–7.

[93] UNHRC, 'Report of the Special Rapporteur on the Promotion and Protection of Human Rights and Fundamental Freedoms while Countering Terrorism' (4 February 2009) UN Doc A/HRC10/3 [53].

[94] European Commission for Democracy through Law, 'Opinion on the International Legal Obligations of Council of Europe Member States in Respect of Secret Detention Facilities and Inter-State Transport of Prisoners' adopted by the Venice Commission at its 66th Plenary Session (17 March 2005), Op No 363/2005 [45]. See also UNHRC, 'Joint Study on Global Practices in relation to Secret Detention in the Context of Countering Terrorism' (19 February 2010) UN Doc A/HRC/13/42 [41].

[95] Joint Committee on Human Rights, *Allegations of UK Complicity in Torture* (2008–09) HL Paper 152 HC 230 [35].

[96] David Caron, 'The ILC Articles on State Responsibility: The Paradoxical Relationship between Form and Authority' (2002) 96 Am J Intl L 857.

[97] See also Crawford, 'A Retrospect' 889.

general rule prohibiting participation in the wrongful act of another state. The critical absence is an explanation of how the general rule is founded on these primary rules.[98] Nonetheless, Article 16 has taken hold as a rule of customary international law, one that defines acceptable conduct for states in their participation in the wrongdoing of other states.

7.3.5. Assessing the Rule with the Analytical Framework

Chapter 2 set out an analytical framework for understanding the elements of complicity rules. The framework structures the analysis around the forms of complicity prohibited, the nexus between the accomplice's act and the principal's wrong, and the fault required of the accomplice. It will be seen that the rule in Article 16 includes an additional element: the double obligation requirement.

7.3.5.1. The Conduct Element

The conduct element of complicity under Article 16 is broad. Article 16 prohibits states from giving aid or assistance that facilitates another state's commission of an internationally wrongful act. There is no inchoate responsibility under Article 16—the assisted state must in fact commit the wrongful act.[99] The commentary lists financing, the provision of an essential facility, the provision of means for the closing of an international waterway, facilitating the abduction of persons on foreign soil, and assisting in the destruction of property belonging to third state nationals as examples of actions that fulfil the conduct element of the test.[100] These examples demonstrate its breadth.

In the light of this breadth, it is sometimes asked if Article 16 is contingent on the provision of a certain kind of aid.[101] This question should not be confused with a separate but related question: what is the required relationship between the aid or assistance and the wrongful act of the assisted state?[102] This latter question might be thought of as the nexus issue; it is the key to the operation of Article 16. On the former question, all *kinds* of aid and assistance fall within the rule.[103] Lowe argues that it may include technical or financial assistance, the non-application of mandatory sanctions, and even the provision by states of credit or investment guarantees that facilitate

[98] Nolte and Aust, 'Equivocal Helpers' 8. See also Tams, 'All's Well that Ends Well' 794.
[99] ARSIWA Commentary on Art 16 [5]. [100] ARSIWA Commentary on Art 16 [1].
[101] See Lowe, 'Responsibility for the Conduct of Other States' 5.
[102] See Nolte and Aust, 'Equivocal Helpers' 10.
[103] Crawford, *State Responsibility: The General Part* 402.

investments by their companies in other states.[104] This is surely correct. There is no principled reason for limiting the kind of aid or assistance that might implicate Article 16. The commentary does not do so.

There are two outstanding issues concerning the forms of complicity prohibited by the rule in Article 16. First, the commentary on Article 16 focuses on the provision of assistance as the sole mode of complicity—the various ways that a state may *help* another state in its commission of an internationally wrongful act.[105] Likewise, in its consideration of Article 16 in the *Bosnian Genocide* case, the ICJ refers specifically to the 'provision of means to enable or facilitate the commission of the crime…'.[106]

These statements reflect a long-standing assumption in international law that excludes classic forms of complicity based on influencing the principal—inducing, instigation, abetting—from state responsibility for complicity in the wrongs of other states.[107] Ago traced this exclusion to the conclusions of the Board of Commissioners set up under the Convention of 4 July 1831 between France and the United States, and argues that '[t]he decision of a sovereign State to adopt a certain course of conduct is certainly its own, even if it has received suggestions and advice from another state, which it was at liberty not to follow'.[108] This position is widely assumed to be correct as a matter of law.[109] As a result, in the absence of a specific treaty regime,[110] forms of complicity that are clearly established in international criminal law—such as instigation and abetting—probably do not apply to states.[111]

Even if this conclusion is correct as a matter of positive law, it is not clear that it should be so. As much as individuals influence other individuals to commit crimes by instigation or encouragement, states influence the decisions of other states.[112] In its commentary on a previous draft of Article 16, the ILC partially based its rejection of 'incitement' on the idea that the

[104] Lowe, 'Responsibility for the Conduct of Other States' 5–6. See also Talmon, 'A Plurality of Responsible Actors' 218: 'The ILC has made it clear that no particular kind of aid or assistance is necessary in order for this responsibility to arise.'

[105] See Kadish, 'Complicity, Cause and Blame' 342.

[106] *Bosnian Genocide* 419.

[107] See ARSIWA General Commentary on Chapter IV [9]; James Crawford, 'Second Report on State Responsibility' (1999) UN Doc A/CN.4/498/Add.1 (1999) II(1) YILC 3.

[108] Ago, 'Seventh Report on State Responsibility' [62]–[63].

[109] Quigley, 'Complicity in International Law' 80; Nolte and Aust, 'Equivocal Helpers' 13; Christian Dominicé, 'Attribution of Conduct to Multiple States and the Implication of a State in the Act of Another State' in Crawford et al. (eds.) *The Law of International Responsibility* 281, 285; Crawford, *State Responsibility: The General Part* 403.

[110] See the prohibition on direct and public incitement to commit genocide, an inchoate wrong, in Art III(c) of the Genocide Convention. See also *Bosnian Genocide* [167].

[111] See ARSIWA General Commentary on Chapter IV [9].

[112] Influence in this case means influence short of coercion under Art 18 ARSIWA.

'motives of State conduct in international relations cannot be assimilated' to the psychological motives underpinning prohibitions on incitement for individuals in domestic law.[113] But we do not need an assimilation of the motives of states and individuals to recognize that states *do* influence the decisions of other states to commit internationally wrongful acts. Of course, there might be evidentiary difficulties in proving such influence, and the other elements of the complicity rule would knock out both more marginal, and less culpable, forms of influence. But just as a state should not help another state to do what it cannot do itself,[114] so a state should not instigate another state to breach an obligation by which it is also bound.

Moreover, Ago's argument that 'the decision of a sovereign State to adopt a certain course of conduct is certainly its own' is not inconsistent with the operation of doctrines of complicit influence.[115] Complicity does not deny the responsibility of the principal; indeed, it affirms it. For this reason, the ILC is incorrect to suggest that such a prohibition would entail the possibility of the principal state 'avoiding or even reducing its responsibility by alleging "incitement" by another state'.[116] A principled approach to complicity under Article 16 would encompass the provision of complicit influence, not because the rule under Article 16 ought necessarily to track criminal conceptions, but because it is wrong for states to instigate other states to breach their obligations, especially where the putative accomplice state is also bound not to carry out the principal act.

The second issue regarding the forms of complicity prohibited by Article 16 concerns omissions. This issue has less to do with the ILC and more to do with the ICJ's holding in the *Bosnian Genocide* case. In interpreting the primary rule prohibiting complicity in genocide, the court held that 'complicity always requires that some positive action has been taken to furnish aid or assistance to the perpetrators...'.[117] Lanovoy argues that it is not clear that the court's holding applies by implication to Article 16.[118] More likely, as Crawford suggests, the exclusion of complicit omissions from complicity in genocide applies, in the ICJ's own understanding, to the rule in Article 16.[119] This position is supported by the prior holding of the court that it 'sees no reason to make any distinction of substance between "complicity in

[113] (1978) II(2) YILC 100 [6]. See also Nollkaemper, 'The Charles Taylor Judgment'.

[114] ARSIWA Commentary on Art 16 [6].

[115] Ago, 'Seventh Report on State Responsibility' [62]–[63].

[116] Cf (1978) II(2) YILC 100 [6].

[117] *Bosnian Genocide* [432].

[118] Lanovoy, 'Revisiting a Structural Norm' 12.

[119] Crawford, *State Responsibility: The General Part* 403–5.

genocide"...and the "aid or assistance" of a State in the commission of a wrongful act by another State...'.[120]

Moreover, there is heritage to the idea that the distinction between (i) 'participation' in the wrongful acts of another state, and (ii) the direct breach of a due diligence obligation to prevent the occurrence of harm, is founded on the line between acts and omissions; indeed, this was Ago's position in his Seventh Report on State Responsibility. In this regard, it is worth setting out Ago's argument in detail:

> [I]t should be remembered that a case of 'participation' in the internationally wrongful act of another cannot be found in the fact, or rather the sole fact, that a state failed to take the preventive or repressive measures required of it with respect to actions committed in its territory by an organ of another State to the detriment of a third State. By such failure, the State in question breaches an international obligation incumbent on it, which is quite different from the obligation breached on its territory by the organ of the foreign State. The murder of a foreign Head of State by organs of State A on the territory of State B, and the failure of State B in its duty to adopt the necessary measures to prevent such an act if possible...are two different internationally wrongful acts, each the responsibility of a different State. There is, of course, an undeniable link between the two acts...but this link is not sufficient to make one of the acts appear as participation in the other. This does not mean that in specific cases there may not also be participation—in the form of 'assistance' or 'complicity'—of the territorial State in the internationally wrongful act perpetrated on its soil by the foreign State. But there is an additional element, a separate breach besides the mere failure to prevent and punish. As the Commission has previously emphasized, that failure, as such, can certainly not be defined as a form of complicity.[121]

Following the *Bosnian Genocide* case, this appears to be the prevailing position in international law.[122] As a matter of principle, it is a misstep. As argued in Chapter 2, there is no good reason to exclude certain culpable omissions in the face of a specific duty from the ambit of responsibility for complicity. As a matter of basic usage, some omissions do assist in the commission of wrongdoing. Moreover, some omissions are sufficiently wrongful as to link the omitting party to the ensuing harm.[123] In criminal law, the paradigm case of a cleaner intentionally failing to lock a bank so as to facilitate a robbery seems to exemplify the wrong of complicity.[124] In respect of state complicity, the ILC itself cites Article 3(f) of the Definition of Aggression as an

[120] *Bosnian Genocide* [420]. [121] Ago, 'Seventh Report on State Responsibility' [57].

[122] Crawford, *State Responsibility: The General Part* 403.

[123] Fletcher, *Rethinking Criminal Law* 611.

[124] Ashworth, *Principles of Criminal Law* 410–11. See section 2.5.2.2 above.

example of a primary complicity rule.[125] States may allow their territory to be used by an aggressor state by omission—failing to object, for instance.[126]

In a system of law that imposes broad due diligence obligations on states to prevent certain harms from occurring, one difficult question is how to draw out a set of omissions that are so culpable as to not only constitute a breach of that due diligence obligation but also give rise to responsibility for complicity.[127] As argued previously, that distinction should not be drawn solely on the basis of an act/omission distinction. Instead, the other elements of a complicity rule will pull into the ambit of complicity particularly culpable omissions that contribute significantly to the commission of the harm and exclude those that do not. To pick up Ago's example, we might compare:

1. State B, hosting the head of state of State A, fails to exercise due diligence in screening guests attending the head of state's speech. The head of state is assassinated by agents of State C; and
2. State B, hosting the head of state of State A, receives specific warning that agents of State C are present at the speech and are about to assassinate the head of state. State B does nothing.

In the first instance, State B will likely have breached its obligation to exercise due diligence in preventing acts on its territory detrimental to the interest of other states.[128] In the second instance, in addition to any such direct responsibility for the omission, on certain conditions the state's failure should be seen to give rise to a derivative form of responsibility for participation in the principal wrong committed by State C.[129] Assuming State B's omission materially facilitated, or substantially contributed to, the principal wrong and the state had specific knowledge about the proposed attack, its conduct constitutes a complicit omission. This is what complicity rules do—they link the accomplice to the wrong of the principal. Here, the omission is sufficiently culpable as to constitute a form of complicity.[130]

7.3.5.2. The Nexus Element

The second element of any complicity rule concerns the relationship between the aid or encouragement provided and the wrongful act committed. Given

[125] ARSIWA Commentary on Art 16 [8].

[126] See section 7.2.2 above. See also Lanovoy, 'Revisiting a Structural Norm' 9; Nolte and Aust, 'Equivocal Helpers' n 43.

[127] See Lanovoy, 'Revisiting a Structural Norm' 9.

[128] See section 6.2 above; Ago, 'Seventh Report on State Responsibility' [57].

[129] Lanovoy, 'Revisiting a Structural Norm' 10. See also Fletcher, *Rethinking Criminal Law* 422.

[130] Kadish, 'Act and Omission' 70.

the range of actions or omissions that might fulfil the conduct element of complicity, it was argued in Chapter 2 that a substantiality criterion should apply. On first glance, this is the approach of the ILC in respect of Article 16. The commentary specifies as follows:

> There is no requirement that the aid or assistance should have been essential to the performance of the internationally wrongful act; it is sufficient if it contributed significantly to that act.[131]

This standard demands that the assistance materially facilitates the commission of the wrongful act.[132] It excludes assistance that is indirectly or remotely related to that act.[133] This much seems clear. However, in discussing the nature of responsibility under Article 16, the commentary appears to assume that assistance that 'may have been only an incidental factor in the commission of the primary act' might fall within its scope.[134] This clearly suggests a different standard from one of significant contribution or material facilitation.

The standard of material facilitation is to be preferred. For a start, it appears within the paragraphs of the commentary that define the scope of the test. As a matter of textual interpretation, therefore, material facilitation seems to be the standard preferred by the ILC.[135] Second, although the contours of the customary rule may evolve, the instances in which states have condemned other states' complicity inevitably involve something more than incidental contributions. Finally, as to an evaluation of the requisite standard, the potential breadth of the rule in Article 16 should be noted. As a primary rule of international law, Article 16 defines the acceptable bounds of state conduct in cooperating with other states. Given that no limitation is imposed on the kinds of aid included within the first limb of the test, it serves the interests of international cooperation to require a nexus beyond incidental contribution to give rise to international responsibility.[136] Put simply, incidental contribution sweeps too widely. Material facilitation is a standard that catches conduct with a sufficient link to another state's wrongdoing while excluding the incidental relationships that arise from virtually every state interaction.

[131] ARSIWA Commentary on Art 16 [5].

[132] Crawford, 'Second Report on State Responsibility' [180]. See also Lowe, 'Responsibility for the Conduct of Other States' 5.

[133] Nolte and Aust, 'Equivocal Helpers' 10.

[134] ARSIWA Commentary on Art 16 [10].

[135] See Crawford, *State Responsibility: The General Part* 402–3.

[136] See Lowe 'Responsibility for the Conduct of Other States' 5; Nolte and Aust, 'Equivocal Helpers' 12.

7.3.5.3. Fault element

The standard of fault required by Article 16 was a controversial issue during the drafting process.[137] Strict liability was never an option.[138] This builds on the general principle that states may presume that recipient states will use their aid lawfully.[139] The final set of comments from governments on the draft text reveals the United States and United Kingdom's concern that the fault standard be construed narrowly. The US's position was that the 'assisting state must be both aware that its assistance will be used for an unlawful purpose and so intend its assistance to be used'.[140] The UK suggested that it 'be made clear that the "assisting" State must be aware that the act in question is planned and must further intend to facilitate the commission of that act by its assistance'.[141]

How these comments and other discussions in the drafting process relate to the final text is not entirely clear. Textually, Article 16 requires only that the aid or assistance be given 'with knowledge of the circumstances of the internationally wrongful act'.[142] However, the commentary also states that the 'aid or assistance must be given with a view to facilitating the commission of the wrongful act' and that no responsibility arises 'unless the relevant State organ intended, by the aid or assistance given, to facilitate the occurrence of the wrongful conduct…'. The phrase 'with a view to facilitating' suggests a more stringent fault requirement—the textual knowledge standard is subsumed by one of wrongful intent.[143]

In many cases, there will not be a great practical difference between a standard of actual knowledge and one of intent. In his 7th Report, Ago himself appeared to elide the two:

> The very idea of 'complicity' in the internationally wrongful act of another necessarily presupposes an intent to collaborate in the commission of an act of this kind,

[137] See Quigley, 'Complicity in International Law' 108–20.

[138] See Ago, 'Seventh Report on State Responsibility' 58.

[139] ARSIWA Commentary on Art 16 [4]; Lowe, 'Responsibility for the Conduct of Other States' 10.

[140] International Law Commission, 'State Responsibility—Comments and Observations Received From Governments' (2001) UN Doc A/CN.4/515 52.

[141] Ibid. [142] Art 16 ARSIWA.

[143] Nolte and Aust, 'Equivocal Helpers' 14. On the terminology, the boundaries of intent, intention, and knowledge are deeply contested and vary across legal systems. The debate on the fault element in Art 16 ARSIWA corresponds to knowledge/purpose debate discussed in Part A and Part B of this work. In other words, what Crawford calls at different points 'overt intention' and 'actual intent' may be taken to mean a requirement of purpose. See Crawford, *State Responsibility: The General Part* 407. For reasons of consistency with other scholarship in the law of state responsibility, this chapter will use the term intent instead of purpose.

and hence, in the cases considered, knowledge of the specific purpose for which the State receiving certain supplies intends to use them.[144]

In most situations, where a state provides assistance to another state with the actual knowledge that the aid will be used to commit a wrongful act, the state's intent that its aid facilitates that act may be inferred.[145] As Lowe argues, as 'a matter of general legal principle States must be supposed to intend the foreseeable consequences of their acts'.[146]

There may, however, be situations in which the difference in requirements is dispositive. Development aid is a difficult case.[147] State A might provide hundreds of millions of dollars to State B. State B uses some of this money for education, some for health care, some to build infrastructure, and some to purchase weapons. State A knows that State B perpetrates internationally wrongful human rights violations against its citizens, and, in fact, some of the weapons purchased with this aid are used in the commission of those violations. Nolte and Aust suggest that in such a case the aid might have been provided in the knowledge of the circumstances of the wrongful act but not with a view to facilitating it.[148]

There is little practice resolving the ambiguity of the text and commentary.[149] In the *Bosnian Genocide* case, the ICJ failed to set out precisely the fault element for complicity in genocide—and possibly Article 16 ARSIWA by implication. Instead, the court would only say that 'at the least' complicity requires knowledge.[150] Strangely, some scholars have taken this holding to imply that, in general, complicity requires more than knowledge.[151] This is not a natural interpretation of the judgment.

There is also no agreement among scholars. Nolte and Aust favour the commentary's prescription of wrongful intent on the basis that a broader standard may discourage beneficial forms of international cooperation.[152] Crawford is broadly in agreement, though his position is partly informed by considerations of the ILC's institutional role.[153] Lowe favours a standard based on knowledge.[154] Quigley, writing about the earlier draft Article 27,

[144] Ago, 'Seventh Report on State Responsibility' 58.

[145] See Talmon, 'A Plurality of Responsible Actors' 218–19; Crawford, *State Responsibility: The General Part* 408.

[146] Lowe, 'Responsibility for the Conduct of Other States' 8.

[147] See Nolte and Aust, 'Equivocal Helpers' 14–15.

[148] Ibid 15.

[149] See though Lowe, 'Responsibility for the Conduct of Other States' 8.

[150] *Bosnian Genocide* [421].

[151] See Aust, *Complicity and the Law of State Responsibility* 236; Crawford, *State Responsibility: The General Part* 407.

[152] Ibid 14–15.

[153] Crawford, *State Responsibility: The General Part* 408.

[154] Lowe, 'Responsibility for the Conduct of Other States' 8.

argues that a restrictive standard of culpability based on wrongful intent would undermine the entire purpose of the prohibition of complicity.

As a matter of interpretation, the text itself should be the starting point. Of course, as the rule develops in customary international law, a more stringent standard might evolve. More broadly, in line with the general position of this work, a standard of knowledge is to be preferred. The main argument for the higher standard of wrongful intent is that a lower fault element might unduly limit trade and interstate cooperation.[155] This is not entirely convincing. First, it bears repeating that knowledge is quite different from a standard of strict liability or even negligence—a significant form of culpability is still required. It is an overstatement to suggest that a rule prohibiting knowing assistance that materially facilitates wrongdoing would be unworkable or render interstate cooperation hazardous.[156]

Second, states that are concerned about potential international responsibility in their provision of assistance may mitigate this risk through conditions or more targeted aid. The assisting state may know that the assisted state is in ongoing breach of obligations in one particular area of administration, but may nonetheless want to grant aid for other worthy projects. By imposing a burden on assisting states to ensure that its aid is used lawfully, a standard of knowledge promotes the twin goals of compliance and cooperation. Cooperation is beneficial. Compliance with international law is also beneficial. A standard of knowledge promotes compliance without unduly hampering cooperation.

Even if a standard of knowledge does become entrenched in international practice, much will still turn on how the requirement is interpreted.[157] In the final round of comments from governments on the draft articles, the Netherlands proposed that Article 16 be changed to read: 'That State does so when it knows *or should have known* the circumstances of the internationally wrongful act.'[158] The Commission did not take up this proposal.

In practice, the standard of knowing participation means awareness with something approaching practical certainty as to the circumstances of the principal wrongful act.[159] Dilution from that standard—the slide into reckless assistance—starts to become inconsistent with the essential derivative

[155] Nolte and Aust, 'Equivocal Helpers' 14–15; Aust, *Complicity and the Law of State Responsibility* 239–41.

[156] Cf Aust, *Complicity and the Law of State Responsibility* 239–40.

[157] For discussion, see section 2.5.4 above.

[158] PC Tange, 'Netherlands State Practice for the Parliamentary Year 2000–2001' (2002) 33 Netherlands Y Intl L 191, 237 (emphasis added).

[159] See section 2.5.4 above.

nature of complicity[160] and may indeed undermine valuable international cooperation.[161] Somewhere around the line between knowing and reckless participation is the idea of wilful blindness. Lowe argues that an international tribunal would not allow a state to evade responsibility by deliberately failing to inquire into the circumstances of an assisted act where there are clear indications that its assistance would be employed unlawfully.[162] This is almost certainly correct as a matter of law and in principle—wilful blindness, narrowly interpreted, is a justified extension to the category of legal knowledge.[163] Beyond that, international law does not yet recognize a general due diligence obligation conditioning the provision of aid or assistance to another state.[164]

7.3.6. The Double Obligation Requirement

7.3.6.1. The ILC's Approach

In addition to the elements of the rule set out above, Article 16 demands that the act committed by the principal state would also be internationally wrongful if committed by the complicit state. Where the rule is one of customary international law, both parties will most likely be bound by the obligation. However, with respect to treaty law, this element may limit the scope of the rule. For example, no responsibility arises under Article 16 if China assists the United Kingdom in violating rights guaranteed by the European Convention on Human Rights that extend beyond customary international law.[165] Likewise, a third state may facilitate the breach of a bilateral treaty without incurring responsibility vis-à-vis the injured state.

Chapter 2 of this work considered different ways of thinking about the justification for complicity rules in a legal system. On one level, we can see complicity as a moral claim. If it is wrong to act in certain way, it is wrong to assist or encourage that act.[166] On another level, we may confine our analysis to legal wrongs—assume only that the principal committed a legal wrong

[160] Ibid. [161] Aust, *Complicity and the Law of State Responsibility* 240.

[162] Lowe, 'Responsibility for the Conduct of Other States' 10.

[163] See section 2.5.4.4 above.

[164] Talmon, 'A Plurality of Responsible Actors' 218–19; Lowe, 'Responsibility for the Conduct of Other States' 10. Of course, specific primary rules might themselves impose a due diligence standard on the provision of aid or assistance, either as a specific complicity rule or as a kindred form of direct responsibility such as the principle of *non-refoulement*.

[165] See Crawford, *State Responsibility: The General Part* 410 in respect of obligations of similar content from different sources.

[166] Gardner, 'Complicity and Causality' 133.

against the victim. Here, in assessing whether a complicity rule is justified, it is helpful to distinguish two sets of relationships between the three parties:

A. V has a right exigible against both P and A. P, helped by A, violates the correlative duty;
B. V has a right exigible against P only. P, helped by A, violates the correlative duty.[167]

The rule in Article 16 responds only to the first situation. Certainly, there is a principled reason for prohibiting complicity here—as the commentary puts it, 'a State cannot do by another what it cannot do by itself'.[168]

The question, however, is whether the double obligation requirement unduly limits the rule by excluding the second situation—that is, where A is not bound not to do the act that constituted P's violation. The inclusion of the double obligation requirement is purportedly based on the *pacta tertiis* rule, reflected in Articles 34 and 35 of the VCLT.[169] It is fundamental that '[a] treaty does not create either obligations or rights for a third State without its consent'.[170]

Two arguments may be raised here. First, it is not clear that the *pacta tertiis* rule is a ground for *distinguishing* situations A and B set out above. To explain, consider two alternatives:

1. States A1, P1, and V1 adopt a multilateral treaty (T1) under which each of them agrees not to produce in excess of a certain quantity of steel each year. State P1, assisted by State A1, breaches the obligation;
2. States P2 and V2 adopt a bilateral treaty (T2) under which each of them agrees not to produce in excess of a certain quantity of steel each year. State P2, assisted by State A2, breaches the obligation.

As noted above, responsibility under Article 16 arises only in the first situation, the purported basis of the distinction being that the bilateral treaty in the second situation cannot give rise to obligations binding State A, whereas this issue does not arise in respect of the multilateral treaty in the first situation. The flaw in this argument is the assumption that the obligation that gives rise to responsibility for State A1 in the first situation is its obligation under the multilateral treaty to refrain from producing steel in excess of a certain quantity. This assumption is wrong. The multilateral treaty does not

[167] See generally Hohfeld, 'Fundamental Legal Conceptions' 718–19.
[168] ARSIWA Commentary on Art 16 [6]. [169] Ibid.
[170] Art 34 VCLT. See Malgosia Fitzmaurice, 'Third Parties and the Law of Treaties' (2002) 6 Max Planck YB of United Nations L 37, 38.

prohibit *complicity* in the production of excess steel but rather the act of producing excess steel. In this instance, P1's responsibility arises as a result of its breach of the multilateral treaty; A1's responsibility arises as a result of its breach of Article 16.

In respect of the second situation, the ILC sees the *pacta tertiis* rule as precluding the possibility of A2's responsibility for complicity. But just as in the first situation, any responsibility imposed on the assisting state would likewise arise under Article 16, rather than for breaching the obligation under the bilateral treaty, a treaty to which, as the ILC rightly points out, it is not party. In other words, in both situations the treaty defines the range of appropriate conduct for the principal state vis-à-vis the victim state and Article 16 defines the range of appropriate conduct for the assisting state vis-à-vis the victim state. Strictly speaking, there is no reason to distinguish the two alternatives on the basis of the VCLT.

This argument is, however, a little misleading: it does not follow from the absence of a basis to distinguish the two situations on account of the *pacta tertiis* rule that responsibility should arise for complicity where the assisting state is not bound by the obligation breached by the principal state. The desirability of such responsibility must be independently established. As noted above, in those situations where the assisting state *is* bound by the same obligation, there is a principled reason for prohibiting its participation in the principal's legal wrong: states should not be able to do by another what they cannot do themselves.[171] The question is whether there are principled and policy reasons for extending responsibility for complicity to situations where the assisting state is not so bound.[172]

7.3.6.2. A General Complicity Rule in the Law of State Responsibility?

It was noted above that, strictly speaking, the *pacta tertiis* rule does not provide a reason to distinguish between situations in which the assisting state is, and is not, bound by the obligation breached by the principal state. We should not deny, however, the relevance of the *pacta tertiis* rule to determining whether international law should adopt a general complicity rule—that

[171] ARSIWA Commentary on Art 6 [6].

[172] To be sure, this is not quite the same question as whether the ILC erred in not extending responsibility beyond the double obligation requirement. The latter question also implicates concerns about the ILC's institutional role within the international legal system, the prudence of proceeding cautiously in developing the rules of state responsibility, and the incongruity of the primary nature of Art 16 within a system of secondary rules of state responsibility. See Lowe, 'Responsibility for the Conduct of Other States' 8; Crawford, *State Responsibility: The General Part* 409.

is, one not conditioned by such a double obligation requirement. It is relevant because of the derivative nature of complicity.[173] Complicity rules do not operate independently of the various substantive obligations binding principal actors. Whenever a principal state undertakes an obligation to do or not do a certain act, the freedom of third states bound by a complicity rule is inevitably affected. As a simple example, imagine State P is under no obligation to State V not to produce in excess of a certain amount of steel. It is at liberty to produce as much steel as it wishes. State A is free to assist State P's steel production. Now imagine State P undertakes in a treaty with State V not to produce in excess of that amount of steel. If State A is bound by a general complicity rule, it is prohibited from assisting State P's breach of its obligation.

In this sense, a prohibition on complicity in respect of a breach of the treaty between States P and V does implicate the *pacta tertiis* rule. There is little doubt as to the customary status of the rule.[174] It is underpinned by the principles of independence and equality of states, and is a consequence of the consensual character of treaty relations.[175] Important as these principles are, particularly in the law of treaties,[176] they are not the only values operating in the international legal system. As Chinkin puts it, there is 'inevitably a friction between the rigid *pacta tertiis* rule and the progressive development of normative standards'.[177]

It is here where the analogy drawn in Chapter 2 to inducing breach of contract in domestic legal systems is helpful. First, the *pacta tertiis* rule is itself a principle drawn from the Roman law of obligations.[178] Manifest in modern rules of privity of contract, the principle has been said to protect the 'very freedom of individual action which the common law exists largely to secure',[179] a municipal echo of the values underpinning the rule in international law, though of course concerning a different legal subject. Second, the brief digression into the inducement tort in Chapter 2 illustrated that the desirability of a complicity rule cannot be settled by appeal to a fundamental principle in one area of law—in municipal law, privity in the law of contract; in international law, the *pacta tertiis* rule in the law of treaties. What matters are principled and policy reasons shaped by the conflicting needs and purposes of the legal system itself.[180]

[173] See ARSIWA General Commentary on Chapter IV [7].

[174] Eric David, 'Article 34—General Rule Regarding Third States' in Olivier Corten and Pierre Klein (eds.) *The Vienna Convention on the Law of Treaties: A Commentary—Volume I* (OUP 2011) 887, 888–9.

[175] Ibid 888; Chinkin, *Third Parties in International Law* 26.

[176] Lowe, 'Responsibility for the Conduct of Other States' 7.

[177] Chinkin, *Third Parties in International Law* 5.

[178] Ibid 26.

[179] Sayre, 'Inducing Breach of Contract' 687.

[180] See section 2.3.2 above. See also Aust, *Complicity and the Law of State Responsibility* 252.

In this respect, the double obligation requirement is an undue limitation on the operation of a prohibition on complicity in international law. This weakness in Article 16 may be approached from two directions. First, by allowing third state complicity in these instances, Article 16 fails to give due weight to the relationship between the principal state and the victim state. Here, again, the analogy to inducing breach of contract is helpful. Simester and Chan suggest that promises change the relationship between the two parties to the promise.[181] Drawing on Raz, they argue that in addition to the performance right arising thereunder, the promise creates for the promisee a 'right to preemptive status in the promisor's reasoning'.[182] By inducing P to breach her promise to V, the inducer undermines something of intrinsic value—the relationship between the two parties to the promise.[183]

This argument builds on the moral presuppositions of Raz's idea of promises, namely 'the desirability of special bonds between people and the desirability of special relations that are voluntarily shaped and developed by the choice of participants'.[184] In place of people, we might substitute the state. When states voluntarily undertake obligations to each other, it creates a special relationship *inter se*. Between the parties, that relationship is sustained by the foundational principle of *pacta sunt servanda*.[185] Although the obligations voluntarily undertaken by the principal parties do not bind a third party, the value of that relationship itself is worthy of protection. That protection may be provided by a complicity rule.

The second direction from which to approach the flaw engendered by the double obligation requirement starts from the needs of the legal system as a whole rather than the specific value of the relationship between the principal parties. Lanovoy argues that:

> [T]he opposability of the obligation on the aiding or assisting State and on the aided or assisted State perpetuates a particular vision of reciprocal normativity without asking whether it is still suitable in the modern state of international law.[186]

On this basis, a rule that recognizes the broader community interest in compliance with international law would be desirable. Just as the municipal tort of inducing breach of contract is seen as an assertion of 'society's interest

[181] Simester and Chan, 'Inducing Breach of Contract' 151.

[182] Ibid. See Joseph Raz, 'Promises and Obligations' in PMS Hacker and Joseph Raz, *Law, Morality, and Society—Essays in Honour of H.L.A. Hart* (Clarendon 1977) 210.

[183] Simester and Chan, 'Inducing Breach of Contract' 151–2.

[184] Joseph Raz, 'Promises in Morality and Law' (1981–1982) 95 Harv L Rev 916, 928.

[185] See Art 26 VCLT; Jean Salmon, 'Article 26: *Pacta Sunt Servanda*' in Corten and Klein, *The VCLT: A Commentary—Volume I* 659.

[186] Lanovoy, 'Revisiting a Structural Norm' 31.

in commercial stability and contractual integrity',[187] so a broader complicity rule would protect the international community's interests in the stability of international relations and the integrity of treaty commitments. It would protect the validity of international legal obligations.[188] In this respect, international law would 'endeavour for its own legality'.[189]

To bind together those two objections to the double obligation requirement, a practical example from outside of the treaty context may be helpful. Lowe considers the position of a persistent objector to extended security zones in the law of the sea.[190] State A—the persistent objector—assists State P to wrongfully engage in military activities within the extended security zone of State V. The action is wrongful because State P has acquiesced in such claims, rendering it bound vis-à-vis State V.[191] The double obligation requirement in Article 16 would exclude State A's responsibility on the basis of its persistent objector status.

Lowe rightly asks why this should be the rule.[192] State A, the persistent objector, assisted the principal state's violation of its obligations. Assuming State A acted with knowledge and made a substantial contribution to the wrong, it should be responsible. It should not be responsible for the wrong committed by P, but rather for its own acts of assistance. The demand for responsibility in this instance is supplied by the logic of complicity: both the wrongs we do, and the wrongs we help or encourage others to do, matter.[193]

7.3.7. Evaluating the Structure of the Rule in Article 16

Chapter 2 of this work argued that complicity is a particular way of contributing to wrongdoing. Whether the subject is an individual or a state, there are principled reasons for holding accomplices responsible for their own contribution to the principal's wrong. The wrong of the principal should not be imputed or attributed to the accomplice.

This is how the rule in Article 16 is structured. Although at some point complicity crosses over into joint commission,[194] the position under Article 16 is made clear in the commentary:

> In accordance with article 16, the assisting State is responsible for its own act in deliberately assisting another State to breach an international obligation by which they are both bound. It is not responsible, as such, for the act of the assisted State.[195]

187 Danforth, 'Tortious Interference with Contract' 1491.

188 Lanovoy, 'Revisiting a Structural Norm' 34. 189 Ibid 32.

190 Lowe, 'Responsibility for the Conduct of Other States' 7–8. 191 Ibid.

192 Ibid. 193 Ibid 13; Gardner, 'Complicity and Causality' 132.

194 See Crawford, *State Responsibility: The General Part* 325–61; Lowe, 'Responsibility for the Conduct of Other States' 4.

195 ARSIWA Commentary on Art 16 [10].

In the attribution of responsibility, Article 16 is a non-imputational complicity rule.

The consequences of that responsibility as a matter of international law raise difficult questions.[196] Duties of cessation and non-repetition would apply.[197] There are few difficulties here.[198] Reparation must be paid.[199] Calculating the form and scale of reparation is complex.[200] Here, analogies to domestic prohibitions of wrongful participation are not particularly helpful.

The challenge is to locate the rule in Article 16 within the ordinary principles of reparation set out in Articles 31 and 35–37 ARSIWA.[201] Article 31 reads as follows:

1. The responsible State is under an obligation to make full reparation for the injury caused by the internationally wrongful act.
2. Injury includes any damage, whether material or moral, caused by the internationally wrongful act of a State.

The causal language in Article 31 is immediately evident. As argued in Chapter 2, complicity is best understood as a form of indirect causal contribution to wrongdoing.[202] The principal causes the injury; the accomplice makes a causal contribution to the principal's causing the injury.[203] Accomplices make 'a difference to the difference that principals make'.[204]

On this basis, when State A provides State B with weapons with a view to facilitating State B's bombing of a factory in State C, State A makes a causal contribution to State's B's causing of the injury. How, then, might the complicit state's share of responsibility be determined, a question most pertinent to claims of compensation?[205] Aust's suggestion that no abstract formula will work seems to be correct.[206] In providing guidance, the ILC introduces some confusion:

[W]here the assistance is a necessary element in the wrongful act in absence of which it could not have occurred, the injury suffered can be concurrently attributed

[196] See generally Pierre d'Argent, 'Reparation, Cessation, Assurances and Guarantees of Non-Repetition' SHARES Research Paper 34 (2014); For a discussion of the possibility of the injured state taking countermeasures against the assisting state, see Christian Tams, 'Countermeasures against Multiple Responsible Actors' SHARES Research Paper 35 (2014).

[197] Art 30 ARSIWA

[198] Aust, *Complicity and the Law of State Responsibility* 274.

[199] Art 31 ARSIWA.

[200] Aust, *Complicity and the Law of State Responsibility* 274–6.

[201] See ibid 274.

[202] See section 2.5.3 above.

[203] Gardner, 'Moore on Complicity and Causality' 437–8.

[204] Gardner, 'Complicity and Causality' 128.

[205] Art 36 ARSIWA. See Aust, *Complicity and the Law of State Responsibility* 278.

[206] Aust, *Complicity and the Law of State Responsibility* 276.

to the assisting and the acting State. In other cases, however, the difference may be very material: the assistance may have been only an incidental factor in the commission of the primary act, and may have contributed only to a minor degree, if at all, to the injury suffered. By assisting another State to commit an internationally wrongful act, a State should not necessarily be held to indemnify the victim for all the consequences of the act, but only for those which . . . flow from its own conduct.[207]

There are two problems here. To understand them, it is necessary to return to the normative framework set up in Chapter 2. There, it was argued that it is helpful to distinguish three kinds of differentiation regarding participation in wrongdoing:

A. doctrinal differentiation;
B. differentiation in the attribution of responsibility; and
C. differentiation in the consequences of responsibility.

Doctrinal differentiation distinguishes among participants in wrongdoing at the level of legal doctrine. In respect of complicity, the law recognizes the category of accomplice and prescribes certain doctrinal requirements of conduct and fault. This is clearly the case with Article 16.

Differentiation in the attribution of responsibility distinguishes among participants in wrongdoing at the stage of conviction or responsibility. In a differentiated system the accomplice is held responsible for its own contribution to the principal's wrong, rather than for the wrong of the principal. The commentary on Article 16 makes clear that the assisting state is responsible for its own act and not for the act of the principal acting state.[208]

Differentiation in the consequences of responsibility distinguishes between accomplices and principals in the imposition of sanction or remedy for wrongful conduct. It might be thought that differentiation of this kind flows from differentiation in the attribution of responsibility. This is not always the case. It is entirely conceivable, though not defensible, that accomplices are held responsible *as accomplices*, but are then sanctioned or punished as though they committed the wrong.

Here, then, is the first problem in the passage. The commentary on Article 16 emphasizes that the assisting state is responsible for its own act. However, it provides that where that assistance is an essential part of the acting state's wrong, the injury may be concurrently attributed to the assisting and acting

207 ARSIWA Commentary on Art 16 [10] (footnote omitted). 208 Ibid.

states.[209] Concurrent attribution of this kind comes perilously close to undermining Article 16's organizing principle of differentiation in the attribution of responsibility. Of course, if states act jointly, they may be held responsible in accordance with Article 47 ARSIWA.[210] But 'responsibility for aiding and assisting wrongdoing is not at all the same as joint responsibility'.[211] The distinction between principalship and accomplice liability is essential to a proper accounting for wrongdoing.[212]

The second problem in the passage lies in what the ILC does not say. Beyond suggesting that the assisting state will not ordinarily be responsible for all the consequences of the acting state's wrongful act, it does not provide any guidelines for determining the consequences of the complicit state's responsibility. To emphasize, it is crucial that the complicit state is held responsible for its own wrongdoing—that is, its contribution to the injury caused by the acting state. What that quantum looks like will be left to the practice of states and decisions of international institutions.[213] In terms of compensation, a guiding principle of relative culpability may be useful. The scale of the assistance within the context of the wrongful act and the assisting state's foresight of the damage incurred will be central.[214]

This approach presupposes a rejection of joint and several liability as a general principle in cases of complicity. The normative claim of this work argues for differentiation at each of the three levels set out above. In contrast, joint and several liability abolishes differentiation in the consequences of responsibility. There are principled reasons, underpinned by the idea of sovereignty, for holding states responsible for, and sanctioning them in terms of, their own wrongdoing.[215] It is doubtful that any policy grounds for joint and several liability in respect of the implementation of international responsibility outweigh these principled reasons.[216] Moreover, it is not the case that the principle of relative culpability always means that the complicit state will be responsible to a lesser degree than the principal state. There may be situations in which the assisting state is more culpable than the acting state. The essential logic of Article 16—and non-imputational complicity rules

[209] ARSIWA Commentary on Art 16 [10].

[210] Art 47 ARSIWA; Lowe, 'Responsibility for the Conduct of Other States' 10–11.

[211] Lowe, 'Responsibility for the Conduct of Other States' 11.

[212] Gardner, 'Complicity and Causality' 132.

[213] Lowe, 'Responsibility for the Conduct of Other States' 12; Aust, *Complicity and the Law of State Responsibility* 295.

[214] See Lowe, 'Responsibility for the Conduct of Other States' 12.

[215] See Nollkaemper and Jacobs, 'Shared Responsibility in International Law' 386; section 2.4.1 above.

[216] Aust, *Complicity and the Law of State Responsibility* 296.

more generally—allows for a differentiated assessment of responsibility. As Quigley puts it: 'The path to assessing higher or lower damages against a complicit State is left open by the concept that the act of a complicit State is a wrong separate from that of the principal State.'[217]

7.3.8. Complicity and the Monetary Gold Principle

States attempting to invoke the responsibility of a complicit state under Article 16 before an international tribunal may face a procedural problem. The *Monetary Gold* principle acts as a bar to jurisdiction where, in order to resolve the matter before it, the court must determine the lawfulness of the conduct of a third state without its consent.[218] The wrongfulness of the principal state's conduct is an essential part of Article 16. On this basis, the prospect for enforcing Article 16 before an international tribunal is diminished.[219]

Space precludes a detailed assessment of different interpretations of the *Monetary Gold* principle and its relationship with Article 16.[220] It should be reiterated that the principle only operates as a bar to admissibility before international tribunals.[221] The responsibility of states for complicity persists and may be invoked in the absence of enforcement before an international tribunal.[222] This is not to downplay the detrimental effect of the absence of enforcement on the international legal system generally, or the damage it may do to the promise of Article 16.[223] However, as Lowe puts it:

> The bonds that tie us most effectively are those of which we are least aware, those with which we comply out of sheer habit. If I am right in believing that Article 16

[217] Quigley, 'Complicity in International Law' 129. See also *Taylor* (Appeals Chamber Decision) [666].

[218] *Monetary Gold* 32. See also *East Timor (Portugal* v. *Australia)* [1995] ICJ Rep 90.

[219] ARSIWA Commentary on Art 16 [11].

[220] See generally Aust, *Complicity and the Law of State Responsibility* 296–318; André Nollkaemper, Martins Paparinskis, Freya Baetens, Lorand Bartels, Ilias Plakokefalos, 'Themed Section: Procedural Aspects of Shared Responsibility in International Adjudication' (2013) 4 J Intl Dispute Settlement 277–405.

[221] ARSIWA Commentary on Art 16[11]. For a discussion of the potential impact of *Monetary Gold* on the possibility of the injured state taking countermeasures against the assisting state, see Tams, 'Countermeasures against Multiple Responsible Actors' 19–20.

[222] Ibid; Aust, *Complicity and the Law of State Responsibility* 317–18. See also Crawford, 'Second Report on State Responsibility' [174]:

> Diplomatic protests have been made in cases of wrongful assistance given to another State, and this is proper, since States are entitled to assert complicity in the wrongful conduct of another State even though courts may be incompetent to rule on the charge in the absence of that other State.

[223] See Aust, *Complicity and the Law of State Responsibility* 311.

> ascribes responsibility to States, in some circumstances at least, for unlawful acts that are facilitated by the provision of foreign aid... it is likely that before very long it will become a matter of routine in donor States to review the legality of conduct of the recipient State that is materially facilitated by that aid. Such a bureaucratisation of the monitoring of compliance with international law, partial as it might be, would make a significant contribution to the entrenchment of the rule of law in the international community.[224]

The bureaucratization of the monitoring of compliance with international law is minimally affected by the *Monetary Gold* principle as a procedural bar to the question of jurisdiction much further down the line. As Article 16 becomes part of the day-to-day processes and practices of international law, it has the potential to radically change the ways in which states interact.

7.3.9. Article 16, the Prohibition on Complicity in Aggression, and Peremptory Norms of International Law

The first part of this chapter assessed the rule of international law prohibiting state complicity in aggression. The current part did the same for the rule reflected in Article 16. As this analysis makes clear, the relationship between the two is not one between a primary rule and a secondary rule, but one between a specific primary rule and a general primary rule.[225] The prohibition on complicity in aggression forbids a specific form of state complicity in a specific international wrong. The rule reflected in Article 16 prohibits broader forms of complicity in any international wrong of another state, so long as the obligation at stake is opposable against the complicit state.

The relationship between the two is similar to the relationship between other primary rules of international law. The prohibition on complicity in aggression, alongside any other specific primary complicity obligations binding states,[226] subsists as an independent obligation regulating state conduct. Different elements of these rules may evolve,[227] and Article 16 may be used as a reference point for other complicity rules.[228] New rules might arise, imposing stricter standards on states in respect of matters of particularly grave concern.[229] Together, these rules are a crucial part of, in Aust's phrase, a 'network of rules' relating to states' obligations arising in respect of conduct of other actors.[230]

[224] Lowe, 'Responsibility for the Conduct of Other States' 14.
[225] See also Aust, *Complicity and the Law of State Responsibility* 188–90.
[226] See ibid 97–191. [227] Nolte and Aust, 'Equivocal Helpers' 16–17.
[228] See *Bosnian Genocide* [420]. [229] Nolte and Aust, 'Equivocal Helpers' 17.
[230] Aust, *Complicity and the Law of State Responsibility* 376.

This network of rules is supplemented by additional obligations that states bear in respect of breaches of peremptory norms of international law, as reflected in Chapter III ARSIWA.[231] There is an extensive literature concerning the existence and implications of peremptory norms.[232] A peremptory norm of international law is one 'accepted and recognized by the international community of States as a whole as a norm from which no derogation is permitted and which can be modified only by a subsequent norm of general international law having the same character'.[233] The prohibitions on genocide, aggression, slavery, and torture are commonly understood to be norms of this character.[234]

Article 41 ARSIWA sets out the particular consequences of serious breaches of peremptory norms. These consequences, almost entirely,[235] entail obligations on non-responsible states.[236] In the first place, all states are under an obligation to cooperate in bringing to an end the serious breach.[237] Second, Article 41(2) prescribes that:

> No State shall recognize as lawful a situation created by a serious breach within the meaning of article 40, nor render aid or assistance in maintaining that situation.[238]

The second clause of Article 41(2) supplements the prohibition on aid and assistance in Article 16, dealing 'with conduct "after the fact" which assists the responsible state in maintaining' the situation created by the breach.[239]

[231] Chapter III ARSIWA.

[232] See Christian Tomuschat and Jean-Marc Thouvenin, *The Fundamental Rules of the International Legal Order: Jus Cogens and Obligations Erga Omnes* (Martinus Nijhoff 2006); Alexander Orakhelashvili, *Peremptory Norms in International Law* (OUP 2006); Ulf Linderfalk, 'The Effect of *Jus Cogens* Norms: Whoever Opened Pandora's Box, Did You Ever Think About the Consequences?' (2007) 18 Eur J Intl L 853.

[233] Art 53 VCLT.

[234] See Eric Suy, 'Article 53—Treaties Conflicting with a Peremptory Norm of General International Law ('*jus cogens*')' in Olivier Corten and Pierre Klein (eds.) *The Vienna Convention on the Law of Treaties: A Commentary—Volume II* (OUP 2011) 1224; ARSIWA Commentary on Art 40 [4], [5]; Lowe, *International Law* 58–60.

[235] The obligation of non-recognition applies to *all* states, including the responsible state. See ARSIWA Commentary on Art 41 [9]:

> Under article 41, paragraph 2, no State shall recognize the situation created by the serious breach as lawful. This obligation applies to all States, including the responsible State. There have been cases where the responsible State has sought to consolidate the situation it has created by its own 'recognition'. Evidently, the responsible State is under an obligation not to recognize or sustain the unlawful situation arising from the breach.

[236] See Christian Tams, 'Do Serious Breaches Give Rise to Any Specific Obligations of the Responsible State?' (2002) 13 Eur J Intl L 1161.

[237] Art 41(1) ARSIWA.

[238] Art 41(2) ARSIWA.

[239] ARSIWA Commentary on Art 41[11].

In contrast to conventional rules of complicity that respond to participation in a particular wrongful act, Article 41(2) defines the principal wrong more broadly as the situation created by the serious breach.

There are interesting questions about the scope of Article 41(2) and its relationship with Article 16.[240] For present purposes, it is sufficient to note that the rules, together with the specific primary rule prohibiting complicity in aggression by the provision of territory, are mutually reinforcing.[241] A state that allows its territory to be used for an act of aggression is itself responsible for an act of aggression. As argued above, this rule is not conditioned by a substantiality requirement in the nexus between the complicit act and the principal wrong—any grant of territory, no matter where the territorial state lies in relation to the victim state, should be sufficient for responsibility.[242] The general rule, Article 16, prohibits a much broader range of complicit conduct but is subject to a nexus requirement of substantial contribution.[243] It will ordinarily be the case that territorial complicity of the kind prohibited by the specific rule will also give rise to responsibility under Article 16, though it is possible to envisage immaterial or insignificant complicity of this kind that does not engage Article 16. As the principal act will also constitute a violation of the peremptory rule prohibiting aggression, all states owe obligations of non-assistance in maintaining the situation.[244]

7.4. Conclusion

States invade other states. They commit human rights abuses, violate arms treaties, and breach environmental obligations. Other states help. Understood solely as a system of bilateral relationships, international law would not respond adequately to complicity as a particular way of contributing to wrongdoing—it would ask states to pay attention only to the wrongs they commit and not to the wrongs they help other states to commit.[245]

The international legal system is no longer marked by the absence of state complicity rules. The developments analysed in this chapter reflect a move from the specific to the general—from a prohibition on a specific form of

[240] See Aust, *Complicity and the Law of State Responsibility* 338–52.

[241] Nolte and Aust, 'Equivocal Helpers' 16; Nina Jørgensen, 'The Obligation of Non-Assistance to the Responsible State' in Crawford et al. (eds.) *The Law of International Responsibility* 687, 692.

[242] See section 7.2.2 above.

[243] ARSIWA Commentary on Art 16 [5].

[244] Art 41(2) ARSIWA. See Nolte and Aust, 'Equivocal Helpers' 16–17.

[245] Lowe, 'Responsibility for the Conduct of Other States' 13; Gardner, 'Complicity and Causality' 132.

complicity in a specific international wrong to a prohibition on aid or assistance in the commission of any international wrong by the recipient state. It is not the end of the road—in particular, influence as a form of complicity, responsibility for complicit omissions, and the double obligation requirement demand further attention. Nonetheless, Article 16 is an important step towards a principled approach to state complicity in the wrongs of other states.

8

State Complicity, Non-State Actors, and Attribution

8.1. Introduction

The previous chapter considered how international law prohibits state complicity in the commission of an internationally wrongful act by another state, analysing a specific and general complicity rule. States are not, of course, the only actors on the international plane that cause harm to the interests of other states and/or individuals. Non-state actors launch cross-border attacks, pollute rivers, and commit genocide.[1]

Quite often, non-state actors carrying out these acts do so with the support of a state. That is to say, the state often stands in a complicit relationship with the non-state actor. In some instances, state responsibility will arise on the basis of a discrete due diligence obligation to protect against harms caused by non-state actors. Less often, international law imposes direct obligations of non-participation on states. More generally, though, the historical failure of international law to regulate the conduct of non-state actors directly limited the possibility of state responsibility for complicity in these situations. There is simply no international wrong for the state to be complicit in. This follows from the historical normative structure of the international legal system.[2]

The next chapter (Chapter 9) shows how the increased regulation by international law of the conduct of non-state actors has opened up the possibility of states bearing complicity obligations in respect of that conduct. The current chapter addresses an entirely different way that international law addresses state support for the conduct of non-state actors. Here, the putative claim is that a *complicit relationship* between the state and non-state actor is sufficient to attribute the latter's conduct to the state. As will be seen, attribution in international law ordinarily requires an agency relationship.

[1] See Hakimi, 'State Bystander Responsibility' 341.

[2] De Frouville, 'Attribution of Conduct' 276.

In two contexts—state support for terrorist armed attacks and state support for human rights violations in the Inter-American system—there is a claim that this agency standard has been relaxed to entail a standard based on complicity. This is not quite complicity in the sense defined in Chapter 2. Under such an attributional rule, the state is not held derivatively responsible in relation to another actor's wrongdoing; rather, the conduct of that other actor becomes state conduct on the basis of its acts of support or assistance.

This chapter argues that such a claim should be rejected in both cases. In respect of terrorist armed attacks, it will be seen that there is a better interpretation of the international legal materials, one that does not lower the standard for attribution. In respect of human rights violations in the Inter-American system, it will be argued that there are good reasons for maintaining the general standard based on agency in the rules of attribution. Complicity cannot be properly accounted for by relaxing the rules of attribution in international law.

8.2. Attribution in International Law—Baselines

It is foundational in international law that state responsibility requires the attribution of conduct to the state.[3] The search for attribution is the search for a relationship or connection between the state, as a legal person, and the person or group carrying out the conduct.[4] For, as the PCIJ observed in the *German Settlers in Poland Advisory Opinion*: 'States can act only by and through their agents and representatives.'[5]

As a basic rule, states are responsible for the conduct of their own organs.[6] The corollary of this rule is the non-attribution of conduct of non-state actors to the state.[7] As the ILC explains, non-attribution in this instance both limits the responsibility of the state and recognizes the autonomy of non-state persons acting on their own account.[8] De Frouville argues that non-attribution 'ensues above all from a theoretical requirement: attribution can only occur in relation to an autonomous person and autonomy requires that only acts resulting from an exercise of free will can be attributed to it'.[9] Nonetheless, international law does attribute, in limited circumstances, the

[3] Art 2 ARSIWA. [4] ARSIWA Commentary on Art 2 [5].

[5] *Certain Questions Relating to Settlers of German Origin in the Territory Ceded by Germany to Poland* (Advisory Opinion) [1923] PCIJ Series B, No 6 [34].

[6] Art 4 ARSIWA. [7] ARSIWA General Commentary on Chapter II [2], [3].

[8] Ibid. [9] De Frouville, 'Attribution of Conduct' 261.

conduct of non-state actors to the state where there is a sufficient connection between them.

Traditionally, the nature of that connection entails an agency relationship.[10] Attribution, in this sense, may occur under the test of complete dependence or strict control[11]—rendering the non-state actor a de facto state organ[12]—or the subsidiary[13] test of direction or control of specific conduct.[14] Both of these tests constitute rules of customary international law[15] and denote the search for a relationship of principal to agent.[16]

A complicit relationship is thus, on a traditional understanding of the rules of attribution, insufficient to render the conduct of the assisted party conduct of the state. This point was made by Brownlie, acting for the government of Serbia and Montenegro, in the proceedings of the ICJ in the *Bosnian Genocide* case:

> Professor Pellet refers to the assistance and support given to Republika Srpska but not to the issue of control. This is precisely the distinction which the Court made in the *Nicaragua* case. The financing, organizing, training, supplying and equipping of the *contras* did not constitute control.[17]

The court affirmed the need for control, thus rejecting the idea that a complicit relationship may be sufficient to attribute the conduct of non-state groups to the state.[18] Moreover, the court held that, in general, the rules for attributing conduct to a state do not vary according to the nature of the wrongful act.[19] As a default position, the tests for attribution remain the same whether the non-state group is committing genocide, violations of the laws of war, or environmental harms.[20] However, the court left open the possibility that clearly expressed *lex specialis* could impose a different standard, potentially of a less demanding nature than that reflected in ARSIWA, under which conduct of a non-state actor may be attributed to the state.[21]

[10] See Becker, *Terrorism and the State* 43–79; Chinkin, *Third Parties in International Law* 142.

[11] *Military and Paramilitary Activities in and against Nicaragua (Nicaragua* v. *United States)* (Merits) [1986] ICJ Rep 14 [109]; *Bosnian Genocide* [392]. See also Stefan Talmon, 'The Responsibility of Outside Powers for Acts of Secessionist Entities' (2009) *58* ICLQ 493, 499.

[12] Art 4 ARSIWA.

[13] Talmon, 'Responsibility of Outside Powers' 502.

[14] Art 8 ARSIWA; *Nicaragua* [115]; *Bosnian Genocide* [397]

[15] *Bosnian Genocide* [385] with respect to Art 4 and [398] with respect to Art 8. See also *Armed Activities* [160].

[16] Becker, *Terrorism and the State* 43–79; Chinkin, *Third Parties in International Law* 142.

[17] *Bosnian Genocide* (Verbatim Record) CR 2006/16 (Ian Brownlie) [116].

[18] *Bosnian Genocide* [396]–[407]. It should be noted that at the top end of the spectrum, complicity merges into agency. See, for instance, the reference to instigation in paragraph [2] of the commentary to Art 8 ARSIWA.

[19] Ibid [401].

[20] Ibid.

[21] Ibid. See also Art 55 ARSIWA.

This chapter considers two putative rules that are said to impose a different standard: state complicity in terrorist armed attacks and state complicity in human rights violations in the Inter-American system.

8.3. State Participation in Terrorist Attacks and the Rules of Attribution

8.3.1. Introduction

As noted above, traditionally the attribution of conduct to a state has been defined by the search for a relationship of principal to agent—notions of dependence, instruction, direction, and control are determinative.[22] A complicit relationship, in its myriad forms, is ordinarily insufficient to attribute the conduct of the non-state actor to the state.[23] However, an idea persists that the rules of attribution differ in respect of terrorist attacks. This claim is bound up with the requirement of armed attack in the law of self-defence. If an armed attack must be attributable to a state in order to trigger the right of self-defence, then the basis on which the hostile actions of terrorist groups are attributable to the complicit state becomes a central question in the law of self-defence. If an armed attack need not be attributable to the state in order to trigger the right of self-defence, then the international practice set out below puts less pressure on the rules of attribution. The need to show that the state was complicit in the terrorist attack emanating from its territory is diminished.[24]

8.3.2. The Approach of the ICJ

The ICJ has adopted an inter-state reading of the law of self-defence. This requires that the conduct of the non-state actor be attributable to the state to trigger the right to self-defence.

In *Nicaragua*, the ICJ used Article 3(g) of the Definition of Aggression as a yardstick for interpreting the meaning of the term 'armed attack'.[25] In applying Article 3(g), it minimized the application of the final clause of the provision: 'The sending by or on behalf of a State of armed bands, groups,

[22] Arts 4, 8 ARSIWA.

[23] See section 8.2 above. See also *Bosnian Genocide* (Verbatim Record) CR 2006/16 (Ian Brownlie) [116].

[24] There remains a residual role for ideas of complicity—see section 8.3.6 below.

[25] *Nicaragua* [195].

irregulars or mercenaries, which carry out acts of armed force against another State of such gravity as to amount to the acts listed above, *or its substantial involvement therein*.'[26] Nonetheless, it implicitly left open the possibility that substantial state involvement in the conduct of the armed bands could both breach the prohibition of aggression *and* constitute an armed attack for the purposes of self-defence.[27] However, in the *Wall Advisory Opinion*, after setting out Article 51 of the UN Charter the ICJ stated:

> Article 51 of the Charter thus recognizes the existence of an inherent right of self-defence in the case of armed attack by one State against another State. However, Israel does not claim that the attacks against it are imputable to a foreign State.
>
> ...
>
> Consequently, the Court concludes that Article 51 of the Charter has no relevance in this case.[28]

This is a clear statement of the inter-state reading of the law of self-defence.[29] This interpretation was not unanimous. Judges Higgins, Kooijmans, and Buergenthal point out that there is nothing in the text of Article 51 that demands that the armed attack be attributable to a state.[30] Kooijmans and Buergenthal, in particular, place some weight on the fact that Security Council Resolutions 1368 and 1373 refer to the right of self-defence without referring to an armed attack by a state.[31] Higgins, in line with her long-standing academic criticism of this interpretation, simply believes the inter-state reading to be incorrect.[32]

In the *Armed Activities* case, the ICJ added a degree of confusion to its prior interpretations. On the one hand, the court stated that it had no need to address whether international law allows for a right of self-defence in response to large-scale attacks by irregular forces.[33] On the other hand, it specifically found that the legal and factual circumstances for the exercise of self-defence by Uganda were not made out *because* the

[26] Art 3(g) Definition of Aggression (emphasis added).

[27] See Tom Ruys, *'Armed Attack' and Article 51 of the UN Charter: Evolutions in Customary Law and Practice* (CUP 2010) 415–19.

[28] *Legal Consequences of the Construction of a Wall in the Occupied Palestinian Territory* (Advisory Opinion) [2004] ICJ Rep 136 [139].

[29] See also *Armed Activities* [146]. In quoting Art 3(g) of the Definition of Aggression, the court omits the 'substantial involvement' clause of the provision.

[30] *Wall Advisory Opinion* (Separate Opinion of Judge Higgins) [33]; (Separate Opinion of Judge Kooijmans) [35]; (Declaration of Judge Buergenthal) [6].

[31] Separate Opinion of Judge Kooijmans [35]; Declaration of Judge Buergenthal [6].

[32] Separate Opinion of Judge Higgins [33]; Rosalyn Higgins, *Problems and Process: International Law and How We Use It* (Clarendon 1994) 250–1.

[33] *Armed Activities* [147].

attacks against it by armed bands are not attributable to the Democratic Republic of the Congo.[34] However, if the attacks were attributable to the DRC, then it would be an ordinary application of the right of self-defence against armed attacks by states. Given that the attacks were not attributable, the consequent question is whether international law permits the exercise of self-defence in any event. The court implicitly answers this in the negative.[35]

There is an argument that the court's restrictive interpretation has been overtaken by the practice of states. This point is well put by Judge Simma in his Separate Opinion in the *Armed Activities* case.[36] Indeed, over the last 30 years, states have asserted the right to use force against terrorist targets in other states in situations where the conduct of those non-state actors would not be attributable to the state under the ordinary rules of attribution in the law of state responsibility.[37] There are two ways to interpret this emergent norm, the first of which is particularly relevant to the operation of ideas of complicity in international law:

1. a new rule of attribution is operating in the context of state responsibility for the attacks of terrorist groups. This rule of attribution is based on a complicit relationship, rather than one of agency or control, such that an armed attack by a non-state group executed with the support of the state becomes conduct of the state. This preserves the inter-state reading of the law of self-defence; or
2. the inter-state reading of Article 51 and its customary analogue no longer represents international law.

8.3.3. State Practice in the 1980s and 1990s

Although both interpretations find some support, a review of state practice from the last 30 years indicates that the better interpretation is the latter: the inter-state reading of Article 51 and its customary analogue no longer represents customary international law. In assessing the practice, it makes sense to start with the Schultz Doctrine, developed and propounded by the United States under President Reagan.[38] A central element of the US's approach to

[34] Ibid [146]–[147].

[35] Jörg Kammerhofer, 'The Armed Activities Case and Non-State Actors in Self-Defence Law' (2007) 20 Leiden J Intl L 89, 96.

[36] *Armed Activities* (Separate Opinion of Judge Simma) [11]. See also Separate Opinion of Judge Kooijmans [16]–[35].

[37] See generally Ruys, *Armed Attack' and Article 51* 419–510.

[38] See Ruys, *Armed Attack and Article 51* 421–8.

terrorism was the claim that force could be used 'against states that support, train, and harbor terrorists or guerillas'.[39] Following the terrorist attacks on Rome and Vienna Airports in 1985, President Reagan made the following statement:

> By providing material support to terrorist groups which attack U.S. citizens, Libya has engaged in armed aggression against the United States under established principles of international law, just as if [it] had used its own armed forces.[40]

The clearest manifestation of the Schultz Doctrine in practice is perhaps the attacks by the United States on Sudan and Afghanistan following the 1998 embassy bombings in Kenya and Tanzania.[41] There was no assertion that the bombings were carried out by state actors; rather, it was asserted that Afghanistan and Sudan had harboured and supported terrorists.[42] Nonetheless, in its letter informing the Security Council of its actions, the US specifically invoked Article 51 of the UN Charter and referred to the bombings as 'armed attacks against United States embassies and United States nationals'.[43] The response of other states was mixed.[44]

Scholars have detailed other incidents of state practice throughout the 1990s.[45] For instance, in 1992 and 1995, Senegal attacked suspected rebel

[39] US Secretary of State George Schultz, 'Low-Intensity Warfare: the Challenge of Ambiguity' (15 January 1986) reprinted in (1986) 25 ILM 204, 206. See also Ruys, *Armed Attack and Article 51* 422–3.

[40] President Ronald Reagan, 'The President's News Conference' (7 January 1986) Public Papers of Ronald Reagan. See also Schultz, 'Low-Intensity Warfare' 206:

> There is substantial legal authority for the view that a state which supports terrorist or subversive attacks against another state, or which supports or encourages terrorist planning and other activities within its own territory, is responsible for such attacks. Such conduct can amount to an ongoing armed aggression against another state under international law.

[41] Ruys, *Armed Attack and Article 51* 426.

[42] President Bill Clinton, 'Address to the Nation on Military Action against Terrorist Sites in Afghanistan and Sudan' (20 August 1998) Public Papers of Bill Clinton. See also Sean Murphy, 'Contemporary Practice of the United States Relating to International Law—1998' (1999) 93 Am J Intl L 161, 162; Ruth Wedgwood, 'Responding to Terrorism: The Strikes Against Bin Laden' (1999) 24 Yale J Intl L 559.

[43] Letter dated 20 August 1998 from the Permanent Representative of the United States of America to the United Nations addressed to the President of the Security Council, UN Doc S/1998/780 (20 August 1998).

[44] Jules Lobel, 'The Use of Force to Respond to Terrorist Attacks: The Bombing of Sudan and Afghanistan' (1999) 24 Yale J Intl L 537, 538; Murphy, 'Contemporary Practice—1998' 164–5; Ruys, *Armed Attack and Article 51* 426–7.

[45] See Ruys, *Armed Attack and Article 51* 428–33; Tom Ruys and Sten Verhoeven, 'Attacks by Private Actors and the Right of Self-Defence' (2005) 10 J Confl & Sec L 289, 294–6; Christine Gray, *International Law and the Use of Force* (3rd edn. OUP 2008) 132–43.

bases in Guinea-Bissau.[46] In 1993, Tajikistan and Russia asserted their right to respond against armed groups operating from Afghanistan, partly on the basis of alleged Afghan participation in the attacks.[47] In 1995, Thailand crossed the Burmese border in response to attacks by non-state groups operating out of Burma.[48] A year later, Sudan alleged that Eritrea had supported, encouraged, hosted, and sponsored rebel groups hostile to it, and described Eritrea's conduct as a series of aggressive acts.[49]

Since the first Gulf War, Turkey has repeatedly targeted Kurdistan Workers Party interests within Iraq without Iraq's consent.[50] In 1995, Turkey defended its use of force on the basis that Iraq had failed to prevent its territory from being used as a staging ground for terrorist attacks, and argued that, consequently, its measures could not be regarded as a violation of Iraq's sovereignty.[51] Cross-border operations of this kind followed throughout the late 1990s to a mixed response from states and international institutions.[52]

Even before the attacks of September 11, 2001, and the response of the international community thereto, the practice surveyed above may illustrate a 'norm-shaping dynamic going on behind the sound and fury of... Charter-invoking claims and counterclaims'.[53] Nonetheless, a new norm had not fully emerged—states did express condemnation of many of these

[46] See Gray, *International Law and the Use of Force* 140.

[47] Letter dated 15 July 1993 from the Permanent Representative of Tajikistan to the United Nations addressed to the Secretary General, UN Doc S/26092 (16 July 1993); Letter dated 15 July 1993 from the Permanent Representative of the Russian Federation addressed to the Secretary General, UN Doc S/26110 (19 July 1993). See Gray, *International Law and the Use of Force* 140; Ruys, *Armed Attack and Article 51* 428.

[48] Keesing's (1995) 40554; Gray, *International Law and the Use of Force* 140.

[49] Letter dated 13 May 1996 from the Chargé d'Affaires AI of the Permanent Mission of the Sudan to the United Nations addressed to the President of the Security Council, UN Doc S/1996/358 (21 May 1996). See also Ruys, *Armed Attack and Article 51* 428–9; Letter dated 4 December 1996 from the Permanent Representative of the Sudan to the United Nations addressed to the President of the Security Council, UN Doc S/1996/1007 (5 December 1996): 'The flagrant support of the Eritrean regime to Sudanese terrorist groups, in particular the so-called Sudanese National Alliance, and the facilities it provides for their terrorist activities inside Eritrea is a violation of the Charter of the United Nations and constitutes a threat to regional and international peace and security.'

[50] See Gray, *International Law and the Use of Force* 140–3; Thomas Franck, *Recourse to Force—State Action against Threats and Armed Attacks* (CUP 2002) 63–4; Ruys, *Armed Attack and Article 51* 429–33.

[51] Letter dated 24 July 1995 from the Chargé d'Affaires AI of the Permanent Mission of Turkey to the United Nations addressed to the President of the Security Council, UN Doc S/1995/605 (24 July 1995).

[52] Gray, *International Law and the Use of Force* 142; Ruys, *Armed Attack and Article 51* 431–3.

[53] Franck, *Recourse to Force* 55.

operations[54] and the prevailing inter-state reading of the law of self-defence probably remained in place.

8.3.4. A New Era of Terrorism

The response of the international community to the attacks of September 11, 2001, is often seen as evidence of the crystallization of the emergent norm discussed above.[55] The attacks were carried out by operatives from Al-Qaeda, acting with the support of the Taliban authorities in Afghanistan.[56] In the immediate aftermath of the attacks, the Security Council affirmed the right of states to exercise self-defence against terrorist attacks.[57] The General Assembly condemned the attacks.[58] NATO and the Organization of American States invoked their collective self-defence provisions.[59] On 7 October 2001, the United States commenced military action against Afghanistan in the exercise of the right to self-defence triggered by the armed attacks against it.[60] A survey of responses from states indicates widespread support for the United States' military action.[61]

This support was given despite the fact that under the ordinary rules of state responsibility it is unlikely that the conduct of Al-Qaeda was attributable to Afghanistan.[62] Interpretations by scholars of the effect of the invasion

[54] See the statements of Iran, Iraq, Libya, Pakistan, Russia, and Yemen with respect to US bombings of targets in Afghanistan and Sudan—Murphy, 'Contemporary Practice—1998' 164–5; Letter dated 6 June 2000 from the Permanent Representative of South Africa to the United Nations (as Chair of the Coordinating Bureau of the Non-Aligned Movement) addressed to the Secretary General, UN Doc A/54/917; S/2000/580 [137] (16 June 2000).

[55] Michael Schmitt, 'Responding to Transnational Terrorism under the *Jus ad Bellum*: A Normative Framework' in Michael Schmitt and Jelena Pejic (eds.) *International Law and Armed Conflict: Exploring the Faultlines—Essays in Honour of Yoram Dinstein* (Martinus Nijhoff 2007) 157, 165.

[56] See Sean Murphy, 'Contemporary Practice of the United States Relating to International Law—2001' (2002) 96 Am J Intl L 237–55.

[57] UNSC Res 1368 (12 September 2001) UN Doc S/Res/1368. See also Gray, *International Law and the Use of Force* 193.

[58] UNGA Res 56/1 (18 September 2001) UN Doc A/Res/56/1.

[59] North Atlantic Treaty Organization, 'Statement by the North Atlantic Council' (12 September 2001) reprinted in (2001) 40 ILM 1267; Organization of American States, 'Resolution on Terrorist Threat to the Americas' (21 September 2001) reprinted in (2001) 40 ILM 1273. See also Gray, *International Law and the Use of Force* 193; Dinstein, *War, Aggression and Self-Defence* 228–9.

[60] Letter dated 7 October 2001 from the Permanent Representative of the United States of America to the United Nations addressed to the President of the Security Council, UN Doc S/2001/946 (7 October 2001). See also Letter dated 7 October 2001 from the Chargé d'Affaires AI of the Permanent Mission of the United Kingdom of Great Britain and Northern Ireland addressed to the President of the Security Council, UN Doc S/2001/947 (7 October 2001).

[61] Murphy, 'Contemporary Practice of the United States—2001' 248–9.

[62] Ruys, *Armed Attack and Article 51* 440; Sean Murphy, 'Terrorism and the Concept of "Armed Attack" in Article 51 of the UN Charter' (2002) 43 Harv J Intl L 41, 46; Dinstein, *War, Aggression and Self-Defence* 228.

of Afghanistan on the law of self-defence have varied. Few discount the impact of the invasion entirely.[63] Dinstein argues that the response of the international community dispelled 'all lingering doubts' that armed attacks may emanate from non-state actors.[64] Gray is more cautious, but nonetheless asserts that under certain conditions a right of self-defence does exist against attacks by non-state actors.[65] Franck's position is that a state may invoke Article 51 to take forcible action against a state harboring or supporting terrorism, but that the 'quasi-jury' of the Security Council, General Assembly, and International Court of Justice must evaluate the basis of the victim state's claim.[66]

More recent practice repeats the pre-September 11 pattern: the response of the international community to various incursions and statements has been mixed. In 2002, Australian Prime Minister John Howard asserted his country's right to use pre-emptive unilateral force against terrorist bases in neighbouring South East Asian countries.[67] This statement was condemned by Malaysia, Thailand, and the Philippines.[68] In 2003, Israel attacked terrorist targets within Syria. Despite the emphasis placed by Israel on Syria's complicity, all members of the Security Council other than Russia, the United Kingdom, and United States condemned the attacks.[69] The response of states to Israel's 2006 invasion of Lebanon was more supportive, at least with respect to the right of self-defence.[70] In 2007 and 2008, Turkey attacked militants, weapons stores, and bases located in northern Iraq affiliated with the PKK in response to cross-borders attacks by the PKK against Turkey. In this case, the international response was essentially one of condonation.[71] Finally, Colombia acted against FARC targets

[63] See Ruys, *Armed Attack and Article 51* 442.

[64] Dinstein, *War, Aggression and Self-Defence* 227. See also Schmitt, 'Responding to Transnational Terrorism' 165; Frederic Kirgis, 'Israel's Intensified Military Campaign against Terrorism' Am Soc Intl L Insight (December 2001); Michael Byers, 'Terrorism, the Use of Force and International Law after 11 September' (2002) 51 ICLQ 401, 408–9.

[65] Gray, *International Law and the Use of Force* 199.

[66] Franck, *Recourse to Force* 67.

[67] Tom Allard, 'Pre-emptive Strikes: PM Weights UN Rules Change' *Sydney Morning Herald* (6 December 2002) <http://www.smh.com.au/articles/2002/12/05/1038950147512.html> accessed 23 December 2014; See also Myint Zan, 'Comment: John Howard's "Pre-emptive Strike Thesis"' (2003) 7 J of South Pac L 4. Of course, Howard's remarks raise the issue of pre-emption too, which under conventional interpretations of international law are unlawful.

[68] See Zan, 'Pre-emptive Strike Thesis' 4.

[69] UN Doc S/PV.4836 (5 October 2003). See also Ruys, *Armed Attack and Article 51* 447–8.

[70] Ruys, *Armed Attacks and Article 51* 449–57; Tams, 'Use of Force against Terrorists' 379.

[71] Tom Ruys, '*Quo Vadit Jus ad Bellum*?: A Legal Analysis of Turkey's Military Operations against the PKK in Northern Iraq' (2008) 9 Melb J Intl L 334, 339–45.

in Ecuador in 2008, prompting condemnation by the OAS and a muted response from other states.[72]

The law of self-defence remains in a state of flux on this question. The invasion of Afghanistan is the high-point in international recognition of the right of self-defence in response to attacks by non-state actors. Subsequent incidents have demonstrated that the international community is still working out the existence and contours of the emergent norm. Interpreting the practice, however, has important implications for the operation of ideas of complicity in international law.

8.3.5. The Basis of the Emergent Norm

If it is the case that states may use force in response to attacks emanating from another state but which are not, on the application of the ordinary rules of state responsibility, attributable to that state, how might this be explained in accordance with existing understandings of the regulation of the use of force? As noted above, there are two possible interpretations. The first posits that a new rule of attribution, defined by complicity rather than agency, has arisen or is in the process of arising. Under this new rule, the armed attack of a private terrorist group is attributed to the participating state—that is, the state providing weapons and financial aid, logistical support, or safe harbour.[73] The second interpretation posits that this practice has brought about a change within the law of self-defence specifically—that there is no requirement that an armed attack be attributable to the state to trigger the right of self-defence.[74] It is not that the conduct of the non-state actor is attributed to the state, but rather that the armed attack need not come from the state to allow the victim state to act in self-defence.

Some evidence may be found to support the attributional interpretation. The Bush Doctrine, in particular, appears to put forward a new attributional rule.[75] In his address to a Joint Session of Congress on 20 September 2001, President Bush stated: 'By aiding and abetting murder, the Taliban regime is

[72] Permanent Council of the Organization of American States, OAS Doc CP/RES.930 (1632/08) (5 March 2008); Tams 'Use of Force against Terrorists' 380. See also Ruys '*Quo Vadit Jus ad Bellum*' 358.

[73] Tams, 'Use of Force against Terrorists' 385; Carsten Stahn, 'Terrorist Acts as "Armed Attack": The Right to Self-Defence, Article 51 (1/2) of the UN Charter, and International Terrorism' (2003) 27 Fletcher For of World Aff 35, 37.

[74] Kimberley Trapp, *State Responsibility for International Terrorism* (OUP 2009) 45–62; Ruys, *Armed Attack and Article 51* 493; Dinstein, *War, Aggression and Self-Defence* 224–30; Thomas Franck 'Terrorism and the Right of Self-Defence' (2001) 98 Am J Intl L 839, 840.

[75] Steven Ratner, 'Jus ad Bellum and Jus in Bello after September 11' (2002) 96 Am J Intl L 905, 908.

committing murder.'[76] This is echoed in the United States' National Security Strategy of September 2002: 'We make no distinction between terrorists and those who knowingly harbor or provide aid to them.'[77] In 2006, following Katyusha rocket attacks by Hezbollah, Israel characterized its actions as a 'direct response to an act of war from Lebanon' and held the government of Lebanon responsible.[78] Although Israel's statements are somewhat ambiguous,[79] they may be read as invoking a new attributional rule.

However, on the whole, most of the evidence points to the interpretation that denies armed attacks must be attributable to the state to trigger the right of self-defence.[80] In the vast majority of cases, the state using force has not considered the host state to be the author of the attack, and, indeed, has limited its response to terrorist targets.[81] In the case of the Turkish strikes in Northern Iraq in 2007 and 2008, for instance, a note to the United Nations Human Rights Council implicitly denies that Turkey viewed Iraq as the author of the terrorist attacks:

> The counter-terrorism operation carried out by the Turkish Armed Forces in northern Iraq was limited in scope, geography and duration. It targeted solely the PKK/KONGRA-GEL terrorist presence in the region... Turkey remains a staunch advocate of the territorial integrity and sovereignty of Iraq.[82]

In addition to accounting more accurately for the practice, there are three other reasons for favouring the non-attributional interpretation of the emergent norm. First, there is value in maintaining the coherence of the framework of secondary attributional rules in international law. Clearly expressed *lex specialis* may, in rare cases, give rise to varying rules of attribution.[83] However, in deciding whether conduct may be attributable to the

[76] President George W Bush, Address to a Joint Session of Congress and the American People (20 September 2001).

[77] National Security Strategy of the United States (September 2002) 5.

[78] UN Doc S/PV.5489, 6.

[79] Compare Tams 'Use of Force against Terrorists' 379 and Raphaël Van Steenberghe, 'Self-Defence in Response to Attacks by Non-state Actors in the Light of Recent State Practice: A Step Forward?' (2010) 23 Leiden J Intl L 183, 194.

[80] Trapp, *State Responsibility for International Terrorism* 59. See also Daniel Bethlehem, 'Self-Defense against an Imminent or Actual Armed Attack by Non-State Actors' (2012) 106 Am J Intl L 770.

[81] Ruys, *Armed Attack and Article 51* 493.

[82] Note Verbale dated 26 March 2008 from the Permanent Mission of Turkey to the United Nations Office at Geneva addressed to the Secretariat of the Human Rights Council, UN Doc A/HRC/7/G/15 (28 March 2008). See also Ruys '*Quo Vadit Jus ad Bellum*' 345. It is doubtful that the last clause quoted above makes any legal sense.

[83] *Bosnian Genocide* [401].

state, it is helpful to apply the same rules across different substantive areas of international law.[84]

Second, in terms of the normative claim of this work, we should be wary of holding actors responsible for conduct that they, or their agents, did not, in fact, commit. When the actor is an individual, this claim is sustained by the principle of culpability.[85] When the actor is a state, the claim is underpinned by the principle of sovereignty.[86] Of course, ideas of commission or perpetration are themselves in need of interpretation, and we may wish to build into them a judgment about responsibility.[87] But there is a significant step in attributing the conduct of a principal actor to an accomplice state on the basis of the state's complicity. Such a step denies the status of complicity as a particular way of contributing to wrongdoing.

Third, to the extent that states should be able to strike terrorist targets in states that are harbouring or supporting terrorist groups engaged in armed attacks, they should also be able to strike such targets where the state is simply unable to carry out its due diligence obligations to prevent its territory from being used for such attacks.[88] This is a matter of the internal logical consistency of the law of self-defence. A weak state may be unable to control the activities of terrorist groups operating on its territory. Such a failure to act probably cannot be seen as complicity and, on the attributional interpretation of the law of self-defence, the failure would not entitle the targeted state to respond. However, from the perspective of the state subject to the terrorist attacks, there is no meaningful difference in the harm it suffers. The second interpretation, which allows states to use force in response to armed attacks not attributable to the host state, at least provides internal coherence to the rule.

8.3.6. The Residual Role of Complicity

If the inter-state reading of armed attack has disappeared, why is it that states invoking the right of self-defence sometimes accuse the host state of some form of complicity in the terrorist attacks?[89] The answer is found in the

[84] See Marko Milanović, 'Self-Defense and Non-State Actors: Indeterminacy and the Jus ad Bellum' (*EJIL:Talk!*, 21 February 2010) <http://www.ejiltalk.org/self-defense-and-non-state-actors-indeterminacy-and-the-jus-ad-bellum/> accessed 23 December 2014.

[85] See section 2.4.1 above.

[86] See Nollkaemper and Jacobs, 'Shared Responsibility in International Law' 386; section 2.4.1 above.

[87] See section 2.4.1 above.

[88] See Trapp, *State Responsibility for International Terrorism* 80–2.

[89] See Trapp, *State Responsibility for International Terrorism* 58–9; Van Steenberghe, 'Self-Defence' 199; Ruys, '*Quo Vadit Jus ad Bellum*' 357.

ordinary *jus ad bellum* principle of necessity, applicable to both the customary and Charter rights of self-defence.[90] Except in cases of state failure, without a nexus to the host state, whether that be the provision of financial support, the supply of weapons, or guarantee of safe harbour, the use of force against that state is unlikely to be necessary.[91] The principle of necessity requires that avenues of cooperation be first pursued; without some responsibility of the host state, the doctrine of necessity thus constrains the targeted state's response.[92] Where a state stands in a complicit relationship to the attack, the requirement of necessity is more easily fulfilled.

8.3.7. Conclusion

States that support or harbour terrorist groups will likely violate the obligation to protect within their territory the rights of other states.[93] Here, their participation is caught within that broader due diligence obligation. They will also likely violate direct obligations prohibiting state support for terrorism. Security Council Resolution 1373, for instance, obligates state to: 'Refrain from providing any form of support, active or passive, to entities or persons involved in terrorist acts...'[94] There are also a number of sectoral treaties on terrorism under which complicity may give rise to direct responsibility.[95]

In addition, in an era of renewed focus on terrorism, we have seen a further claim that the idea of complicity is operating in the rules of attribution in international law. This claim posits that a complicit relationship is sufficient to render the non-state actor's conduct state conduct. This claim is not, however, the best interpretation of the relevant state practice. The better view is that the emergent norm allows states to use force in response to attacks by non-state actors. Complicity plays a residual role in informing the principle of necessity.

[90] *Nicaragua* [176]; *Nuclear Weapons* [41].

[91] Kimberley Trapp, 'The Use of Force against Terrorists: A Reply to Christian J. Tams' (2009) 20 Eur J Intl L 1049, 1053. Cf Kammerhofer, 'The Armed Activities Case' 99.

[92] Trapp, *State Responsibility for International Terrorism* 59. See also *Armed Activities* (Separate Opinions of Judges Simma and Kooijmans). It should be noted that the principle of proportionality also bears on determinations of whether state infrastructure, rather than the non-state groups only, may be targeted. See Kimberley Trapp, 'Back to Basics: Necessity, Proportionality, and the Right of Self-Defence against Non-State Terrorist Actors' (2007) 56 ICLQ 141, 145–55.

[93] *Island of Palmas; Corfu Channel.*

[94] UNSC Res 1373 [2(a)].

[95] See generally Trapp, *State Responsibility for International Terrorism*; Crawford, *State Responsibility: The General Part* 159–60.

8.4. State Participation in Human Rights Violations and the Rules of Attribution

8.4.1. Introduction

As argued above, in the law of state responsibility the attribution of conduct of non-state actors to the state is rooted in agency, not complicity. For attribution on the basis that the non-state actor is a *de facto* organ of state, a standard of complete dependence is required.[96] For attribution of specific conduct of a non-state actor to the state, effective control is required.[97] Under this approach, short of effective control by the state, human rights violations committed by a non-state actor with the assistance of a state official are not attributable to the state itself. However, there is a claim that certain rules of attribution in the context of international human rights law constitute *lex specialis* with respect to the general rules of state responsibility set out above. Just as in respect of terrorist attacks, this approach seeks to attribute the conduct of a non-state actor to the state on the basis of a complicit relationship, rather than any conception of agency.

This idea of a *lex specialis* regime of attribution based on complicity has developed within the Inter-American human rights system. As a starting point, the Inter-American system follows the basic structure of negative and positive obligations common to international human rights law.[98] In *Velasquez Rodriguez*, the Inter-American Court of Human Rights interpreted Article 1(1) of the American Convention[99] as imposing obligations on states to (i) 'respect the rights and freedoms recognized by the Convention' and (ii) 'ensure the full and free exercise' of those rights.[100] This entails obligations to refrain from violating such rights and to take a range of positive measures to prevent, investigate, and punish human rights violations that are not attributable to the state.[101]

In assessing an allegation that a state failed to respect the rights guaranteed by the American Convention, attribution (or imputability, in the language of the court) plays a central role. At its core, as in the general law of state responsibility, is the attribution of the conduct of either *de facto* or *de jure* state

[96] See section 6.2 above. [97] Ibid.

[98] See UNHRC, 'General Comment 31' [6]–[8]; *Velasquez Rodriguez* [161]–[167]; *Ireland* v. *United Kingdom* [239].

[99] American Convention on Human Rights (adopted 22 November 1969, entered into force 18 July 1978) 1144 UNTS 123.

[100] *Velasquez Rodriguez* [165]–[166]. [101] Ibid.

organs and officials to the state.[102] In many cases, the attribution requirement is easily satisfied: it is evident that those who perpetrated the violations were state agents or were under the direct control of the state. However, the Inter-American system has also dealt with instances where the state has supported a non-state actor in its perpetration of human rights violations. It is in these cases that the putative *lex specialis* rule of attribution has arisen.

It should be noted at this point that state participation of this kind, at least where the principal harm is territorial, would constitute a breach of the state's positive obligations to take measures to prevent violations committed by non-state actors, an obligation conditioned by a due diligence standard.[103] In such cases, it is not that the conduct of the non-state actor is itself imputable to the state; rather, the state's own omission in failing to act diligently to prevent it gives rise to responsibility.[104] The *lex specialis* rule of attribution analysed in this section is an attempt by the institutions of the Inter-American system to supplement, in cases of culpable state participation, state responsibility for violations of a positive obligation with the *attribution* of the non-state actor's conduct to the state.

8.4.2. Sources of the Rule

The source of the attributional rule is a dictum of the Inter-American Court in the *Paniagua Morales* case.[105] The case concerned acts of abduction, detention, inhuman treatment, torture, and murder perpetrated in Guatemala in 1987 and 1988. Evidence indicated that members of the state's Treasury Police committed the acts in question. In setting out the law on imputability, the court stated:

> The sole requirement is to demonstrate that the State authorities supported or tolerated infringement of the rights recognized in the Convention. Moreover, the State's international responsibility is also at issue when it does not take the necessary steps under its domestic law to identify and, where appropriate, punish the authors of such violations.[106]

Given that the case concerned conduct of *de jure* state officials,[107] this assertion was broader than was needed to resolve the case. Nonetheless, it seems to suggest that a complicit relationship—support or toleration—is sufficient to impute conduct of non-state actors to a state.

[102] See *Velasquez Rodriguez* [169]–[172]. [103] Ibid [172]. [104] Ibid.
[105] *Paniagua Morales* et al. (8 March 1998) Inter-Am Ct H (Ser C) No 37.
[106] Ibid [91]. [107] See ibid [93].

The Inter-American Commission subsequently applied the court's statement in *Paniagua Morales* in the *Riofrío* matter.[108] In this case, the petitioners asserted that the state of Colombia sponsored, permitted, and covered up the massacre of 13 individuals by paramilitaries in the municipality of Riofrío. In setting out the law on attribution under the Convention, the Commission stated:

> Before turning to the analysis of the alleged violations of the standards of the American Convention, it must be ascertained whether the acts of the individuals implicated in the incident in violating such fundamental rights as the rights to life and humane treatment are attributable to the State of Colombia and therefore call into question its responsibility in accordance with international law. In this regard, the Inter-American Court has noted that it is sufficient to show that the infringement of the rights recognized in the Convention has been supported or tolerated by the government.[109]

This, then, is an explicit assertion that support or toleration of private human rights violations by state officials is sufficient for attribution of those private acts to the state.

Recently, this question arose again in the *Mapiripán Massacre* case.[110] The case concerned a massacre carried out by paramilitaries in the Colombian municipality of Mapiripán in 1997. Evidence indicated widespread state involvement in the killings.[111] In its submissions to the court, the Commission argued that a complicit relationship was sufficient for attribution:

> [T]he acts of private individuals involved in said acts can be attributed to the State and, therefore, entail its responsibility in accordance with international law, for which it is sufficient to prove that there has been support or tolerance by the public authorities in the breach of the rights embodied in the Convention...[112]

In contrast, Colombia sought to distinguish the acts and omissions of its own agents—for which it accepted responsibility—from those of the paramilitaries. Indeed, it argued that the attribution of the acts of the paramilitaries 'to the State as if they were its agents... would be contrary to international law'.[113] Here, Colombia was referring to the rules of attribution in customary international law, as reflected by the ILC in Chapter II of ARSIWA.[114] Colombia distinguished this set of secondary rules from the primary rules defining the

[108] *Riofrío Massacre* (6 April 2001) Inter-Am C HR, Report No 62/01. See John Cerone, 'Human Dignity in the Line of Fire: The Application of International Human Rights Law During Armed Conflict, Occupation, and Peace Operations' (2006) 39 Vand J Intl L 1447.

[109] *Riofrío Massacre* [48].

[110] *Mapiripán Massacre* (15 September 2005) Inter-Am Ct HR, Series C No 134 (2005).

[111] Ibid [96]. [112] Ibid [98.a]. [113] Ibid [97.b]. [114] Ibid [97.d].

content and duration of the obligations imposed by the Convention on state parties.[115]

Colombia's submission is interesting in its express denial that the Inter-American Convention prescribes a *lex specialis* rule of attribution based on complicity. Its position is that state responsibility for the conduct of non-state actors is governed by the agency relationship set out in *Nicaragua* and reflected in Article 8 ARSIWA.[116] This is to say, attribution in international human rights law is the same as the default rules of attribution in international law. In the case at hand, Colombia submitted that because 'there were no instructions or effective control by the State...' the conduct of the non-state group was not attributable to it.[117]

In its assessment of Colombia's responsibility, the court explicitly rejected Colombia's argument and asserted that the rule of attribution in the Convention constitutes *lex specialis* with respect to the general law of state responsibility.[118] Setting out the content of the special rule of attribution, the court is not entirely clear on the standard it requires. It may be said that the following factors, many of which are iterations of the same general idea of state involvement, contributed to the attribution of the private conduct of the paramilitaries to the state: (a) the massacre was carried out with 'full knowledge, logistic preparations and collaboration by the Armed Forces'; (b) the 'massacre could not have been prepared and carried out without the collaboration, acquiescence, and tolerance' of the Armed Forces; and (c) the 'link' between the Armed Forces and paramilitaries.[119] Running through these factors, and through the presentation of the evidence, is the idea that the state was complicit in the massacre. A complicit relationship, in the court's interpretation, is sufficient for attribution.

A similar approach, albeit one concerning state complicity in the wrongdoing of another state, may be found in the recent case of *El-Masri* v. *Macedonia* before the European Court of Human Rights.[120] The case concerned the rendition, detention, and torture of Khaled El-Masri, a German national, by the Central Intelligence Agency of the United States, and the state of Macedonia's involvement therein. El-Masri was (i) arrested, detained, and ill-treated in Macedonia by Macedonian agents, (ii) handed over to a CIA rendition team at Skopje Airport, where he was tortured, and (iii) rendered to Afghanistan, where he was detained for four months.[121]

[115] Ibid [97.c]. [116] Ibid [97.d]. [117] Ibid [97.e]. [118] Ibid [107].

[119] Ibid [120]–[123].

[120] *El-Masri* v. *The Former Yugoslav Republic of Macedonia* (App 39630/09) (Judgment of 13 December 2012).

[121] Ibid [195]–[223].

The inhuman and degrading treatment of El-Masri by Macedonian agents in (i) raises few legal difficulties—these are attributable acts of ill-treatment by state agents. Likewise, Macedonia's role in the removal of the applicant in (iii) entails a straightforward application of the *non-refoulement* obligation stemming from *Soering*.[122] More interesting is the court's approach to the torture of El-Masri at the airport by the CIA rendition team:

> The Court must first assess whether the treatment suffered by the applicant at Skopje Airport at the hands of the special CIA rendition team is imputable to the respondent State. In this connection it emphasises that the acts complained of were carried out in the presence of officials of the respondent State and within its jurisdiction. Consequently, the respondent State must be regarded as responsible under the Convention for acts performed by foreign officials on its territory with the acquiescence or connivance of its authorities.[123]

In other words, Macedonia's complicity in the conduct of another state—the US—was sufficient to attribute the foreign state's conduct to it.[124] This holding was reaffirmed in the recent cases of *Al Nashiri* v. *Poland* and *Husayn (Abu Zubaydah)* v. *Poland*.[125] These cases under the European Convention on Human Rights replicate the approach of the Inter-American institutions to the question of attribution in international law.

8.4.3. Understanding the Attributional Approach

The question in these cases is whether the conduct at issue is attributable to the state. The prescribed test entails the search for a complicit relationship—collaboration, support, or coordination.[126] This approach

[122] Ibid [212]–[222]. See also André Nollkaemper, 'The ECtHR Finds Macedonia Responsible in Connection with Torture by the CIA, but on What Basis?' (*EJIL:Talk!*, 24 December 2012) <http://www.ejiltalk.org/the-ecthr-finds-macedonia-responsible-in-connection-with-torture-by-the-cia-but-on-what-basis/> accessed 23 December 2014.

[123] *El-Masri* [206]. See [235] and [240] with respect to Art 5 ECHR. See also *Mohammed Alzery* v. *Sweden* (10 November 2006) UNHRC, CCPR/C/88/D/1416/2005 [11.6] for a similar approach arising out of a similar set of facts: 'On the issue of the treatment [of] the author at Bromma airport, the Committee must first assess whether the treatment suffered by the author at the hands of foreign agents is properly imputable to the State party under the terms of the Covenant and under applicable rules of State responsibility. The Committee notes that, at a minimum, *a State party is responsible for acts of foreign officials* exercising acts of sovereign authority on its territory, if such acts are performed with the consent or acquiescence of the State party.' (emphasis added).

[124] See also *Ilaşcu and Others* v. *Moldova and Russia* (App 48787/99) (2005) 40 EHRR 1030. Cf Art 17 ARSIWA.

[125] *Al Nashiri* v. *Poland* (App 28761/11) (Judgment of 24 July 2014) [452], [517]; *Husayn (Abu Zubaydah)* v. *Poland* (App 7511/13) (Judgment of 24 July 2014) [449], [512].

[126] See *Riofrío Massacre* [48]; *Mapiripán Massacre* [120]–[123].

attempts to address state complicity in the rules of attribution in international law.[127]

This approach is misguided. First, on their own terms, certain of the cases seem to betray a degree of conceptual confusion regarding the relationship between secondary rules of attribution and primary obligations—either positive or negative—binding states in international law. A state commits an internationally wrongful act when (a) an act or omission is attributable to it under international law *and* (b) that act or omission breaches an international obligation of the state.[128] These are two separate and necessary stages of inquiry.

Some of the decisions seem to misunderstand how attribution operates in the context of positive obligations.[129] Claims relating to positive obligations implicate omissions on the part of the state: the state failed to prevent a violation, or punish private actors who committed it, or take steps to ensure fulfilment of the right. Here, of course, attribution plays a necessarily diminished role—by its very nature a failure on the part of the state to fulfil a positive obligation is conduct of that state. All of the legwork in such a case is done in determining the specific content of the positive obligation to take action and whether it was discharged.

The confusion in the Inter-American approach may be found in the Commission's use in *Riofrío* of the holding of the court in *Paniagua Morales*. The latter case concerned Guatemala's responsibility for actions of its own Treasury Police. The court's test for determining international responsibility was somewhat ambiguous.[130] In the *Riofrío* matter, the Commission applied this test to determine whether or not the actions of non-state actors were attributable to the state of Colombia.[131] A flawed premise seems to underlie the Commission's approach—that *to engage the responsibility of the state under the Convention* it is necessary to impute the conduct of the non-state actor to it. But responsibility under the Convention may be engaged by the state's failure to ensure the full and free exercise of rights where those rights are violated by private parties. There is no need to find that the acts of the private party are attributable to state—the relevant state official's failure to act is the attributable act.[132]

There is another, more charitable, explanation of how this rule developed, one that denies that the court is confused about the question of attribution

[127] See Cerone, 'Human Dignity in the Line of Fire' 1459–62. [128] Art 2 ARSIWA.

[129] See Cerone 'Human Dignity in the Line of Fire' 1462–4; Hakimi, 'State Bystander Responsibility' 354.

[130] See *Paniagua Morales* [90]–[91]. [131] *Riofrío Massacre* [48].

[132] See Hakimi, 'State Bystander Responsibility' 353–4.

in respect of positive obligations. It is most evident in the *Mapiripán Massacre* case. Faced with the mountain of evidence of the state's involvement, the court refused to rule that Colombia was responsible only for failing to protect against harm by private actors—that is, for breach of its positive obligations to protect against violations of the rights at issue. Rather, it was *complicit*—the state's participation constituting a particular way of contributing to the principal wrong. A nod towards this understanding may be seen in the judgment of the court,[133] and, more forcefully, in the separate opinion of Judge Cançado Trindade.[134]

Indeed, Judge Cançado Trindade specifically engages Colombia's objection to the attribution of the massacre itself to the state. In the first place, he quotes, perhaps disingenuously given the subsequent work of the commission and requirements of Article 8 ARSIWA, a suggestion by Ago in his Fourth Report on State Responsibility that state 'participation' or 'complicity' may be a sufficient basis for the attribution of private conduct to the state.[135] Leaving aside this appeal to the authority of Ago, the real source of Judge Cançado Trindade's objection subsequently becomes evident:

> There is no way to avoid finding the respondent State responsible for conduct in violation of human rights in the *cas d'espèce* ... To attempt to do this, under the circumstances of the instant case, would involve a fruitless and *in abstracto* interpretive exercise, devoid of meaning and of juridical value. There is no way to avoid recognizing both the failings and omissions of the public State authorities regarding prevention and conclusive investigation of the violations committed in the instant case, and the support or collaboration provided, directly or indirectly, by public State authorities to the paramilitary, in committing grave violations of human rights under the American Convention.[136]

The issue for Cançado Trindade is simple: in the light of Colombia's evident participation in the harms at issue, it is not sufficient that responsibility arises only in respect of the state's failure to discharge its positive obligations to prevent the harms from arising. Its complicity must be censured and sanctioned by attributing the conduct of the non-state actors to the state.

As in the context of terrorism, there are problems with this approach. First, in line with the normative claim of this work, we should be wary of holding

[133] *Mapiripán Massacre* [120]–[123].

[134] *Mapiripán Massacre* (Separate Opinion of Judge Cançado Trindade).

[135] Ibid [12]. See Roberto Ago, 'Fourth Report on State Responsibility—The Internationally Wrongful Act of the State, Source of International Responsibility' (1978) UN Doc A/CN.4/264 (1978) II YILC 72 [64].

[136] *Mapiripán Massacre* (Separate Opinion of Judge Cançado Trindade) [14].

any actor responsible for wrongdoing that it, or its agents, did not, in fact, commit. At stake here is the principle of sovereignty. The tests for attribution reflected in Articles 4 and 8 ARSIWA, bounded as they are by the search for an agency relationship, reflect this claim. It is a significant leap to render an actor that financed or supported a human rights violation responsible for that human rights violation itself. Such a leap denies the status of complicity as a particular way of contributing to wrongdoing.

Second, the approach to attribution in the Inter-American system denies the value of maintaining coherence in the secondary rules of attribution in international law. In matters of this kind, international actors and courts are asking the same question: which acts are state acts? Applying a set of secondary rules across most, if not all, primary rules develops a coherent and certain framework for assessing issues of international responsibility. In other words, short of overwhelming imperative, the attributional rules should not be 'primary rule-dependent'.[137]

That said, the approach of the Inter-American institutions is understandable. Although the nature of complicity demands that accomplices are not held responsible for the wrongs of their principals, it also demands that complicity—as a particular way of contributing to such wrongdoing—is prohibited on its own terms. That is to say, we should not be satisfied with sweeping up instances of *complicit* conduct into a broader due diligence obligation to protect against harm. There is a grave difference between a state failing to put in place the appropriate structures in its police service so as to diligently prevent violations of the right to life and a state providing weapons to a non-state actor in the knowledge that they will be used to kill civilians. Faced with evidence of Colombia's participation in the massacre at Mapiripán, the court chose to condemn that participation by using it, contrary to the general rule in international law, as a ground for attributing the conduct of the non-state group to the state.

In addition, it may be that the normative claim of this work carries most weight when the complicit relationship arises between two legal subjects of the same status—individual complicity in the conduct of another individual or state complicity in the conduct of another state. In the present instance, we are dealing with the participation of a state in the conduct of a non-state actor. The difference is entailed not in the fact that the relationship is between two different subjects, but rather in the different nature of that subjectivity in international law. The state is the subject granted primary regulatory

[137] See Milanović, 'Self-Defense and Non-State Actors'.

authority by international law.[138] To consider the state is not only to consider its obligations, but also its powers. In the context of such institutional power, to hold the state responsible for complicity might seem to underweight its culpability.[139]

This is an interesting argument. Nonetheless, it is not sufficient to displace the principled demand that actors be held responsible only for their own wrongdoing or that of their agents. Moreover, complicity is not necessarily a lesser or more 'marginal' form of responsibility than responsibility for the principal wrong.[140] Recognizing complicity as a discrete way of contributing to wrongdoing also opens up the possibility of viewing a certain actor's complicit contribution as more culpable even than the principal's wrongdoing, depending on the circumstances of the case.[141]

In cases of state participation of this kind, rather than loosening the test for attribution, a better solution might be for treaty bodies to interpret the obligation-imposing clauses of their respective instruments to impose obligations of non-participation on state parties. There is no reason that, for instance, the obligation in Article 1 ECHR to 'secure to everyone within their jurisdiction the rights and freedoms' defined therein cannot be interpreted to include a prohibition on participation in rights violations carried out by other actors.[142] Such an obligation would capture a form of culpability falling between direct state perpetration and a failure to exercise due diligence to prevent the commission of rights violations.

This interpretive solution, which reads the obligation to refrain from participating in the rights violations of others into the respective conventions, would not be unprecedented. The development of the prohibition on *non-refoulement* under the European Convention on Human Rights and International Covenant on Civil and Political Rights is somewhat analogous.[143] Article 3 ECHR provides: 'No one shall be subjected to torture or to inhuman or degrading treatment or punishment.'[144] As is the case with other rights, states are under an obligation to refrain from violating the right and to take a range of positive measures to secure its fulfilment.[145] *Soering* v. *United*

[138] Lowe, *International Law* 138.

[139] Amoroso, 'Moving towards Complicity as a Criterion of Attribution' 992–3.

[140] Cf Amoroso, 'Moving towards Complicity as a Criterion of Attribution' 993. See section 2.4.2 above.

[141] See Quigley, 'Complicity in International Law' 129.

[142] Art 1 ECHR.

[143] International Covenant on Civil and Political Rights (adopted 16 December 1966, entered into force 23 March 1976) 999 UNTS 171.

[144] Art 3 ECHR.

[145] Robin White and Clare Ovey, *Jacobs, White, and Ovey—The European Convention on Human Rights* (5th edn. OUP 2010) 99–102.

Kingdom and the line of cases following it establish an additional negative obligation under Article 3: states must refrain from extraditing or deporting a fugitive where there are substantial grounds for believing that the fugitive faces a real risk of torture or inhuman or degrading treatment or punishment in the requesting or recipient country.[146] This obligation has also been read into Article 7 ICCPR.[147]

The point is not that the obligation of *non-refoulement* is a complicity rule—it arises independently of, and prior to, any subsequent violation in the recipient state. Rather, it demonstrates how a certain right—the right against torture and inhuman and degrading treatment—can be interpreted to give rise to an additional obligation other than the obligation to refrain from direct perpetration of human rights violations. By interpreting the respective instruments to specifically prohibit state participation in violations of human rights by other actors, international human rights institutions would accurately capture and condemn a common form of state culpability in relation to the breach of the right.

Such an interpretation would bolster the modern understanding of rights as giving rise to a tripartite division of correlative duties. In Shue's formulation, basic rights correlate with three duties:

1. Duties to avoid depriving;
2. Duties to protect from deprivation; and
3. Duties to aid the deprived.[148]

Shue's typology grounds contemporary understandings of human rights as giving rise to obligations to respect, protect, and fulfil.[149] The virtue of this approach, in its departure from traditional understandings of rights as negative liberties, cannot be overstated. However, it may be further strengthened by recognizing an additional duty of non-participation, falling between the duty to avoid depriving and the duty to protect from deprivation. International human rights law would thereby accurately capture a morally significant and discrete way that states contribute to the commission of rights violations.

146 *Soering* v. *United Kingdom* [89]; *Chahal* v. *United Kingdom* (App 22414/93) (1996) 23 EHRR 413.

147 UNHRC, General Comment 20 [9].

148 Henry Shue, *Basic Rights—Subsistence, Affluence, and U.S. Foreign Policy* (2nd edn. Princeton University Press 1996) 52.

149 See Hakimi, 'State Bystander Responsibility' 346–7.

8.5. Conclusion

In international law, the rules of attribution in respect of the conduct of non-state actors are marked by a search for an agency relationship between the state and non-state actor. In two contexts, there is a claim that a complicit relationship, rather than one based on agency, is sufficient to attribute the conduct of the non-state actor to the state. Both should be rejected.

These putative attributional rules are conceptually distinct from complicity in international criminal law, and, indeed, state complicity in the wrongdoing of another state. Unlike the latter two instances, these rules do not seek to tie the accomplice to a separate wrong committed by a principal actor. Instead, they attribute the conduct of the principal actor to the state and, in doing so, give rise to state responsibility for that conduct in terms of the state's own primary obligations.

By their very nature, attributional rules of this kind cannot comply with the normative claim of this work. The normative claim demands that accomplices are held responsible for, and labelled in terms of, their own acts of contribution to the principal's wrong. Responsibility of this kind does not fit easily with the historical structure of international law, simply because of the absence of regulation of the conduct of the non-state actor. Trying to accommodate what looks like ordinary forms of complicity—aid, assistance, or support—within the secondary rules leads to incoherence in the rules of attribution and renders states responsible for conduct that they, or their agents, did not commit.

A better solution would be to interpret the rights guaranteed by human rights instruments as imposing a correlative duty of non-participation in violations of human rights carried out by other actors. In this way, states would be held responsible for their own contribution to wrongdoing.

9

State Complicity and the Obligations of Non-State Actors

9.1. Introduction

It is worth recapping the analysis up to this point. From a starting point marked by an absence of complicity rules, international law has come to prohibit state complicity in the wrongdoing of other states. Specific primary rules such as the prohibition of territorial complicity in aggression subsist alongside the general prohibition on aid or assistance reflected in Article 16 ARSIWA.

Where states participate in harms caused by non-state actors, conceptual problems arise for complicity. The traditional absence of regulation by international law of the conduct of non-state actors meant that there was no wrong on the international plane for the participating state to be complicit in. As noted in Chapter 8, some instances of state participation will be captured under a direct obligation of non-participation or under broader due diligence obligations binding states in various areas of international law. But generally, in these cases, complicity, as a particular way of contributing to wrongdoing, could not be properly sanctioned by international law.

The previous chapter set out one way in which ideas of complicity bear on international law's regulation of state participation in harms caused by non-state actors. Under this approach, what looks like a complicit relationship between the state and the non-state actor would give rise to the attribution of the non-state actor's conduct to the state. This is not accomplice liability in the strict sense, as the state's responsibility is not derived from the non-state actor's wrong. Rather, it takes a factual relationship of complicity as sufficient for attribution. This is a contested and undesirable development.

This chapter analyses a quite different development in the regulation of state complicity. States are no longer the sole bearers of international obligations. Now that other legal subjects bear international obligations, it is possible to articulate a state's responsibility for participating in the violation of those obligations in terms of complicity.[1] In other words, the non-state actor may be responsible for international wrongdoing as a principal; the participating state may be linked to that wrongdoing as an accomplice. The clearest example in this regard is the prohibition on state complicity in genocide.

The prohibition on state complicity in genocide is a specific complicity rule. This chapter assesses the content of that rule within the analytical framework of the work and evaluates its structure. This chapter also raises the possibility that the evolution from specific rules to a general rule seen in respect of state complicity in the wrongdoing of another state will be repeated here. Wherever international law imposes obligations on non-state actors, so state complicity in violations thereof would give rise to international responsibility.

9.2. State Complicity in Genocide—A Specific Rule

9.2.1. Introduction

The Convention on the Prevention and Punishment of the Crime of Genocide—adopted by the General Assembly in 1948 and ratified by the required 20 states in 1950—envisaged a system of domestic criminalization and punishment of genocide. Article I of the Convention provides:

> The Contracting Parties confirm that genocide, whether committed in time of peace or in time of war, is a crime under international law which they undertake to prevent and to punish.[2]

There is no textual reference in the Convention to an obligation prohibiting states from committing genocide, let alone complicity in genocide. Article IX of the Convention, however, makes provision for the International Court of Justice to resolve disputes arising between state parties. In the *Bosnian Genocide* case, the Court was called upon to determine what obligations the Convention imposes on state parties, including whether a complicity obligation exists.

Briefly, the factual foundation of the complicity question in the case lay in the provision by the Federal Republic of Yugoslavia of political, financial, and military aid to authorities of Republika Srpska—a non-state entity in Bosnia and Herzegovina. This aid was used in the commission of genocide by the army of Republika Srpska against the adult male Muslim population

[1] De Frouville, 'Attribution of Conduct' 277.

[2] Art I Genocide Convention.

of Srebrenica. Thus, one question was whether the FRY was complicit in the genocide perpetrated by Republika Srpska.[3]

9.2.2. The Reasoning of the ICJ

The ICJ found that the Genocide Convention did indeed impose an obligation on states not to be complicit in genocide.[4] The moves made by the Court in this respect are important and have potential ramifications for the interpretation of treaty obligations in other areas of international law.[5] Against the respondent's objection that duties in the Convention relate only to genocide 'when this crime is committed by individuals',[6] the Court found that states are themselves bound by an obligation not to commit genocide. By its reasoning, this prohibition flows from two sources: (i) by categorizing genocide as 'a crime under international law', logically states must be undertaking not to commit the act so described, and (ii) the obligation to prevent genocide imposed by the Convention necessarily implies an obligation not to perpetrate genocide.[7]

The Court then applied this reasoning to the other punishable acts listed in Article III of the Convention, namely conspiracy, direct and public incitement, and attempt to commit genocide, as well as complicity in genocide:

> That conclusion must also apply to the other acts enumerated in Article III. Those acts are forbidden along with genocide itself in the list included in Article III. They are referred to equally with genocide in Article IX and without being characterized as 'punishable'; and the 'purely humanitarian and civilizing purpose' of the Convention may be seen as being promoted by the fact that States are subject to that full set of obligations, supporting their undertaking to prevent genocide.[8]

On the basis of this reasoning, state parties to the Genocide Convention are obligated to refrain from acts constituting complicity in genocide. It does not matter if the genocide is attributable to another state or committed by a non-state actor. Customary international law also imposes a discrete obligation on states not to commit genocide.[9] In principle, the content of the customary obligation may differ from that imposed by the Convention. However, the Convention and interpretations thereof will serve as the main

[3] *Bosnian Genocide* [418]–[424]. [4] Ibid [167].
[5] See Trapp, *State Responsibility for International Terrorism* 144. [6] Ibid [156].
[7] Ibid [166]. [8] Ibid [167].
[9] John Quigley, *The Genocide Convention: An International Law Analysis* (Ashgate 2006) 80; Paola Gaeta, 'On What Conditions Can a State Be Held Responsible for Genocide?' (2007) 18 Eur J Intl L 631, 632.

reference point for determinations of the customary obligation.[10] Customary international law should be seen to prohibit complicity in genocide too.

9.2.3. Criticism of the Court's Approach

Both the first stage—the finding that the Convention prohibits states from committing genocide—and the second stage—the extension of this finding to the other punishable acts listed in Article III—of the Court's reasoning have been criticized. In respect of the first stage, the Joint Declaration of Judges Shi and Koroma in the case explicitly rejects the majority's finding that Article I, read in the light of the purpose and objects of the Convention, may found the obligation not to commit genocide:

> Hence, Article I of the Convention has to be interpreted in the light of Article VI and the attempt in the Judgment to sever Article I of the Convention from Articles IV, V, VI, VII and VIII, in order to reach the outcome stated in the Judgment, is to us legally unsustainable and contrary to the object and purpose of the Convention, the meaning of the text of the Convention and the real intention of the parties.[11]

Their argument is premised on the essential criminal nature of the Convention. This approach is echoed in the separate opinions of Judges Owada[12] and Tomka.[13] Academic criticism, most notably by Gaeta, has argued that the Court's approach to Article I is at odds with both the historical context of the Genocide Convention and ordinary methods of treaty interpretation.[14]

This criticism has some merit. The Convention does not expressly impose an obligation on states not to commit genocide and is, indeed, primarily concerned with individual responsibility through domestic criminalization. This much is conceded even by those scholars who support the imposition of state responsibility for genocide under the Convention.[15] Moreover, some of the arguments relied on by the Court are weak. For instance, the Court appears to place some weight on the fact that there is no conceptual difficulty in interpreting the Convention to impose both individual criminal liability and state responsibility; this potential duality of responsibility is affirmed in both the Rome Statute and ARSIWA.[16] This point is strongly rebutted by

[10] See *Krstić* (Trial Chamber Judgment) [541].

[11] *Bosnian Genocide* (Joint Declaration of Judges Shi and Koroma) [4].

[12] *Bosnian Genocide* (Separate Opinion of Judge Owada) [38]–[56].

[13] *Bosnian Genocide* (Separate Opinion of Judge Tomka) [40]–[45].

[14] Gaeta, 'On What Conditions' 633.

[15] See Antonio Cassese, 'On the Use of Criminal Law Notions in Determining State Responsibility for Genocide' (2007) 5 J Intl Crim Just 875, 876–7.

[16] *Bosnian Genocide* [173], referencing Art 25(4) Rome Statute and Art 58 ARSIWA.

Judge Owada: the question is not whether international law envisages potential duality of responsibility—a proposition few argue against—but whether the Genocide Convention itself does so.[17]

The Court's central argument is teleological. It seems right that interpreting Article I to prohibit states from committing genocide would serve the purpose of liberating mankind from the scourge of genocide.[18] Likewise, the Court's interpretation imposes a coherent set of obligations on state parties in relation to genocide.[19] In relying so heavily on the object and purpose of the Convention, the Court, in essence, makes this a matter of the permissible breadth of teleological interpretation. The *travaux préparatoires* are ambiguous at best.[20] It may be argued that rather than using the object and purpose of the Convention to interpret the content of obligations imposed thereunder, the Court infers an entirely discrete obligation.[21] The obligation to prevent wrongful conduct is distinct from the obligation not to perpetrate or support it. Of course, where a state is complicit in, or indeed perpetrates, the wrong it is required to prevent, international responsibility for the breach of its obligation to prevent will arise.[22] But, as a matter of law if not logic, that is a different proposition from implying an obligation not to perpetrate wrongful conduct from the obligation to prevent it.

The Court's teleological construction leads it to rely less directly on the wording of Article IX, which provides a stronger textual argument for the imposition of state responsibility under the Convention. Article IX, the compromissory clause, grants jurisdiction to the ICJ in matters 'relating to the interpretation, application or fulfillment of the present Convention, including those relating to the responsibility of a State for genocide or for any of the other acts enumerated in article III . . .'.[23] The clause 'including those relating to the responsibility of a State . . .' was adopted as an amendment to the working draft on the proposal of the United Kingdom and Belgium.[24] Of course, as a compromissory clause, Article IX does not itself impose substantive obligations on states. However, to the extent that the *travaux préparatoires* concerning the obligations imposed by the operative articles of the Convention are ambiguous, this direct reference to state responsibility may be seen as dispositive.[25] Although this issue was always going to be a difficult

[17] *Bosnian Genocide* (Separate Opinion of Judge Owada) [56].

[18] See Cassese, 'On the Use of Criminal Law Notions' 877.

[19] Ibid 877–8.

[20] See *Bosnian Genocide* [164]–[165], [176]–[178]; Separate Opinion of Judge Owada [59]–[71]; Schabas, *Genocide in International Law* 491–9; Nina Jørgensen, 'State Responsibility and the 1948 Genocide Convention' in Guy Goodwin-Gill and Stefan Talmon (eds.) *The Reality of International Law—Essays in Honour of Ian Brownlie* (OUP 1999) 273, 290.

[21] Gaeta, 'On What Conditions' 639.

[22] *Bosnian Genocide* [382].

[23] Art IX Genocide Convention.

[24] Schabas, *Genocide in International Law* 496–7.

[25] Marko Milanović, 'State Responsibility for Genocide' (2006) 17 Eur J Intl L 553, 566.

question of interpretation, greater reliance on Article IX would have been more convincing.

The second stage of the Court's reasoning—extending the obligations on states to include the other enumerated acts in Article III of the Convention—has also been criticized by scholars, although not as widely as the first stage. Most notably, Cassese questions 'this remarkable extension of contracting states' obligations under the Convention. It simply and tersely refers to the object and scope of the Convention. Can this means of interpretation justify such a sweeping conclusion?'[26] Without answering this question directly, Cassese suggests that this expansive approach is inconsistent with the Court's more restrained answers to other questions of international responsibility, particularly its rejection of the *Tadić* test of overall control.[27]

Cassese's criticism of the second stage of the Court's reasoning is better read as an argument for a more expansive approach to the test of control necessary for attribution rather than as a plea for restrained interpretation of the obligations imposed by the Genocide Convention. Surely, if one accepts, as Cassese does,[28] a reading of the Convention that imposes an obligation on state parties not to commit genocide, it would be paradoxical not to accept that such an obligation exists also in respect of the other related acts set out therein. This reading is confirmed by the textual reference to the other acts enumerated in Article III in the clause added to Article IX by the amendment offered by the United Kingdom and Belgium.[29] All of the legwork of the Court's approach lies in the first stage—finding that the Genocide Convention provides for state responsibility for genocide itself. Once the Court made this ruling, it was always going to find that the Convention prohibits state incitement, conspiracy, attempts, and complicity.

9.2.4. The Content of the Rule—The Court's Approach

When, then, will state responsibility for complicity in genocide arise? In the first place, the Court holds that complicity certainly 'includes the provision of means to enable or facilitate the commission of the crime'.[30] Developing this idea, the Court turns to Article 16 ARSIWA, which prohibits the provision by one state to another of aid or assistance in the commission of an internationally wrongful act:

> The Court sees no reason to make any distinction of substance between 'complicity in genocide', within the meaning of Article III, paragraph (e), of the Convention,

[26] Cassese, 'On the Use of Criminal Law Notions' 878.
[27] Ibid 878.
[28] Ibid 877.
[29] Art IX Genocide Convention.
[30] *Bosnian Genocide* [419].

and the 'aid or assistance' of a State in the commission of a wrongful act by another State within the meaning of the aforementioned Article 16... In other words, to ascertain whether the Respondent is responsible for 'complicity in genocide' within the meaning of Article III, paragraph (e)... it must examine whether organs of the respondent State, or persons acting on its instructions or under its direction or effective control, furnished 'aid or assistance' in the commission of the genocide in Srebrenica, in a sense not significantly different from that of those concepts in the general law of international responsibility.[31]

Clearly, the Court locates the prohibition of complicity in genocide within the general law of international responsibility for aid and assistance. Concerning the conduct prohibited by the complicity rule, the Court refers to the 'quite substantial aid of a political, military and financial nature provided by the FRY to the Republika Srpska' and its army.[32] The flow of aid preceded and continued during the genocide at Srebrenica.

The level of fault required by the primary rule prohibiting complicity in genocide proved more problematic. Indeed, the Court appeared unsure of how to approach the simple question whether the accomplice needs to share in the specific intent of the principal or if, instead, knowledge of that intent is sufficient.[33] The Court failed to answer the question, holding that 'at the least' the complicit organ or actor must have acted knowingly; it did not decide if knowledge was, in and of itself, sufficient.[34] It was on this basis that the claim failed: it was not established beyond doubt that the FRY continued its provision of aid with knowledge that the 'perpetrators had the specific intent characterizing genocide, namely, the intent to destroy, in whole or in part, a human group, as such'.[35]

Two points may be made at this stage. First, there are doubts about the accuracy of the Court's factual finding that it was not established beyond doubt that the FRY continued its provision of aid with knowledge that the perpetrators of the genocide were acting with requisite specific intent.[36] Vice President Al-Khasawneh, in his dissenting opinion, argues that Belgrade was fully aware of General Mladić's activities in Srebrenica.[37] The evidence set out by Judge Keith reinforces this.[38] Given this evidence, and the close relationship between the FRY and General Mladić, it is arguable that an inference of knowledge should have arisen.

Second, it is strange that the Court chose not to resolve the requisite level of culpability required for state complicity in genocide.[39] It remains unclear

[31] Ibid [420]. [32] Ibid [422]. [33] Ibid [421]. [34] Ibid.
[35] Ibid [422]. [36] See Cassese, 'On the Use of Criminal Law Notions' 882.
[37] *Bosnian Genocide* (Dissenting Opinion of Vice President Al-Khasawneh) [48]–[55].
[38] *Bosnian Genocide* (Declaration of Judge Keith) [8]–[16].
[39] See Milanović, 'State Responsibility for Genocide: A Follow-Up' 681.

whether knowledge of the perpetrator's specific intent or a shared specific intent is required. If the Court had drawn an inference of knowledge from the relationship and meetings between President Milosević and General Mladić, this question, which the Court failed to answer, would have been dispositive of Serbia's legal responsibility for complicity in genocide.

9.2.5. Assessing the Rule within the Analytical Framework

9.2.5.1. Introduction

The analytical framework set out in Chapter 2, as well as the assessment of complicity in international criminal law in Chapter 4, provide a rich source for insights into the operation of the rule prohibiting state complicity in genocide. At the outset, it is worth reiterating the Genocide Convention's criminal law underpinnings—in Article I 'the Contracting Parties confirm that genocide... is a crime under international law which they undertake to prevent and to punish'.[40] The international crime of genocide and accessorial modes of responsibility therein have been fleshed out over the last 20 years in international practice, case law, and scholarship. This raised a methodological question for the ICJ in interpreting the prohibition on state complicity. Should it draw on international criminal law to determine the meaning of complicity or, as Cassese puts it, interpret complicity as an 'autonomous and self-sufficient public international law' concept?[41]

9.2.5.2. The Conduct Element

To reiterate, the court was faced in the *Bosnian Genocide* case with text that prescribed simply that 'complicity in genocide' was a punishable act.[42] In construing the meaning of complicity, its first move was to look to Article 16 ARSIWA rather than to doctrines of complicity developed in international criminal law.[43] This is the basis of the holding that the meaning of complicity in the context of genocide did not differ significantly from the provision of 'aid or assistance' under Article 16.[44] The question, then, is how the idea of aid or assistance under Article 16 fits with ordinary understandings of the scope of complicity.

Drawing as it does on Article 16, the ICJ's approach seems to deny the possibility of complicity by encouragement or abetment—influence in Kadish's terminology.[45] The court gives the example of the 'provision of means to

[40] Art I Genocide Convention.

[41] See Cassese, 'On the Use of Criminal Law Notions' 879.

[42] Art III(e) Genocide Convention. [43] *Bosnian Genocide* [419]. [44] Ibid [420].

[45] Kadish, 'Complicity, Cause and Blame' 342.

enable or facilitate the commission of the crime...'.[46] As explained previously, in the ILC's conception, the rule reflected in Article 16 comprises different forms of physical assistance—its examples include providing means for the closure of an international waterway, facilitating the abduction of a person on foreign soil, and financing the wrongful activity.[47] By looking to Article 16 rather than to international criminal law, the ICJ adopts a limited interpretation of complicity, seemingly ignoring that complicity ordinarily comprises both the provision of assistance to the principal *and* influence on the decision of the principal to commit the wrong.[48]

On one level, this approach is understandable: there is heritage to the idea that influence does not constitute state complicity in international law. As explained in Chapter 7, Roberto Ago traced this position to the conclusions of the Board of Commissioners set up under the Convention of 4 July 1831 between France and the United States regarding potential claims against France for the spoliation of property of US citizens.[49] However, the idea that cases of complicit state influence should not give rise to responsibility is generally predicated on the assumption that the principal actor in these instances is another state. This is evident in Ago's own words: '[t]he decision of a sovereign State to adopt a certain course of conduct is certainly its own, even if it has received suggestions and advice from another state, which it was at liberty not to follow.'[50]

Even if it is right that international law should not be concerned with cases of influence between sovereign states,[51] it does not follow that a state that influences the decision of a non-state actor to commit an international wrong should escape responsibility for complicity.[52] As an analogy, we might look to the obligations of non-participation encompassed by the prohibition on the use of force and the principle of non-intervention, both of which include classical modes of complicity by influence. Under the former, states are obligated to refrain from '*encouraging* the organization of irregular forces

[46] *Bosnian Genocide* [419].

[47] ARSIWA Commentary on Art 16 [1]. See section 7.3.5.1 above.

[48] Where the principal is another state, some extreme forms of influence—namely direction and control (Art 17 ARSIWA) or coercion (Art 18 ARSIWA)—may give rise to responsibility. Where the principal is a non-state actor, there is a chance that heightened forms of instigation will result in attribution under Art 8 ARSIWA. In this respect, see ARSIWA Commentary on Art 8[2]. There remains the possibility of state responsibility for the inchoate wrong of incitement to commit genocide. See Art III(c) Genocide Convention; *Bosnian Genocide* [167].

[49] Ago, 'Seventh Report on State Responsibility' [62]. See section 7.3.5.1 above.

[50] Ibid [63]. See also ARSIWA General Commentary on Part IV [9]; Quigley, 'Complicity in International Law' 80.

[51] In this respect, see section 7.3.5.1 above.

[52] See Nollkaemper, 'The Charles Taylor Judgment'.

or armed bands, including mercenaries, for incursion into the territory of another State' and '*instigating* ... acts of civil strife or terrorist acts in another State'.[53] Under the principle of non-intervention, states may not '*foment* [or] *incite*... subversive, terrorist or armed activities directed towards the violent overthrow of the regime of another State'.[54] In addition, the forms of state participation addressed in UN General Assembly Resolutions on terrorism ordinarily include both instigation and encouragement.[55]

Clearly, then, international law does indicate concern for the influence of states on the conduct of non-state actors.[56] As international law develops to recognize increased possibilities of principal wrongdoing by non-state actors, so the ways in which states might participate in that wrongdoing should be adequately sanctioned. This would include not simply the provision of assistance—or help, in Kadish's terminology—but also complicit influence.[57]

A second issue arising under the conduct element concerns the court's treatment of omissions. After disposing of the claim that Serbia was complicit in the genocide, the court went on to consider the differences between the complicity obligation and the obligation to prevent genocide.[58] In addition to a difference in the kind of knowledge required of the state for responsibility, the court found that:

> [C]omplicity always requires that some positive action has been taken to furnish aid or assistance to the perpetrators of the genocide, while a violation of the obligation to prevent results from mere failure to adopt and implement suitable measures to prevent genocide from being committed. In other words, while complicity results from commission, violation of the obligation to prevent results from omission...[59]

The simplicity of the court's approach, though not unappealing, should be resisted. As argued previously, complicity by omission is doctrinally and normatively supported in both municipal[60] and international criminal law.[61] Think of the cleaner who, in breach of his duty to lock up a bank,

[53] Declaration on Friendly Relations (emphasis added); *Armed Activities* [162]. See Trapp, *State Responsibility for International Terrorism* 28–32.

[54] Ibid (emphasis added).

[55] See UNGA Res 40/61 (9 December 1985) UN Doc A/RES/40/61; UNGA Res 44/29 (4 December 1989) UN Doc A/RES/44/29; UNGA Res 49/60 (9 December 1994) UN Doc A/RES/49/60; UNGA Res 51/210 (17 December 1996) UN Doc A/RES 51/210; UNGA Res 53/108 (26 January 1999) UN Doc A/RES/53/108.

[56] See also Common Article 1 to the Geneva Conventions of 1949 (12 August 1949) 75 UNTS 31, 75 UNTS 85, 75 UNTS 135, 75 UNTS 287, and *Nicaragua* [220]; Art III(c) Genocide Convention and *Bosnian Genocide* [167].

[57] Kadish, 'Complicity, Cause and Blame' 342.

[58] *Bosnian Genocide* [432].

[59] Ibid.

[60] See section 2.5.2.2 above.

[61] See section 5.2 above.

intentionally leaves the door open so as to facilitate a break-in.[62] He did not simply fail in his duty to lock the door; he was complicit in the robbery.

So should it be with state complicity in genocide.[63] Many more omissions will violate the obligation to prevent genocide than constitute complicity. Fleshed out, the obligation to prevent genocide requires that states take a range of positive measures. It is conditioned by a due diligence standard,[64] and limited by practical and legal restraints binding the state, including resource concerns, geographical proximity, and the state's other legal obligations.[65] But in some circumstances, a particularly culpable and proximate omission, where both the *mens rea* and nexus requirements are met, should also be seen to constitute complicity in genocide.[66] Here, the state is more directly tied to the harm that results.[67] In this way, international law will accurately condemn and sanction the increased culpability entailed in a complicit omission.

9.2.5.3. The Nexus Element

Chapter 2 argued that, in general, a substantiality requirement ought to condition complicity rules.[68] In the *Bosnian Genocide* case, the ICJ paid little attention to the connection between the complicit state's assistance and the principal's wrong, though in its factual assessment it does refer to 'the *quite substantial aid* of a political, military and financial nature provided by the FRY to the Republika Srpska and the VRS...' in the lead up to Srebrenica.[69] As noted above, the court found that the concept of complicity in the prohibition on state complicity in genocide does not differ significantly from the concept of aid or assistance in the law of state responsibility.[70] For this reason, it can implicitly be read to endorse the nexus requirement in the Article 16. Although the text of Article 16 is silent on the level of contribution, the Commentary provides as follows:

> There is no requirement that the aid or assistance should have been essential to the performance of the internationally wrongful act; it is sufficient if it contributed significantly to that act.[71]

[62] See Ashworth, *Principles of Criminal Law* 410–11.

[63] See Cassese, 'On the Use of Criminal Law Notions' 883–7. For the same argument in respect of Art 16 ARSIWA, see section 7.3.5.1 above.

[64] Ibid [430].

[65] Ibid.

[66] See Nina Jørgensen, 'Complicity in Genocide and the Duality of Responsibility' in Bert Swart, Alexander Zahar, and Göran Sluiter (eds.) *The Legacy of the International Criminal Tribunal for the Former Yugoslavia* (OUP 2011) 247, 268–70.

[67] Fletcher, *Rethinking Criminal Law* 422–3.

[68] See section 2.5.3 above.

[69] *Bosnian Genocide* [422] (emphasis added).

[70] Ibid [420].

[71] ARSIWA Commentary on Art 16 [5]. On the ambiguity in the commentary, see section 7.3.5.2 above.

This standard of significant contribution is similar to that imposed by international criminal law—the accomplice's assistance or encouragement must have a substantial effect on the principal's commission of the crime.[72]

9.2.5.4. The Fault Element

As noted above, in the *Bosnian Genocide* case the Court strangely failed to determine authoritatively the requisite fault element for state complicity in genocide.[73] Instead, the Court held that 'at the least' the complicit actor must have acted knowingly; it did not determine if knowledge was sufficient.[74] In determining the appropriate standard, there is again the methodological question as to whether we should look to Article 16 ARSIWA or the requirement of fault in international criminal law.[75]

As explained in Chapter 7, there is an ongoing dispute as to whether a standard of knowledge or wrongful intent is required for the rule reflected in Article 16 ARSIWA. The text requires only that the aid or assistance be given 'with knowledge of the circumstances of the internationally wrongful act…'.[76] In interpreting the text, the Commentary suggests that the aid or assistance 'must be given with a view to facilitating the commission of the wrongful act'.[77] As argued above, there are good reasons to prefer a standard of knowledge in this context.[78]

A similar debate arises in international criminal law. In customary international law and the case law of the ad hoc tribunals, a standard of knowledge is preferred, even if that standard is sometimes reduced to recklessness in practice.[79] Here, amongst different formulations of a similar idea, the test is best expressed as requiring that the complicit party made a 'conscious decision to act in the knowledge that he thereby supports the commission of the crime'.[80] Article 25(3)(c) of the Rome Statute, on the other hand, requires that assistance be given 'for the purpose of facilitating the commission' of the crime.[81]

As it stands, the standard of fault for the specific primary rule prohibiting state complicity in genocide is not clear. If the fault requirement for the general rule reflected in Article 16 ARSIWA evolves in state practice to entail a

[72] See *Tadić* (Appeals Chamber Judgment) [229]; *Simić* (Appeals Chamber Judgment) [85]; *Mrkšić, Šljivančanin* (Appeals Chamber Judgment) [81].

[73] See Milanović, 'State Responsibility for Genocide: A Follow-Up' 681.

[74] Ibid.

[75] See Cassese, 'On the Use of Criminal Law Notions' 882–3.

[76] Art 16 ARSIWA.

[77] ARSIWA Commentary on Art 16 [5].

[78] See section 7.3.5.2 above; Lowe, 'Responsibility for the Conduct of Other States' 8.

[79] See section 4.3.3 above.

[80] *Kunarac, Kovač, Vuković* (Trial Chamber Judgment).

[81] Art 25(3)(c) Rome Statute.

standard of wrongful intent, there is a chance that this may be taken to affect the fault required for the specific rule prohibiting state complicity in genocide. This would be a misstep. Doctrinally, there is no reason that specific primary rules of complicity cannot impose a lower standard than the rule in Article 16.[82] Moreover, as this work has consistently argued, there are good reasons to condition complicity rules with a standard of knowledge. Here, this is not so much because a standard of knowledge would cohere with that in international criminal law, but rather because of the independent normative attraction of knowledge. In general, the culpability of the knowing participant in genocide, especially given the gravity of the principal act, is not all that different from the participant who acts with wrongful intent. Even if that claim is open to dispute, it is certainly the case that knowing participation in the wrongs of others should generally be sufficient to inculpate an actor in relation to that wrong.

9.2.6. Evaluating the Structure of the Rule

Non-imputational complicity rules render accomplices responsible for their own contribution to the principal's wrong rather than for the wrong of the principal. As argued in Chapter 2, this structure of complicity is normatively desirable.

Like the rule reflected in Article 16 ARSIWA, the prohibition on state complicity in genocide is clearly a non-imputational rule. The methodological assumptions of the ICJ in the *Bosnian Genocide* case make little sense if Serbia's putative complicity would have rendered it responsible *for* the genocide perpetrated at Srebrenica by Republika Srpska. Rather, such complicity, unproven in the judgment of the court, would have given rise to responsibility for complicity in genocide.[83] The complicit state is held responsible for its contribution to the principal's wrong.

9.2.7. Conclusion

States commit genocide. Sometimes they fail to take reasonable measures, informed by ideas of proximity and due diligence, to prevent acts of genocide from occurring. But in other instances, states *participate* in acts of genocide committed by another actor. That is to say, states are sometimes complicit in genocide.

[82] Nolte and Aust, 'Equivocal Helpers' 16–17.

[83] See *Bosnian Genocide* [471].

If genocide were not recognized to be internationally wrongful without reference to the status of the principal perpetrator, it would be impossible to express a state's responsibility for participation in the conduct of non-state actors in terms of complicity. There would be no principal legal wrong for the state to be complicit in. International law's traditional structure would impede the imposition of responsibility for complicity. Instead, international law's recognition of the wrong of genocide enables the articulation of responsibility in terms of complicity. Here, international law understands complicit conduct as a particular way of contributing to wrongdoing, falling between direct state perpetration and a failure to exercise due diligence in preventing the wrong from occurring.

9.3. A General Rule?

The obligation not to commit genocide is not the only obligation imposed by international law on non-state actors. The tantalizing prospect is that the evolution set out in Chapter 7 regarding state complicity in the wrongful acts of other *states*—the move from specific complicity rules to a general rule—will be repeated here.[84] As international law comes to recognize additional kinds of wrongdoing by non-state actors, so a general complicity rule would restrain state participation in the commission of that wrongdoing.[85]

This would be an important step in the development of the international legal system. Indeed, the seriousness of the obligations that international law imposes on non-state actors supplies the logic for a complicity rule. Such a rule might be thought of as a non-state analogue to the rule reflected in Article 16. On this basis, it might read:

> A State which aids or assists a non-state actor in the commission of an internationally wrongful act by the latter is internationally responsible for doing so if:
> (a) the State does so with knowledge of the circumstances of the internationally wrongful act; and
> (b) the act would be internationally wrongful if committed by the State.[86]

As in the rule reflected in Article 16, this non-state analogue would prohibit all forms of complicity based on the provision of assistance. Ideally, it would also prohibit forms of complicit influence that have a substantial effect on the principal's commission of the wrong, though that would take it beyond the confines of its analogue in Article 16.[87]

[84] See Vogel, 'Twelve Models' 160 in respect of evolution of this kind in municipal criminal law.
[85] De Frouville, 'Attribution of Conduct' 277.
[86] Cf Art 16 ARSIWA.
[87] See section 9.2.5.2 above.

The rule might be of particular relevance to state participation in violations of international humanitarian law by non-states groups.[88] Indeed, such a non-state analogue to Article 16 was recently cited by Austria in a brief arguing against the lifting of the arms embargo against Syria.[89] Although there is debate about the scope and theoretical underpinning of the obligations imposed by the law of armed conflict on non-state groups,[90] the existence of a core of obligations is not controversial.[91] These are obligations with which each party to a non-international armed conflict must comply.[92]

No doubt difficult questions would arise in respect of the requirement of knowledge and the nexus between the accomplice state's assistance and principal non-state actor's wrong. This is nothing new for complicity. Clause (b) ensures that the complicity rule is limited to instances where the state is prohibited from doing the principal act. As the ILC puts it in the Commentary on Article 16: 'a State cannot do by another what it cannot do by itself.'[93]

A rule of this kind might become a useful restraint on the ways that states participate in wrongdoing committed by non-state actors. It would also resolve an irony in the development of the rule reflected in Article 16. By the time the International Law Commission's Articles on State Responsibility were adopted and started to ground themselves in the international legal system—50 years after drafting commenced—states had increasingly been joined by powerful non-state actors as potential violators of fundamental international norms. The rule reflected in Article 16 speaks only to the ways in which states participate in wrongdoing committed by other states. The rule proposed above would be a start towards remedying this gap.

[88] See also Common Article 1 to the Geneva Conventions of 1949: 'The High Contracting Parties undertake to respect and *to ensure respect* for the present Convention in all circumstances' (emphasis added); *Nicaragua* [220].

[89] Syria: Austrian Position on Arms Embargo (as of 13 May 2013) available at <http://www.ft.com/cms/1721c482-bcbc-11e2-b344-00144feab7de.pdf> accessed 23 December 2014.

[90] See Antonio Cassese, 'The Status of Rebels under the 1977 Geneva Protocol on Non-International Armed Conflict' (1981) 30 ICLQ 416; Sandesh Sivakumaran, 'Binding Armed Opposition Groups' (2006) 55 ICLQ 369.

[91] For an overview, see Cassese, *International Law* 429–34; Andrew Clapham, 'The Rights and Responsibilities of Non-State Actors: The Legal Landscape & Issues Surrounding Engagement' (February 2010) Ownership of Norms Project—Towards a Better Protection of Civilians in Armed Conflict 6–21; Annyssa Bellal, Gilles Giacca, and Stuart Casey-Maslen, 'International Law and Armed Non-State Actors in Afghanistan' (2011) 93 Intl Rev of the Red Cross 47.

[92] See Common Article 3 to the Geneva Conventions of 1949. See generally Liesbeth Zegveld, *The Accountability of Armed Opposition Groups in International Law* (CUP 2002).

[93] ARSIWA Commentary on Art 16 [6].

9.4. Conclusion

The implications of such a non-state analogue to Article 16 should not be overstated. Once complicity is adopted as the doctrinal tool through which to regulate the ways that states participate in harms caused by non-state actors, persisting limitations on non-state subjectivity in international law will continue to inhibit its operation.[94] For this reason, direct, non-derivative forms of state responsibility will continue to play a prominent role in constraining the ways that states interact with non-state actors. However, a general complicity rule, subsisting alongside specific prohibitions on state complicity, would graft onto any increases in the subjectivity of, and obligations borne by, non-state actors on the international plane. This could only contribute to compliance with international law.

[94] Amoroso, 'Moving towards Complicity as a Criterion of Attribution' 994.

PART D

CONCLUSION

10

Conclusion

The claim of complicity is simple—we should not help or influence others to do wrong.[1] Whenever complicity is prohibited, certain questions of scope and form need to be resolved. To this end, this work proposed an analytical framework in which complicity rules may be assessed and defended a normative claim as to how they should be structured. The framework organized the analysis around the forms of complicity prohibited, the nexus between the accomplice's act and principal's wrong, and the fault required of the accomplice. The normative claim demands that accomplices are held responsible for, and labelled in terms of, their own contribution to the principal's wrong.

This analysis allows the following conclusions to be drawn. International criminal law prohibits individual complicity in the international crimes of others in a comprehensive way. The central doctrines—instigation and aiding and abetting—are marked by the breadth of complicit conduct prohibited, encompassing all forms of help and influence, an underused nexus requirement, and a standard of knowledge that sometimes reduces to recklessness in practice. There is clearly doctrinal differentiation among participants in wrongdoing, but this doctrinal differentiation is not carried over into differentiation in the attribution of responsibility.

The comprehensive nature of complicity in international criminal law follows from the initial broad proscriptions of various forms of participation in crime.[2] These broad proscriptions, which borrow from municipal criminal law, have allowed judges at international criminal tribunals to systematically develop complicity in international criminal law. This process may be contrasted with the incremental way in which prohibitions on state complicity have arisen in international law.

In respect of state complicity in the internationally wrongful acts of other states, what we see is a move from specific complicity rules to a general rule. This move tracks the historical evolution of municipal criminal law doctrines

[1] Kadish, 'Complicity, Cause and Blame' 342.

[2] Of course, the set of international crimes onto which these comprehensive complicity rules latch is itself narrow.

of complicity, where accomplice liability was often adjunct to the specific crime of murder before migrating to the general part of the criminal law.[3] The prohibition of state complicity in aggression proscribes a specific form of complicity—the provision of territory—in a specific international wrong. The rule reflected in Article 16 ARSIWA, although limited by the double obligation requirement, prohibits general forms of aid or assistance by the accomplice state that facilitate the commission of any internationally wrongful act by the recipient state. Crucially, in the attribution of responsibility, the assisting state is responsible for its own contribution to the principal's wrong, rather than for the principal's wrong itself. The rule reflected in Article 16 ARSIWA represents, as Lowe puts it, a leap in the 'moral sophistication of international law'.[4]

In respect of the ways that states participate in harms caused by non-state actors, there is a conceptual difficulty that doctrines of complicity must overcome. Complicity is essentially derivative—it operates so as to link the accomplice to the wrongdoing committed by the principal.[5] International law's historical normative structure, which imposed obligations only on states, foreclosed the possibility that a state's support for the acts of non-state actors could give rise to responsibility for complicity.[6] This presented a normative gap in the international legal system.[7]

This work assessed two developments relating to state participation in the harms caused by non-state actors, both of which have a bearing on that normative gap. First, there is a claim that a new rule of attribution based on a *complicit relationship*, rather than an agency relationship, has arisen in the context of terrorist attacks. This claim is not the best interpretation of the legal materials and should be rejected on principled and policy grounds. Similarly, certain recent decisions of human rights courts locate the attribution of conduct of non-state actors to the state in a relationship of complicity. As argued in Chapter 8, there are sound reasons to reject this approach.

The second development relating to state participation in the harms caused by non-state actors is more positive. As shown in Chapter 9, as international law has come to impose obligations on non-state actors, so the possibility has arisen for articulating a state's responsibility in connection with the conduct of those actors in terms of complicity. International law now recognizes wrongdoing on the part of the non-state actor to which the state

[3] Vogel, 'Twelve Models' 160.

[4] Lowe, 'Responsibility for the Conduct of Other States' 12.

[5] Kadish, 'Complicity, Cause and Blame' 337.

[6] De Frouville, 'Attribution of Conduct' 276.

[7] Amoroso, 'Moving Towards Complicity as a Criterion of Attribution' 992.

may be linked. The prohibition on state complicity in genocide is the clearest example of a specific complicity rule of this kind. Chapter 9 also raises the possibility that a general rule akin to Article 16 ARSIWA prohibiting aid or assistance to a non-state actor will arise.

International crimes are seldom committed alone. Plans are made, weapons provided, and encouragement rendered. When states go to war, third states allow their territory to be used; others provide military and financial aid. States fund rebel groups, harbour terrorists, and provide credit guarantees for companies engaged in human rights abuses abroad. As a factual relationship, complicity is commonplace. As a matter of law, the rule reflected in Article 16, subsisting specific complicity rules, emerging rules concerning state participation in harms caused by non-state actors, and the criminal law doctrines of instigation and aiding and abetting, demonstrate increasing attention to complicity in international law. Both our own wrongs, and the wrongs in which we are complicit, matter.

Bibliography

BOOKS

Anscombe GEM, *Causality and Determination* (CUP 1971)
Ashworth A, *Principles of Criminal Law* (6th edn. OUP 2009)
Ashworth A and Horder J, *Principles of Criminal Law* (7th edn. OUP 2013)
Aust H, *Complicity and the Law of State Responsibility* (CUP 2011)
Austin JL, *How to Do Things with Words* (OUP 1962)
Barnidge R, *Non-State Actors and Terrorism: Applying the Law of State Responsibility and the Due Diligence Principle* (TMC Asser 2008)
Becker T, *Terrorism and the State* (Hart 2006)
Boas G, Bischoff J, and Reid N, *Forms of Responsibility in International Criminal Law—International Criminal Law Practitioner Library Series: Volume I* (CUP 2007)
Bonafè B, *The Relationship between State and Individual Responsibility for International Crimes* (Martinus Nijhoff 2009)
Brownlie I, *Principles of Public International Law* (7th edn. OUP 2008)
Carty H, *An Analysis of the Economic Torts* (2nd edn. OUP 2010)
Cassese A, *International Law* (2nd edn. OUP 2005)
Chinkin C, *Third Parties in International Law* (OUP 1993)
Crawford J, *Brownlie's Principles of Public International Law* (OUP 2012)
Crawford J, *State Responsibility: The General Part* (CUP 2013)
Cryer R, *Prosecuting International Crimes: Selectivity and the International Criminal Law Regime* (CUP 2005)
D'Ascoli S, *Sentencing in International Criminal Law: The UN ad hoc Tribunals and Future Perspectives for the ICC* (Hart 2011)
Damgaard C, *Individual Criminal Responsibility for Core International Crimes: Selected Pertinent Issues* (Spring 2008)
Dinstein Y, *War, Aggression and Self-Defence* (5th edn. CUP 2012)
Duff A, *Intention, Agency and Criminal Liability—Philosophy of Action and the Criminal Law* (Blackwell 1990)
Duff A, *Criminal Attempts* (OUP 1996)
Fletcher G, *Rethinking Criminal Law* (first published 1978, OUP 2000)
Foster N and Sule S, *German Legal System and Laws* (4th edn. OUP 2010)
Franck T, *Recourse to Force—State Action against Threats and Armed Attacks* (CUP 2002)
Garner B (ed.) *Black's Law Dictionary* (9th edn. West 2009)
Gray C, *International Law and the Use of Force* (3rd edn. OUP 2008)
Hart H and Honoré T, *Causation in the Law* (2nd edn. Clarendon 1985)

Heller K, *The Nuremberg Military Tribunals and the Origins of International Criminal Law* (OUP 2011)
Higgins R, *Problems and Process: International Law and How We Use It* (Clarendon 1994)
Jennings R and Watts A, *Oppenheim's International Law—Volume 1: Peace* (9th edn. Longman 1996)
Jørgensen N, *The Responsibility of States for International Crimes* (OUP 2000)
Keiler J, *Actus Reus and Participation in European Criminal Law* (Intersentia 2013)
Lepora C and Goodin R, *On Complicity and Compromise* (OUP 2013)
Lowe V, *International Law* (OUP 2011)
Mackie J, *The Cement of the Universe: A Study of Causation* (Clarendon 1974)
Meloni C, *Command Responsibility in International Criminal Law* (TMC Asser 2010)
Mettraux G, *International Crimes and the Ad Hoc Tribunals* (OUP 2005)
Mettraux G, *The Law of Command Responsibility* (OUP 2009)
Nagel T, *Mortal Questions* (CUP 1979)
Orakhelashvili A, *Peremptory Norms in International Law* (OUP 2006)
Quigley P, *The Genocide Convention: An International Law Analysis* (Ashgate 2006)
Peel E, *Treitel's Law of Contract* (13th edn. Sweet and Maxwell 2011)
Roxin C, *Täterschaft und Tatherrschaft* (1st edn. Cram, De Gruyter & Co 1963)
Ruys T, *'Armed Attack' and Article 51 of the UN Charter: Evolutions in Customary Law and Practice* (CUP 2010)
Saul B, *Defining Terrorism in International Law* (OUP 2006)
Schabas W, *The UN International Criminal Tribunals—The Former Yugoslavia, Rwanda and Sierra Leone* (CUP 2006)
Schabas W, *Genocide in International Law: the Crime of Crimes* (2nd edn. CUP 2009)
Schabas W, *The International Criminal Court—A Commentary on the Rome Statute* (OUP 2010)
Shue H, *Basic Rights—Subsistence, Affluence, and U.S. Foreign Policy* (2nd edn. Princeton University Press 1996)
Simester S, Spencer J, Sullivan GR, and Virgo G, *Simester and Sullivan's Criminal Law: Theory and Doctrine* (4th edn. Hart 2010) 253
Smith KJM, *A Modern Treatise on the Law of Complicity* (Clarendon 1991)
Stevens R, *Torts and Rights* (OUP 2007)
Tomuschat C and Thouvenin J, *The Fundamental Rules of the International Legal Order: Jus Cogens and Obligations Erga Omnes* (Martinus Nijhoff 2006)
Trapp K, *State Responsibility for International Terrorism* (OUP 2009)
Van Sliedregt E, *Individual Criminal Responsibility in International Law* (OUP 2012)
Weiler J, Cassese A, and Spinedi M (eds.) *International Crimes of State: A Critical Analysis of the ILC's Draft Article 19 on State Responsibility* (Walter de Gruyter 1989)
Werle G, *Principles of International Criminal Law* (TMC Asser 2009)
White R and Ovey C, *Jacobs, White, and Ovey—The European Convention on Human Rights* (5th edn. OUP 2010)
Williams G, *Criminal Law—The General Part* (2nd edn. Stevens & Sons 1961)

Zegveld L, *The Accountability of Armed Opposition Groups in International Law* (CUP 2002)

SECTIONS OF BOOKS

Alexander L, 'Criminal Liability for Omissions: An Inventory of Issues' in Shute S and Simester A (eds.) *Criminal Law Theory: Doctrines of the General Part* (OUP 2002) 121

Ambos K, 'Superior Responsibility' in Cassese A, Gaeta P, and Jones J (eds.) *The Rome Statute of the International Criminal Court: A Commentary—Vol 1* (OUP 2002) 805

Ambos K, 'Article 25—Individual Criminal Responsibility' in Triffterer O (ed.) *Commentary on the Rome Statute of the International Criminal Court: Observers' Notes, Article by Article* (2nd edn. Hart 2008) 743

Arnold R and Triffterer O, 'Article 28—Responsibility of Commanders and Other Superiors' in Triffterer O (ed.) *Commentary on the Rome Statute of the International Criminal Court: Observers' Notes, Article by Article* (2nd edn. Hart 2008) 975

Ashworth A, 'Belief, Intent, and Criminal Liability' in Eekelaar J and Bell J (eds.) *Oxford Essays in Jurisprudence—Third Series* (Clarendon 1987) 1

Ashworth A, 'Taking the Consequences' in Shute S, Gardner J, and Horder J (eds.) *Action and Value in Criminal Law* (Clarendon 1993) 107

Bannelier K, 'Foundational Judgment or Constructive Myth? The Court's Decision as a Precursor to International Environmental Law' in Bannelier K, Christakis T, and Heathcote S (eds.) *The ICJ and the Evolution of International Law: The Enduring Impact of the Corfu Channel Case* (Routledge 2012) 242

Bianchi A, 'Enforcing International Law Norms against Terrorism: Achievements and Prospects' in Bianchi A (ed.) *Enforcing International Law Norms against Terrorism* (Hart 2004) 491

Bianchi A, 'State Responsibility and Criminal Liability of Individuals' in Cassese A (ed.) *Oxford Companion to International Criminal Justice* (OUP 2009) 16

Corten O and Klein P, 'The Limits of Complicity as a Ground of Responsibility: Lessons Learned from the Corfu Channel Case' in Bannelier K, Christakis T, and Heathcote S (eds.) *The ICJ and the Evolution of International Law: The Enduring Impact of the Corfu Channel Case* (Routledge 2012) 315

Cryer R, 'General Principles of Liability in International Criminal Law' in McGoldrick D, Rowe P, and Donnelly E (eds.) *The Permanent International Criminal Court: Legal and Policy Issues* (Hart 2004) 233

David E, 'Article 34—General Rule Regarding Third States' in Corten O, and Klein P (eds.) *The Vienna Convention on the Law of Treaties: A Commentary—Volume 1* (OUP 2011) 887

De Frouville O, 'Attribution of Conduct to the State: Private Individuals' in Crawford J, Pellet A, and Olleson S (eds.) *The Law of International Responsibility* (OUP 2010) 257

Dominicé C, 'Attribution of Conduct to Multiple States and the Implication of a State in the Act of Another State' in Crawford J, Pellet A, and Olleson S (eds.) *The Law of International Responsibility* (OUP 2010) 281

Dupuy P, 'International Criminal Responsibility of the Individual and International Responsibility of the State' in Cassese A, Gaeta P, and Jones J (eds.) *The Rome Statute of the International Criminal Court: A Commentary—Vol 2* (OUP 2002) 1085

Dupuy P, 'State Sponsors of Terrorism: Issues of International Responsibility' in Bianchi A (ed.) *Enforcing International Law Norms against Terrorism* (Hart 2004) 3

Eser A, 'Individual Criminal Responsibility' in Cassese A, Gaeta P, and Jones J (eds.) *The Rome Statute of the International Criminal Court: A Commentary—Vol 1* (OUP 2002) 767

Gattini A, 'A Historical Perspective: From Collective to Individual Responsibility and Back' in Nollkaemper A, and van der Wilt H (eds.) *System Criminality in International Law* (CUP 2009) 101

Glazebrook P, 'Structuring the Criminal Code: Functional Approaches to Complicity, Incomplete Offences, and General Defences' in Simester A, and Smith A (eds.) *Harm and Culpability* (Clarendon 1996) 195

Heathcote S, 'State Omissions and Due Diligence: Aspects of Fault, Damage and Contribution to Injury in the Law of State Responsibility' in Bannelier K, Christakis T, and Heathcote S (eds.) *The ICJ and the Evolution of International Law: The Enduring Impact of the Corfu Channel Case* (Routledge 2012) 295.

Hogan B, 'Omissions and the Duty Myth' in Smith P (ed.) *Criminal Law: Essays in Honour of JC Smith* (Butterworths 1987) 85

Jørgensen N, 'State Responsibility and the 1948 Genocide Convention' in Goodwin-Gill G, and Talmon S (eds.) *The Reality of International Law—Essays in Honour of Ian Brownlie* (OUP 1999) 273

Jørgensen N, 'The Obligation of Non-Assistance to the Responsible State' in Crawford J, Pellet A, and Olleson S (eds.) *The Law of International Responsibility* (OUP 2010) 687

Jørgensen N, 'Complicity in Genocide and the Duality of Responsibility' in Swart B, Zahar A, and Sluiter G (eds.) *The Legacy of the International Criminal Tribunal for the Former Yugoslavia* (OUP 2011) 247.

Klein P, 'Attribution of Acts to International Organizations' in Crawford J, Pellet A, and Olleson S (eds.) *The Law of International Responsibility* (OUP 2010) 297

Lauterpacht E, and Bethlehem D, 'The Scope and Content of the Principle of *Non-Refoulement*' in Feller E, Türk V, and Nicholson F (eds.) *Refugee Protection in International Law—UNHCR's Global Consultations on International Protection* (CUP 2003) 87

Ohlin J, 'Incitement and Conspiracy to Commit Genocide' in Gaeta P (ed.) *The UN Genocide Convention: A Commentary* (OUP 2009) 207

Pellet A, 'The ILC's Articles on State Responsibility for Internationally Wrongful Acts and Related Texts' in Crawford J, Pellet A, and Olleson S (eds.) *The Law of International Responsibility* (OUP 2010) 75

Raz J, 'Promises and Obligations' in Hacker P, and Raz J (eds.) *Law, Morality, and Society—Essays in Honour of H.L.A. Hart* (Clarendon 1977) 210

Saland P, 'International Criminal Law Principles' in Lee R (ed.) *The International Criminal Court: The Making of the Rome Statute—Issues, Negotiations, Results* (Kluwer Law International 1999) 189

Salmon J, 'Article 26: *Pacta Sunt Servanda*' in Corten O, and Klein P (eds.) *The Vienna Convention on the Law of Treaties: A Commentary—Volume 1* (OUP 2011) 659

Schmitt M, 'Responding to Transnational Terrorism under the *Jus ad* Bellum: A Normative Framework' in Schmitt M, and Pejic J (eds.) *International Law and Armed Conflict: Exploring the Faultlines—Essays in Honour of Yoram Dinstein* (Martinus Nijhoff 2007) 157

Shute S, 'Knowledge and Belief in Criminal Law' in Shute S, and Simester A (eds.) *Criminal Law Theory: Doctrines of the General Part* (OUP 2002) 171

Suy E, 'Article 53—Treaties Conflicting with a Peremptory Norm of General International Law ("*jus cogens*")' in Corten O, and Klein P (eds.) *The Vienna Convention on the Law of Treaties: A Commentary—Volume II* (OUP 2011) 1224

Talmon S, 'A Plurality of Responsible Actors—International Responsibility for Acts of the Coalition Provision Authority in Iraq' in Shiner P, and Williams P (eds.) *The Iraq War and International Law* (Hart 2008) 185

Ventura M, 'Farewell "Specific Direction": Aiding and Abetting War Crimes and Crimes against Humanity in *Perišić, Taylor, Šainović et al.* and US Alien Tort Statute Jurisprudence' in Casey-Maslen S (ed.) *The War Report 2013* (OUP 20 November 2014)

Werle G, 'General Principles of International Criminal Law' in Cassese A (ed.) *Oxford Companion to International Criminal Justice* (OUP 2009) 54

JOURNAL ARTICLES

Ago R, 'Le Délit International' (1939) 68 (II) Recueil des Cours 419

Akhavan P, 'The Crime of Genocide in the ICTR Jurisprudence' (2005) 3 J Intl Crim Just 989

Allott P, 'State Responsibility and the Unmaking of International Law' (1988) 29 Harv Intl L J 1.

Ambos K, 'Is the Development of a Common Substantive Criminal Law for Europe Possible? Some Preliminary Reflections' (2005) 12 Maastricht J of Eur & Comp L 173

Ambos K, 'Amicus Curiae Brief in the Matter of the Co-Prosecutors' Appeal of the Closing Order against Kaing Guek Eav "Duch" Dated 8 August 2008' (2009) 20 Crim L Forum 353

Ambos K, 'What Does "Intent to Destroy" in Genocide Mean?' (2009) 91 Intl Rev of the Red Cross 833.

Ambos K, 'The First Judgment of the International Criminal Court (*Prosecutor* v. *Lubanga*): A Comprehensive Analysis of the Legal Issues' (2012) 12 Intl Crim L Rev 114

Amoroso D, 'Moving Towards Complicity as a Criterion of Attribution of Private Conducts: Imputation to States of Corporate Abuses in the US Case Law' (2011) 24 Leiden J Intl L 989

Ashworth A, 'The Scope of Criminal Liability for Omissions' (1989) 105 LQR 424

Bagshaw R, 'Can the Economic Torts be Unified?' (1998) 18 OJLS 729

Bantekas I, 'On Stretching the Boundaries of Responsible Command' (2009) 7 J Intl Crim Just 1197

Bellal A, Giacca G, and Casey-Maslen S, 'International Law and Armed Non-State Actors in Afghanistan' (2011) 93 Intl Rev of the Red Cross 47

Berster L, '"Duty to Act" and "Commission by Omission" in International Criminal Law' (2010) 10 Intl Crim L Rev 619

Bethlehem D, 'Self-Defense against an Imminent or Actual Armed Attack by Non-State Actors' (2012) 106 Am J Intl L 770

Beynon H, 'Causation, Omissions and Complicity' (1987) Crim L Rev 539

Bodansky D, and Crook J, 'Symposium: The ILC's State Responsibility Articles—Introduction and Overview' (2002) 96 Am J Intl L 773

Bogdan A, 'Individual Criminal Responsibility in the Execution of a "Joint Criminal Enterprise" in the Jurisprudence of the *ad hoc* International Tribunal for the Former Yugoslavia' (2006) 5 Intl Crim L Rev 63

Bowett D, 'Crimes of State and the 1996 Report of the International Law Commission on State Responsibility' (1998) 9 Eur J Intl L 163

Brownlie I, 'International Law and the Activities of Armed Bands' (1958) 7 ICLQ 712

Byers M, 'Terrorism, the Use of Force and International Law after 11 September' (2002) 51 ICLQ 401

Caron D, 'The ILC Articles on State Responsibility: The Paradoxical Relationship between Form and Authority' (2002) 96 Am J Intl L 857

Carty H, 'Joint Tortfeasance and Assistance Liability' (1999) 19 Legal Stud 489

Cassese A, 'On the Use of Criminal Law Notions in Determining State Responsibility for Genocide' (2007) 5 J Intl Crim Just 875

Cerone J, 'Human Dignity in the Line of Fire: The Application of International Human Rights Law During Armed Conflict, Occupation, and Peace Operations' (2006) 39 Vand J Intl L 1447

Chalmers J, and Leverick F, 'Fair Labelling in Criminal Law' (2008) 71 MLR 217

Clapham A, 'Human Rights Obligations of Non-State Actors in Conflict Situations' (2006) 88 Intl Rev of the Red Cross 491

Clapham A, 'Extending International Criminal Law beyond the Individual to Corporations and Armed Opposition Groups' (2008) 6 J Intl Crim Just 899

Clapham A, 'The Rights and Responsibilities of Non-State Actors: The Legal Landscape & Issues Surrounding Engagement' (February 2010) Ownership of Norms Project—Towards a Better Protection of Civilians in Armed Conflict.

Condorelli L, 'The Imputability to States of Acts of International Terrorism' (1989) 19 Isr YB Human Rights 233

Crawford J, 'The ILC's Articles on Responsibility of States for Internationally Wrongful Acts: A Retrospect' (2002) 96 Am J Intl L 874

Damaška M, 'The Shadow Side of Command Responsibility' (2001) 49 Am J of Comp L 455

Danforth J, 'Tortious Interference with Contract: A Reassertion of Society's Interest in Commercial Stability and Contractual Integrity' (1981) 81 Colum L Rev 1491

D'Argent P, 'Reparation, Cessation, Assurances and Guarantees of Non-Repetition' SHARES Research Paper 34 (2014).

Davies P, 'Accessory Liability for Assisting Torts' (2011) 70 Camb L J 353

Dawson G, and Boynton R, 'Reconciling Complicity in Genocide and Aiding and Abetting Genocide in the Jurisprudence of the United Nations *Ad Hoc* Tribunals' (2008) 21 Harv Human Rights J 241

Dietrich J, 'Accessorial Liability in the Law of Torts' (2011) 31 Legal Stud 231

Dressler J, 'Reassessing the Theoretical Underpinnings of Accomplice Liability: New Solutions to an Old Problem (1985–1986) 37 Hastings LJ 91

Dressler J, 'Reforming Complicity Law: Trivial Assistance as a Lesser Offence' (2008) 5 Ohio State J of Crim L 427

Dubber M, 'Criminalizing Complicity: A Comparative Analysis' (2007) 5 J Intl Crim Just 977

Duff A, '"Can I Help You?" Accessorial Liability and the Intention to Assist' (1990) 10 Legal Stud 165

Duttwiler M, 'Liability for Omission in International Criminal Law' (2006) 6 Intl Crim L Rev 1

Eboe-Osuji, '"Complicity in Genocide" versus "Aiding and Abetting Genocide": Construing the Difference in the ICTR and ICTY Statutes' (2005) 3 J Intl Crim Just 56

Epstein R, 'Inducement of Breach of Contract as a Problem of Ostensible Ownership' (1987) 16 J Legal Stud 1

Eulau P, 'Inducing Breach of Contract: A Comparison of the Laws of the United States, France, The Federal Republic of Germany and Switzerland' (1978) 2 Boston College Intl & Comp L Rev 41

Fitzmaurice M, 'Third Parties and the Law of Treaties' (2002) 6 Max Planck YB of United Nations L 37

Fletcher G, 'Criminal Omissions: Some Perspectives' (1976) 24 Am J Comp L 703

Fletcher G, 'Complicity' (1996) 30 Isr L Rev 140

Franck T, 'Who Killed Article 2(4)? Or: Changing Norms Governing the Use of Force by States' (1970) 64 Am J Intl L 809

Franck T, 'Terrorism and the Right of Self-Defence' (2001) 98 Am J Intl L 839

Gaeta P, 'On What Conditions Can a State Be Held Responsible for Genocide?' (2007) 18 Eur J Intl L 631

Gardner J, 'Complicity and Causality' (2007) 1 Crim L & Phil 127

Gardner J, 'Moore on Complicity and Causality' (2008) U Penn L Rev Pennumbra 432

Giustiniani F, 'The Responsibility of Accomplices in the Case-Law of the Ad Hoc Tribunals' (2009) 20 Crim L Forum 417

Graefrath B, 'Complicity in the Law of International Responsibility' (1996) Rev Belge de Droit Intl 371

Greenawalt A, 'Rethinking Genocidal Intent: The Case for a Knowledge-Based Interpretation' (1999) 99 Colum L Rev 2259

Greenfield D, 'The Crime of Complicity in Genocide: How the International Criminal Tribunals for Rwanda and Yugoslavia Got It Wrong, and Why It Matters' (2008) 98 J Crim L & Criminology 921

Greenwood C, 'International Law and the United States' Air Operation against Libya' (1986/1987) 89 W Va L Rev 933

Hakimi M, 'State Bystander Responsibility' (2010) Eur J Intl L 341

Heller K, 'The *Taylor* Sentencing Judgment: A Critical Analysis' (2013) 11 J Intl Crim Just 835

Hohfeld W, 'Some Fundamental Legal Conceptions as Applied in Judicial Reasoning (1913–1914) 23 Yale L J 16

Hohfeld W, 'Fundamental Legal Conceptions as Applied in Judicial Reasoning' (1916–1917) 26 Yale L J 710

Holá B, Smeulers A, and Bijleveld C, 'International Sentencing Facts and Figures—Sentencing Practice at the ICTY and ICTR' (2011) 9 J Intl Crim Just 411

Horder J, 'Rethinking Non-Fatal Offences against the Person' (1994) 14 OJLS 335

Howarth D, 'Against *Lumley* v. *Gye*' (2005) 68 MLR 195

Husak D, 'Abetting a Crime' (2014) 33 L & Phil 41

Kadish S, 'Complicity, Cause and Blame' (1985) 73 Calif L Rev 323

Kadish S, 'Act and Omission, *Mens Rea*, and Complicity: Approaches to Codification' (1989) 1 Crim L Forum 65

Kadish S, 'Reckless Complicity' (1997) 87 J Crim L & Criminology 369

Kammerhofer J, 'The Armed Activities Case and Non-State Actors in Self-Defence Law' (2007) 20 Leiden J Intl L 89

Keitner C, 'Conceptualizing Complicity in Alien Tort Cases' (2008) 60 Hastings Law Journal 61

Kirgis F, 'Israel's Intensified Military Campaign against Terrorism' Am Soc Intl L Insight (December 2001)

Kutz C, 'Causeless Complicity' (2007) 1 Crim L & Phil 289

Lanovoy V, 'Responsibility for Complicity in an Internationally Wrongful Act: Revisiting a Structural Norm' (SHARES Conference—Foundations of Shared Responsibility in International Law, Amsterdam, 17, 18 November 2011) 1

Lauterpacht E, 'The Contemporary Practice of the United Kingdom in the Field of International Law—Survey and Comment' (1958) 7 ICLQ 514
Leavens A, 'A Causation Approach to Criminal Omissions' (1988) 76 Cal L Rev 547
Lee P, 'Inducing Breach of Contract, Conversion and Contract as Property' (2009) 29 OJLS 511
Lewis D, 'Causation' (1973) 70 Journal of Philosophy 556
Lewis D, 'Causation as Influence' (2000) 97 Journal of Philosophy 182
Lillich R, and Paxman J, 'State Responsibility for Injuries to Aliens Occasioned by Terrorist Activities' (1977) 26 Am Univ L Rev 217
Linderfalk U, 'The Effect of *Jus Cogens* Norms: Whoever Opened Pandora's Box, Did You Ever Think About the Consequences?' (2007) 18 Eur J Intl L 853
Linderfalk U, 'State Responsibility and the Primary-Secondary Rules Terminology—The Role of Language for an Understanding of the International Legal System' (2009) 78 Nordic J Intl L 53
Lobel J, 'The Use of Force to Respond to Terrorist Attacks: The Bombing of Sudan and Afghanistan' (1999) 24 Yale J Intl L 537
Lowe V, 'Responsibility for the Conduct of Other States' (2002) 101 Japanese J Intl L 1
Martinez J, 'Understanding *Mens Rea* in Command Responsibility' (2007) 5 J Intl Crim Just 638
Martinez J, and Danner A, 'Guilty Associations: Joint Criminal Enterprise, Command Responsibility, and the Development of International Criminal Law' (2005) 93 Calif L Rev 75
McChesney F, 'Tortious Interference with Contract versus "Efficient" Breach: Theory and Empirical Evidence' (1999) 28 J of Legal Stud 131
Meloni C, 'Command Responsibility: Mode of Liability for the Crimes of Subordinates or Separate Offence of the Superior?' (2007) 5 J Intl Crim Just 619
Milanović M, 'State Responsibility for Genocide' (2006) 17 Eur J Intl L 553
Milanović M, 'State Responsibility for Genocide: A Follow-Up' (2007) 18 Eur J Intl L 669
Moore M, 'The Metaphysics of Causal Intervention' (2000) 88 Cal L Rev 827
Moore M, 'Causing, Aiding, and the Superfluity of Accomplice Liability' (2007) 156 U Penn LR 395
Murmann U, 'Problems of Causation with Regard to (Potential) Actions of Multiple Protagonists' (2014) 12 J Intl Crim Just 283
Murphy S, 'Contemporary Practice of the United States Relating to International Law' (1999) 93 Am J Intl L 161
Murphy S, 'Contemporary Practice of the United States Relating to International Law—2001' (2002) 96 Am J Intl L 237
Murphy S, 'Terrorism and the Concept of "Armed Attack" in Article 51 of the UN Charter' (2002) 43 Harv J Intl L 41
Nollkaemper A, 'Concurrence between Individual Responsibility and State Responsibility in International Law' (2003) 52 ICLQ 615

Nollkaemper A, 'Internationally Wrongful Acts in Domestic Courts' (2007) 101 Am J Intl L 760

Nollkaemper A, and Nedeski N, 'Responsibility of International Organizations "in Connection with Acts of States"' (2012) 9 Intl Org L Rev 33

Nollkaemper A, and Jacobs D, 'Shared Responsibility in International Law: A Conceptual Framework' (2013) 34 Michigan J Intl L 359

Nollkaemper A, Paparinskis M, Baetens F, Bartels L, Plakokefalos I, 'Themed Section: Procedural Aspects of Shared Responsibility in International Adjudication' (2013) 4 J Intl Dispute Settlement 277

Nolte G, and Aust H, 'Equivocal Helpers—Complicit States, Mixed Messages and International Law' (2009) 58 ICLQ 1

Noyes J, and Smith B, 'State Responsibility and the Principle of Joint and Several Liability' (1998) 13 Yale J Intl L 225

Ohlin J, 'Joint Intentions to Commit International Crimes' (2010–2011) 11 Chicago J Intl L 693

Ohlin J, 'Search for the Hinterman: In Praise of Subjective Theories of Imputation' (2014) 12 J Intl Crim Just 325

Ohlin J, van Sliedregt E, and Weigend T, 'Assessing the Control Theory' (2013) 26 Leiden J Intl L 725

Osiel M, 'The Banality of Good: Aligning Incentives Against Mass Atrocities' (2005) 105 Colum L Rev 1751

Pellet A, 'Can a State Commit a Crime? Definitely, Yes!' (1999) 10 Eur J Intl L 425.

Perlman H, 'Interference with Contract and Other Economic Expectancies: A Clash of Tort and Contract Doctrine' (1982) 49 Uni Chicago L Rev 61

Pisillo-Mazzeschi P, 'Due Diligence and the International Responsibility of States' (1992) 35 German YB Intl L 9

Quigley J, 'Complicity in International Law: A New Direction in the Law of State Responsibility' (1986) 57 British YB Intl L 77.

Ratner S, 'Jus ad Bellum and Jus in Bello after September 11' (2002) 96 Am J Intl L 905

Raz J, 'Promises in Morality and Law' (1981–1982) 95 Harv L Rev 916

Reinisch A, 'Aid or Assistance and Direction and Control between States and International Organizations in the Commission of Internationally Wrongful Acts' (2010) 7 Intl Org L Rev 63

Roberts K, 'The Law of Persecution Before the International Criminal Tribunal for the Former Yugoslavia' (2002) 15 Leiden J Intl L 623

Robinson D, 'How Command Responsibility Got So Complicated: A Culpability Contradiction, Its Obfuscation, and a Simple Solution' (2012) 13 Melb J Intl L 1

Robinson P, 'Imputed Criminal Liability' (1984) 93 Yale L J 609

Robinson P, and John Darley, 'Objectivist v. Subjectivist Views of Criminality: A Study in the Role of Social Science in Criminal Law Theory' (1998) 18 OJLS 409

Rosand E, 'Security Council Resolution 1373, the Counter-Terrorism Committee and the Fight Against Terrorism' (2003) 97 Am J Intl L 333

Roxin C, 'Crimes as Part of Organized Power Structures' (Belinda Cooper tr) (2011) 9 J Intl Crim Just 193.

Ruys T, '*Quo Vadit Jus ad Bellum*?: A Legal Analysis of Turkey's Military Operations against the PKK in Northern Iraq' (2008) 9 Melb J Intl L 334

Ruys T, and Verhoeven S, 'Attacks by Private Actors and the Right of Self-Defence' (2005) 10 J Confl & Sec L 289

Sayre F, 'Inducing Breach of Contract' (1922–1923) 36 Harv L Rev 663

Simester A, 'The Mental Element in Complicity' (2006) 122 LQR 578

Simester A, and Chan W, 'Inducing Breach of Contract: One Tort or Two' (2004) 63 Camb L J 132

Simma B, 'From Bilateralism to Community Interest in International Law' (1994) 250 Recueil des Cours 217

Smith J, 'Some Problems of the Reform of the Law of Offences against the Person' (1978) 31 Curr Leg Prob 15

Smith J, *Gillick* v. *West Norfolk and Wisbech AHA* [1986] Crim LR 113 (note)

Smith KJM, 'The Law Commission Consultation Paper on Complicity: Part 1: A Blueprint for Rationalism' (1994) Crim L Rev 239

Stahn C, 'Terrorist Acts as "Armed Attack": The Right to Self-Defence, Article 51 (1/2) of the UN Charter, and International Terrorism' (2003) 27 Fletcher For of World Aff 35

Stapleton J, 'Law, Causation and Common Sense' (1988) 8 OJLS 111

Stewart J, 'The End of "Modes of Liability" for International Crimes' (2012) *25* Leiden J Intl L 165

Stewart J, 'Overdetermined Atrocities' (2012) 10 J Intl Crim Just 1189

Sullivan R, 'Conduct and Complicity: Liability based on Omission and Risk' (2008) 39 Cambrian L Rev 60

Talmon S, 'The Responsibility of Outside Powers for Acts of Secessionist Entities' (2009) 58 ICLQ 493

Tams C, 'All's Well that Ends Well—Comments on the ILC's Articles on State Responsibility' (2002) Heidelberg J Intl L 759

Tams C, 'Do Serious Breaches Give Rise to Any Specific Obligations of the Responsible State?' (2002) 13 Eur J Intl L 1161

Tams C, 'Countermeasures against Multiple Responsible Actors' SHARES Research Paper 35 (2014)

Tange P, 'Netherlands State Practice for the Parliamentary Year 2000–2001' (2002) 33 Netherlands Y Intl L 191

Trapp K, 'Back to Basics: Necessity, Proportionality, and the Right of Self-Defence against Non-State Terrorist Actors' (2007) 56 ICLQ 141

Trapp K, 'The Use of Force against Terrorists: A Reply to Christian J. Tams' (2009) 20 Eur J Intl L 1049

van der Wilt H, 'Genocide, Complicity in Genocide and International v. Domestic Jurisdiction: Reflections on the *van Anraat* Case' (2006) 4 J Intl Crim Just 239

Van Steenberghe R, 'Self-Defence in Response to Attacks by Non-state Actors in the Light of Recent State Practice: A Step Forward?' (2010) 23 Leiden J Intl L 183

Vest H, 'Problems of Participation—Unitarian, Differentiated Approach, or Something Else?' (2014) 12 J Intl Crim Just 295

Vogel J, 'How to Determine Individual Criminal Responsibility in Systemic Contexts: Twelve Models' (2002) Cahiers de Défense Sociale 151

Waddams S, 'Johanna Wagner and the Rival Opera Houses' (2001) 117 LQR 431

Wasik M, and Thompson M, '"Turning a Blind Eye" as Constituting Mens Rea' (1981) 32 NILQ 328, 330–1

Wedgwood R, 'Responding to Terrorism: The Strikes Against Bin Laden' (1999) 24 Yale J Intl L 559

Weigend T, 'Problems of Attribution in International Criminal Law' (2014) 12 J Intl Crim Just 253

Weinrib E, 'A Step Forward in Factual Causation' (1975) 38 MLR 518

Weisberg R, 'Reappraising Complicity' (2000–2001) 4 Buff Crim L Rev. 217

Werle G, 'Individual Criminal Responsibility in Article 25 ICC Statute' (2007) 5 J Intl Crim Just 953

Williams G, 'Oblique Intention' (1987) 46 Camb LJ 417

Wilson W, 'A Rational Scheme of Liability for Participating in Crime' (2008) Crim L Rev 3

Wolf S, 'The Moral of Moral Luck' (2013) 31 Philosophic Exchange 5

Wright R, 'Causation in Tort Law' (1985) 73 Calif L Rev 1735

Yeager D, 'Helping, Doing, and the Grammar of Complicity' (1996) 15 Crim Just Eth 25

Zan M, 'Comment: John Howard's "Pre-emptive Strike Thesis"' (2003) 7 J of South Pac L 4

BLOG POSTS

Cryer R, 'Command Responsibility at the ICC and ICTY: Two Minds on the Mental Element' (*EJIL:Talk!*, 20 July 2009) <http://www.ejiltalk.org/command-responsibility-at-the-icc-and-icty-in-two-minds-on-the-mental-element/>

Milanović M, 'Self-Defense and Non-State Actors: Indeterminacy and the Jus ad Bellum' (*EJIL:Talk!*, 21 February 2010) <http://www.ejiltalk.org/self-defense-and-non-state-actors-indeterminacy-and-the-jus-ad-bellum/>

Milanović M, 'Danish Judge Blasts ICTY President' (*EJIL:Talk!*, 13 June 2013) <http://www.ejiltalk.org/danish-judge-blasts-icty-president/>

Nollkaemper A, 'The ECtHR Finds Macedonia Responsible in Connection with Torture by the CIA, but on What Basis?' (*EJIL:Talk!*, 24 December 2012) <http://www.ejiltalk.org/the-ecthr-finds-macedonia-responsible-in-connection-with-torture-by-the-cia-but-on-what-basis/>

Nollkaemper A, 'The Charles Taylor Judgment: Disconnecting the Responsibilities of Presidents and States' (*SHARES Blog*, 1 October 2013) <http://www.sharesproject.nl/the-charles-taylor-judgment-disconnecting-the-responsibilities-of-presidents-and-states/>

Ohlin J, 'Why did the ICTY Acquit Stanišić and Simatović?' (*Lieber Code*, 1 June 2013) <http://www.liebercode.org/2013/06/why-did-icty-acquit-stanisic-and.html>

Robinson D, 'Comment on *Opinio Juris* LJIL Symposium on James Stewart, The End of "Modes of Liability" for International Crimes—James Stewart Responds to Darryl Robinson' (*Opinio Juris*, 21 March 2012) <http://opiniojuris.org/2012/03/21/ljil-stewart-responds-to-robinson/>

Stewart J, 'The ICTY Loses its Way on Complicity—Part 1' (*Opinio Juris*, 3 April 2013) <http://opiniojuris.org/2013/04/03/guest-post-the-icty-loses-its-way-on-complicity-part-1/>

Stewart J, 'The ICTY Loses its Way on Complicity—Part 2' (*Opinio Juris*, 3 April 2013) <http://opiniojuris.org/2013/04/03/guest-post-the-icty-loses-its-way-on-complicity-part-2/>

Stewart J, '"Specific Direction" is Indefensible: A Response to Heller on Complicity' (*Opinio Juris*, 12 June 2013) <http://opiniojuris.org/2013/06/12/specific-direction-is-indefensible-a-response-to-heller-on-complicity/>

Stewart J, '"Specific Direction" is Unprecedented: Results from Two Empirical Studies' (*EJIL:Talk!*, 4 September 2013) <http://www.ejiltalk.org/specific-direction-is-unprecedented-results-from-two-empirical-studies/>

NEWSPAPER AND MAGAZINE ARTICLES

Baer R, 'Finding Bin Laden Raises Questions About Pakistan's Complicity' *Time* (New York, 2 May 2011)

Bilandzic B, and Dervisbegovic N, 'Serbs Relieved, Bosnia Dismayed by Genocide Ruling' *Reuters* (Sarajevo, 26 February 2007)

Cassese A, 'A Judicial Massacre' *The Guardian* (London, 27 February 2007)

'Court Clears Serbia of Genocide' *BBC News* (London, 26 February 2007)

de Launey G, 'Momcilo Perisic Hague Acquittal Leaves Little Sense of Justice' *BBC News* (Belgrade, 28 February 2013).

Pflanz M, 'French Leaders Accused of Complicity in Rwanda Genocide' *The Telegraph* (London, 5 August 2008)

Reeves E, 'Arming Khartoum: China's Complicity in the Darfur Genocide' *Sudan Tribune* (Paris, 19 October 2010)

Roth K, 'A Tribunal's Legal Stumble' *The New York Times* (New York, 9 July 2013).

ENGLAND AND WALES LAW COMMISSION

Assisting and Encouraging Crime (Law Com Consultation Paper No 131, 1993)

Inchoate Liability for Assisting and Encouraging Crime (Law Com No 300, 2006)

Participating in Crime (Law Com No 305, 2007)

Index

Complicity in International Law – Index
For page references to cases and other primary authorities, please consult the relevant tables at the beginning of the work.

The manufacturer's authorised representative in the EU for product safety is Oxford University Press España S.A. of el Parque Empresarial San Fernando de Henares, Avenida de Castilla, 2 – 28830 Madrid (www.oup.es/en or product.safety@oup.com). OUP España S.A. also acts as importer into Spain of products made by the manufacturer.

www.ingramcontent.com/pod-product-compliance
Lightning Source LLC
LaVergne TN
LVHW011754200926
848484LV00003B/705
* 9 7 8 0 1 9 8 7 3 6 9 3 6 *